Bodily Discourses

When Students Write About Abuse and Eating Disorders

Michelle Payne

Boynton/Cook Publishers
HEINEMANN
Portsmouth, NH

Boynton /Cook Publishers, Inc.
A subsidiary of Reed Elsevier Inc.
361 Hanover Street
Portsmouth, NH 03801–3912
www.boyntoncook.com

Offices and agents throughout the world

A version of Chapter 2 originally appeared as "A Strange Unaccountable Something: Historicizing Sexual Abuse Narratives" in *Writing and Healing: Toward an Informed Practice,* edited by Charles M. Anderson and Marian M. MacCurdy; Published by the National Council of Teachers of English. © by Michelle Payne.

Library of Congress Cataloging-in-Publication Data
Payne, Michelle.
    Bodily discourses : when students write about abuse and eating disorders / Michelle Payne.
       p.   cm.
    Includes bibliographical references and index.
    ISBN 0-86709-471-0
    1. Sexual abuse victims—Anecdotes.   2. Eating disorders—Anecdotes.   I. Title.
RC560.S44 P39   2000
616.85′8369—dc21   99-058722

Editors: Tom Newkirk and Leigh Peake
Production coordinator: Sonja Chapman
Production service: Denise Botelho, Colophon
Cover design: Linda Knowles
Cover photo by Julie Nelson
Manufacturing: Louise Richardson

Printed in the United States of America on acid-free paper
04   03   02   01   00   DA   1   2   3   4   5

For the students who choose to shelter their battered bodies in language
and the teachers who take them seriously

Contents

Acknowledgments

*T*his project began with the students in the Writing About Female Experience course I taught in 1990, particularly three young women among many in that class who chose to explore the effects of gender and culture on their identities. Their desires to make visible what happened to them and my own desires to have student texts in dialogue with composition and critical theory raised the provocative questions that have driven this book. Working on this project has transformed my teaching and my relationship with theory, and it has taught me how fulfilling professional research can be. Colleagues are often puzzled when I claim that writing my dissertation—on which this book is based—was one of the best experiences I had in graduate school. Each time I returned to read transcripts, analyze papers, make connections to theories, and talk with friends and colleagues, I came away understanding my world and my students' worlds differently. I put this project down now knowing how much more I still have to learn.

Acknowledgment pages never seem adequate to capture all those other voices that permeate the ideas and the writing to which a sole author lays claim, and I can't help but be conscious of this as I list, like other writers before me, all those who collaborated with me. I'd rather tell stories about the ways my thinking changed with each conversation over coffee, each challenge during a conference presentation, and each insight dropped in passing in the mail room. Someday I'll weave those stories into a book and challenge this rather inadequate way of recognizing the social nature of all writing. For now, I capitulate to the conventions and beg my readers'—and my collaborators'—pardon.

I thank all those who taught me how to listen:

The students who agreed to participate, who shared their writing and talked with me about their work—their words guide this project.

The writing instructors who spent time with me, asking me questions and offering me their insights from years of working with students. The discussions we had, as well as the support and encouragement both implied and expressed, were vital to the thinking and writing of this book. I cannot name them all, but I especially thank Bruce Ballenger, Pam Barksdale, Derek Brewer, Leslie Brown, Tim Dansdill, Brock Deither, Sara Dovre Wudali, Alice Fogel, Lucinda Garthwaite, Andrea Harkness, Lysa James, Carol Kountz, Jodi Labonte, Tamara Niedzolkowski, Laurie Quinn, Leaf Seligman, Linda Stewart, Barb Tindall, Sue Wheeler, and Bronwyn Williams, among many others. They are a talented group of teachers, committed to students and sensitive to the complex dynamics of writing about such personal issues as bodily violence. I learned much from them and value the relationships we developed. Many thanks.

I also thank the following: The Graduate School at the University of New Hampshire (UNH) who honored me with a Summer Fellowship in 1993 and a Dissertation Fellowship in 1994, both of which made it possible for me to conduct my classroom research and write without the demands of teaching. It was quite a gift of time and money.

The Office of Research Administration at Boise State University for honoring me with a Faculty Research Grant during the 1998–1999 school year— the time away from teaching enabled me to substantially revise my original manuscript.

The librarians at Rye, New Hampshire Public Library—Marnie Tracey, Kathleen Teaze, Jennifer Sanborn, Tricia Quinn, Wendy Palmer, Stefania Metalious, Pam Jautaikis, Sharon Holsapple, and Susan Brough—who found many articles and books I needed and became an important community to both me and my husband, their colleague.

The staff at King Library of Miami University, Ohio, and at Dimond Library of UNH.

The secretaries in the English Department at UNH—Tory Poulin, Heather Robbins, and Chris Ransom, all of whom helped over the years in more ways than I can name.

Chuck Anderson, who edited the article version of Chapter 2 to make it more concise, focused, and organized, and who (along with Marian Mc-

Curdy) convinced me to publish with their text, *Writing and Healing: Toward an Informed Practice,* and get the rest of my work out. Chuck has been a tremendous mentor.

Irene Heisenberg, who helped me find the strength and confidence to continue this work.

My closest friends, who helped me untangle ideas, make connections, battle my self-doubt, and manage my stress. They helped me care for my body and soul with walks on Long Sands Beach, coffee at the MUB or Café Brioche, long talks on the phone, and many hugs when I needed them.

The many readers of this work: the Dissertation Reading Group at UNH who read many drafts of chapters and provided deadlines and a sense of community I needed. They were excellent readers, and Dr. Sue Schibanoff was a wonderful guide and mentor for us all. My thanks, then, to close friends and reading group members: Rick Agran, Jennifer Beard, Greg Bowe, Susan Bradbury Clay, Gay Lynn Crossley, Gretchen DiGeronimo, Molly Doyle, Mary Hallet, Andrea Harkness, Deborah Hodgkins, Elisa Hopkins, Dot Kasik, Carol Keyes, Anne Malone, Erica Olbreicht, Kathe Simons, Lisa Sisco, and Lisa Stepanski.

The Thesis Reading Group at Boise State University who helped me return to my manuscript and begin anew, challenging me to make my prose more clear, my voice more comfortable, and my persona more consistent: Steve Doran, Stacie Lewton, Sandra Roseburg, and Michael Steele.

My faculty writing group, Bruce Ballenger and Mary Ellen Ryder, whose early feedback helped me focus my arguments and "essay" my way into a better book, and whose friendship made the revisions even more worthwhile and a rather trying year more bearable.

The reviewers whose careful reading, critical perspective, and specific suggestions challenged me to significantly revise an earlier draft.

My brother Michael who cajoled me and my husband into buying mountain bikes in 1994 and thus helped us stay sane. Most mornings before I began to write the first draft of this book, my Cannondale took me all through York and Ogunquit, Maine, keeping me focused, centered, and aware of the coastal beauty I could so easily forget.

My brother Aaron who offered me early lessons in compassion, teaching, and listening.

My sister-in-law Brenda and my nephew Tyler who opened their home to me and my husband for a few months during my Dissertation Fellowship year. Tyler reminded me to wonder and imagine. My mother- and father-in-law, Delbert and Norma Barrett, who also opened their home for us during that year and gave me a desk in their plumbing office on which to write. They also cared for me after back surgery and a long bout with debilitating pain that derailed this project for over a year.

My parents, Tom and Marilyn, whose emotional support throughout my years in graduate school has been so important. They never wavered in their confidence. From them I learned the values of stewardship, of using my talents and interests responsibly to affect my community, and of seeing a project through, no matter how difficult.

I am also grateful to the following people: Patricia Sullivan, who directed the dissertation that is the basis for this book. She spent many hours talking with, encouraging, and prompting me, all with patience and in the midst of being the Director of Composition at UNH. This project began as a seminar paper for Pat's Research Methods course. Her enthusiasm for this project and her confidence in me seemed never to waver, and I value her friendship and support.

Thomas Newkirk whose unfailing confidence in my work and persistent reminders to send my writing out has made this book a reality. His keen insights, broad knowledge of the field, and suggestions for revising this manuscript have guided my thinking and writing for several years now.

Melody Graulich who responded copiously to my work, on many levels, and who insisted I not leave my own experiences out of it. It was in one of her seminars that I began my work on women writing about anorexia. She has been a friend and mentor for years, treating me like a colleague before I had the right to call myself one.

Cindy Gannett who talked with me many hours over coffee or a meal (once at Christmas and during a family gathering!), asking thought-provoking questions and guiding me to books she then let me borrow. Sometimes just the touch of her hand on my arm when I came to see her was enough. And it was in her seminar on journal writing that I first read an excerpt of Abigail Abbot Bailey's memoirs, which I later incorporated into Chapter 2.

Paula Salvio who also met many hours with me in her office, responding to drafts, offering insights and texts, plying me with questions, and leaving me with so much more to think about.

All of these mentors' voices permeate this book and helped make it possible for me to write it in a supportive, challenging environment.

Finally, I thank my husband, Steve Barrett, who was able to give me the most critical feedback of anyone, challenging me to articulate my ideas more clearly, to be more bold in my arguments, and to take myself and my material more seriously. So many nights our walks around Nubble Road in York Beach, Maine, were consumed with talks of both our dissertations, our dialogue enriching each other's perspectives, making connections between our projects that surprised and, at times, disconcerted us. More than anyone, he has been vital to the development of my ideas, and his faith and encouragement have been consistent and loving. He also taught me about balance. I cannot imagine my professional and writing life without Steve as a colleague, friend, and critical reader, or my personal life without him as a lover and partner.

Figuring

Marcia is excited about visiting her uncle. She thinks her mother doesn't want her to go. Sure, Marcia knows her uncle was an alcoholic, but when she had seen him three years before, he had been fine. Marcia is certain he hasn't gone "back to the bottle."

But he has, and though Marcia knows he is drinking, it seems only in moderate form. Marcia doesn't think she will have a problem handling it for a week. However, her visit doesn't even last two days.

Marcia's uncle obviously misses his wife. He constantly tells Marcia how much she looks like her aunt, and how beautiful she is. He offers Marcia his wife's wardrobe, which he has kept. He suggests taking Marcia to her aunt's hairdresser, to have her hair styled in the same fashion as her aunt's. And that evening, he molests her.

—Stephanie, college sophomore, 1990

When I first read Stephanie's essay, I was sitting at a formica table in my three-room apartment, surrounded by a stack of my students' drafts that I needed to return to them the next day. It was probably close to midnight. I was in the midst of finishing my master's thesis, so my own writing had crowded me out of my makeshift office in the back room and into the kitchen, my books and papers taking over almost every inch of that tiny, cinder-block apartment. I was tired, and, as I read Stephanie's essay, I slowly put my pen down and leaned back in my chair. I was amazed at how well her narrative frame controlled this painful, uncontrollable story. I learned later that, in the essay "Marcia" was the writer's friend, but, in reality, Marcia was just a pseudonym for Stephanie. This was a way for the writer to split herself in two, to distance herself from the experience by using the third person. In the essay, Marcia's friend guides her to a counselor and explains to the reader the consequences of this abuse for Marcia's sense of self and for her sexuality.

I decided to lay Stephanie's essay aside so I could return to it when I had figured out what to say. I had received essays before about a student's struggles with a painful experience, but I had never received one about sexual abuse. I needed time. I picked up another draft from the pile and commented on several more. Soon I was reading about another young woman who had been sexually molested as a child. This one was written in the first person and the narrator was expressing her anger with the help of lesbian feminist theory. Like Stephanie, she was using an existing public discourse, an existing writing strategy, to shape and direct her essay. In all, I had received three papers about students' experiences with sexual violence, all three radically different in tone, purpose, and approach. What was going on?

I shouldn't have been surprised—and, in fact, I was only slightly so— after all, these essays were from a "special topics" writing course for first-year students that had been advertised as "Writing About Female Experience" (in the days before feminist arguments about essentialism had prompted me to question such a title). It fulfilled the university's requirement for a second-semester freshman writing course while allowing students to choose a focus. I designed this course as I had my other first-year composition courses: as an investigation of the subject, a sustained class project that, through a sequence of assignments, asked students to write about that seemingly nebulous topic *female experience*. Each assignment asked them to consider this subject from vastly different perspectives—their own experiences, the experiences of classmates, and the ideas of other writers—and then to draw some initial conclusions about what *female experience* means. At the beginning of the course, the students chose the specific subjects they wanted to focus on—such as marriage, sexuality, independence/dependence—and I then organized readings and assignments around those interests. At the students' request, we had just finished a section on sexuality and violence where we had had a rather heated discussion about rape. The twenty-seven women and one man rarely agreed on anything we talked about, so I could never predict what kinds of essay topics would confront me each week. It seemed, though, that these three essays about sexual violence had been triggered by something we had read or that had been said during class discussion.

I had to say something on these drafts. In my comments, my first concern was for the student—how she felt, why she wrote about this, how she wanted me to respond, and what if anything I could do to help her with her writing. These were the same kinds of questions I asked of other students regardless of what their essays were about. Then one day a fellow graduate student asked me how I was going to grade these texts. We were sitting around a large table in the writing center, a gathering point for teaching assistants where we shared our struggles, our teaching ideas, and our questions.

At the time, I explained that I had asked each of these young women how they wanted me to respond to their drafts and how they felt about me evaluating them. All three told me they wanted to work on the pieces as essays, bringing in the writing strategies we were learning in class so their readers might be changed by their essays, prompted to think differently about sexual violence, or to learn how to avoid sexual violence. They wanted the essays evaluated. So I offered these students suggestions and questions that might invite them to revise in several different ways, believing that the very act of trying to shape their stories into language and make meaning of them was important to their development as writers.

However, in the next few years, as I moved into a doctoral program in composition and rhetoric, I still had some lingering questions about whether and how my responses to these student texts were or should be different from my responses to other student essays. While taking a graduate course in research methods and methodology, I decided to research students who wrote about sexual abuse, and I soon discovered how little had been written on the issue. A year after the Writing About Female Experience course ended, I began with Stephanie's essay and those of the other two students from my class and decided to look closely at their writing, to do a textual analysis informed by current research on sexual abuse (primarily from psychology and feminist theory). When I presented my research at the Conference on College Composition and Communication (CCCC) that year, the large audience had many questions, most of which were sensitive to the students' experiences and what I had learned about their writing. I had explored the rather sophisticated moves the writers were making, the ways they were negotiating their identities within the text, and the possible reasons the students wrote about their experiences to begin with. At the end of the session, however, despite my earlier discussion of why evaluation was not the most important issue for us to focus on, someone asked the question again: "So how did you grade these?"

Even if I had told my audience that, as individual essays I might give one an A, the other a B, and the third a B-/C+, I doubt anyone would have been satisfied because this question isn't really about evaluation, about wanting a rubric or set of assurances about standards. It's about anxiety.

I'm Not a Therapist

In my last year as a doctoral student, while I was in the midst of the research for this book, the writing instructors in the program I was studying frequently came by for coffee and a conversation about the students they had who were writing about bodily violence. By this time, I had my own office in the department, so I no longer had to carve out a small space at my dining-room table to do my work. I was now mentoring graduate students, and, during my conversation with them and the full-time instructors, I noticed, not surprisingly, the same kinds of concerns I had had just four or five years before. It seemed that composition theory and research had significantly affected the ways they talked about and taught writing, but not the ways they talked about student essays on painful and personal subjects. Although these teachers were all talking differently now, five years later, about teaching academic discourse, understanding student resistance as "underlife," reading the "big game" essay as part of composing culture and identity, they were still asking the same questions about essays on sexual abuse that my colleagues had been asking years ago. Why hadn't the conversation about these papers been affected by recent developments in the field?

Curiously, within the tightly knit teaching community at the university where I was a graduate student, teachers rarely discuss publicly their struggles with students who write about abuse—experiential knowledge about these student essays is hidden within their offices, rarely integrated into the community discourse. Veteran instructors who mentored new teaching assistants might talk privately about such papers, but I began to perceive that the same kinds of knowledge about these students and their essays were being reproduced every time two people discussed it.

When Jodi, a second-year master's student, knocked on my door to talk with me, she was coming because the director of the writing program had told her I was researching the very questions with which she was struggling. I had begun a study of students who had chosen to write about bodily violence in their composition course, so I was interviewing teachers and students and beginning to draw some conclusions about why students were writing about these issues, what textual patterns I perceived, how their teachers were responding, and what assumptions informed all these questions. One of Jodi's female students had written a draft about the sexual abuse she suffered as a child, and, in the process of reading this draft aloud to her small workshop group (something everyone did during workshop), the young woman had begun to cry and then left the classroom. Jodi wasn't sure whether she had handled the situation well.

"We talked about it before class. I wanted to be sure she understood what she was doing if she took the draft to a more public audience. We talked about the difference between writing that is private and for the self and writing that is more public," Jodi explained. She was sitting forward in her chair as she talked to me, her fingers rubbing her thumb as she talked. "She's been in therapy for several years and felt she was ready to do this. I told her it took courage just to write it down and she needn't feel like she had to share it in a more public way. I was concerned, but I didn't want to tell her not to read the paper because I didn't want to imply that the abuse was something to be ashamed of and kept secret."

"So you're wondering whether you should have responded to her differently, should have been able to prevent what happened in class?" I asked.

"Well, yeah. I'm not a therapist. I don't feel qualified to deal with this, but I don't want to shut her out and tell her never to bring it up again. I mean, how do I respond to a paper like this? Ask her to go into more detail in this paragraph? That doesn't seem right. I can't deal with the paper as a piece of writing. I don't want to hurt her in any way. I'm concerned about her fragility."

As we talked, I told Jodi that she was not alone in the dissonance this student's essay had created for her. Most everyone I have talked with about these essays shares the same conflicts. These types of essays confront teachers with their very *raison d'etre:* If I don't want a student to write about *this* subject, then why do I want her to write about others? On what basis am I deciding what is appropriate in my classroom? In what ways am I using my authority and power? What am I teaching about language and communication? These essays challenge our purposes, our roles, and our power as teachers. Behind questions about evaluation, then, lurks anxiety about what writing teachers do and why they do it. Papers about bodily violence—what I'm defining here as physical or sexual abuse and eating disorders—seem to blur the distinctions between our roles as writing teachers and the roles of therapists. These papers seem to force teachers to define more clearly what they aren't, what issues they are not trained to deal with, and where the boundaries are between their emotional lives and those of their students.

At the same time, these essays confront teachers with conflicts about their ethical and ideological commitments and responsibilities: How does one support the experiences and values of a silenced group and yet respect the personal and private? As Jodi said to me, if she asks the student to write only privately about this issue—or not to write at all—to what extent will she then be part of the conspiracy of silence around abuse? Yet, if she supports the student's desire to talk publicly about it, is she allowing the student to be further exploited—by fellow students, for example, who might shame her by dismissing her experience or not believing it, or by the teacher who might unwittingly silence her with criticism? Jodi's question about how to respond, then, is a complicated one about how power operates in American culture, particularly in terms of what role writing teachers play in supporting or critiquing power structures, both within and outside the classroom. But it is also a question about the responsibility teachers have for how they use their own power.

Some of this power is exercised when a teacher comments on a student paper or talks with the student in conference about it. Like other teachers I've talked with, Jodi is concerned that focusing on style, genre, argument, or detail may be interpreted as insensitivity to the emotional and often traumatic experience the content may describe. As a result, the student may feel dismissed, silenced, or not listened to. The assumption here is that the written product is intimately connected to the student's sense of self in a way that makes her more vulnerable than she would be if she wrote about a sports event, a trip to the mountains, or popular culture. Subjects such as abuse, suicide, death, and divorce, are perceived as more closely connected to a private, more vulnerable sense of self, a self that some believe does not belong in a writing class. To address textual features such as structure in a written piece on these issues is presumably to examine the nonemotional, the abstract, the impersonal. It is, in effect, to examine the ways writers control a paper's content, its unruly tendencies, its tangents, and its vulnerabilities. To ignore them is to ignore, it seems here, one of the objects of a writing course—to teach such means of controlling one's language, defining the boundaries of communication, and making conscious choices about content. In this sense, anxiety about responding to such revealing papers is born out of an impulse—a socially inscribed impulse—to pass on the means of control, to discipline, in the terms Foucault (1978) uses, the unruly and the emotional.

Jodi's questions, then, are not simply questions about practice—What do I say? How do I grade this? Should this student share the essay with her group? They are also questions about the theories that inform Jodi's practice. As writing teachers, we all have a set of theories we rely on as we respond to these essays, theories that are often implicit and seem natural. The kinds of questions Jodi asks challenge her to clarify and reconsider some of those tacit theoretical assumptions that guide her pedagogy. If Jodi's responses seem atheoretical, consider the issue this way: If Jodi's course were shaped by critical pedagogy, seeking to liberate students from oppression, would she have the same concerns? Could a student write about being sexually abused in such a course? Or, if Jodi's purposes were to help students see their experiences as part of larger historical, cultural contexts—as constructed—then how would she respond to this student? I have rarely seen such questions asked about essay topics such as sexual abuse, particularly questions that critically reflect on, or make explicit, the theories behind responses to these essays. In the pages ahead, as I explore some of these questions, I'll argue that student essays about bodily violence—and our responses to them—are like the proverbial canary in a mine: They hint at the gaps in much of our theoretical work. They challenge the limits of postmodern beliefs that reality is constructed, that selves and the physical body are knowable only through language. Psychologists argue, for example, that someone who has been abused has a fragmented sense of identity—an identity postmodern theory celebrates—yet student essays on abuse have rarely been talked about in postmodern terms. Instead, they are often dismissed as products of an expressivist pedagogy or a cultural focus on individual self-expression and confession. This book, then, is as much about the challenges these student essays pose to theoretical knowledge as it is about teachers' practical concerns. These essays and their authors have profoundly changed what I thought I knew. As I share my conclusions and analysis, I hope that we no longer ask *how* to grade an essay about someone who was beaten by her boyfriend but *why* that is a question we would ask.

I suppose it seems obvious why we would ask about grading and responding—teachers are, after all, evaluators, and we can't escape the ethical issues that are raised when a student writes an essay about being beaten and submits it for a grade in her writing class. Even the titles of several recent journal articles on the subject illustrate the important issues:

- "Responding When a Life Depends on It: What to Write in the Margins When Students Self-Disclose" (Marilyn Valentino)
- "Ethical Issues Raised by Students' Personal Writing" (Dan Morgan)
- "Crossing Lines" (Carole Deletiner)
- "The Ethics of Requiring Students to Write About Their Personal Lives" (Susan Swartzlander, Diana Pace, and Virginia Lee Stamler).

As the titles suggest, the articles' purposes are to offer an ethical response to these students and their essays. Except for Deletiner's article, they all provide how-to lists, some with numbered or bulleted suggestions. I have used Valentino's article in my teaching assistant training seminar and in faculty development meetings precisely because she describes concrete, practical strategies that define a teacher's responsibilities within legal and psychotherapeutic terms. New teachers appreciate any straightforward advice that can clarify what seems like a murky and complicated writing or teaching situation.

What strikes me about these articles, however, is the impulse toward closure—posing a problem and then solving it within a handful of pages. Deletiner's piece is one of the few that raises many more questions than it answers, avoiding closure because the questions keep confronting her and her students with contradictions and complexities. She seizes on the boundary-crossing metaphor so prevalent in composition theory and, instead of asking what happens when students cross boundaries with each other and their various cultures, she asks what happens when students and teachers cross their defined *classroom* boundaries. However, as I've talked with graduate teaching assistants, writing faculty, and other academics, I've noticed very little patience with such questions. Instead, there is a tendency to erect boundaries (between teacher and student, writing and therapy, facilitator and evaluator), which is a curious move in the midst of so much postmodern boundary-crossing in the field right now. This impulse toward closure, then, although important, suggests again how much anxiety these essays evoke, especially when we consider the kinds of critical questions we do *not* ask of these papers but that we do of others.

Throughout this book I will try to examine this anxiety. I will explore the answer to two overarching questions:

- What might we learn about our theories and pedagogies from the ways we *read* these students, their essays, and our classrooms?
- What might we learn about our theories and pedagogies from the ways these students *write* their essays?

This means, of course, that I will postpone closure. How we respond to these students is intimately tied to how we understand their texts; their motives; their cultural, familial, and historical contexts, and our own theories of learning and language. Although it is easier and initially more satisfying to follow a list of suggestions such as those Valentino offers, I think our responses to students can be richer and more critically informed when we set aside those answers temporarily and look again at ourselves and our students.

Why Bodily Violence?

I could, of course, research the issues I've raised by looking at any number of student essays that seem particularly personal and private. The teachers in my study, for example, told me that more students wrote about their parents' divorce than about any kind of abuse or eating problem, and essays about divorce can often raise similar kinds of questions for teachers. So why would I focus on students who write about bodily violence?

Because our bodies are not our own anymore.

Or, at least within academic discussions of the body. It is more text than substance, more a product of language than a corporeal presence. These theoretical conversations have rarely been brought to bear on nonliterary writing where the body is a central metaphor or a key character. Throughout graduate school I often heard my colleagues declare that postmodern theory is all well and good to think about, but it has little to do with what happens in their classrooms. As I struggled with this myself, I kept returning to my belief that critical theory need not be alienating or elitist or diametrically opposed to practice. Much of the theory I read described my own sense of the world and I increasingly found it helped me understand and interact with my students more effectively. I began to wonder whether theories on "writing the body" might help me understand my students' writing—and whether their writing could help me understand and further analyze theories on the body.[1] Why *not* see what kind of dialogue might develop in bringing student texts and critical theory together?

A student's essay about physical violence and a textual description of a body ravaged by starvation both capture a central question in feminist theory, the issue of essentialism. The essays themselves make explicit how bodies are written on; understood through language; and shaped by linguistic codes, rhetorical situations, and power struggles. But the subject of the essay, the author's body, has been physically affected, feels pain, and may be in the process of dying. At what point, then, is the body purely text? purely physical? neither? both? Like some feminists, I am unwilling to grant that there is no such thing as man or woman or that biological bodies do not exist as anything other than texts. When I read an essay about a young woman whose boyfriend has trapped her in her dorm room and beaten her repeatedly in spite of her orange belt in karate, I am reading about two people who act on the *beliefs* that there are biological differences between men and women that translate into subordinate power relations, and for whom the pain and blood of the body are real. These young women are read as female and their bodies bear the marks of such a reading. As Lois McNay (1991) argues,

> It is not necessary to posit a single bodily cause of feminine subordination. Once the female sex has come to connote specific feminine characteristics, this "imaginary signification" produces concrete effects throughout diverse social practices. These concrete effects are not the expression of an immutable feminine essence. (128)

If anything, the student essays in this book illustrate the *effects* of essentializing gender and open the possibilities for responding to those effects and the forces that produce them.

Within critiques of essentialism, however, the physical body ceases to exist and becomes instead a collection of social practices and discourses which, as Susan Bordo (1993) points out, "look suspiciously more like 'mind' than 'body'" (35). Bordo's stance on these issues has informed my own reading of these student essays, a position that does not deny biology but is suspicious of locating truth there.

> I view current postmodern theoretical tendencies thoroughly to "textualize" the body . . . as giving a kind of free, creative rein to *meaning* at the expense of attention to the body's material locatedness in history, practice, culture. If the body is treated as pure text, subversive, destabilizing elements can be emphasized and freedom and self-determination celebrated; but one is left wondering, is there a *body* in this text? (38)

Bordo's final question is especially relevant to my own study because if there is no body, then what do we do with pain? with blood? with starvation? As I will illustrate, when students represent in written form the ways they or someone else have violently forced their bodies into pain, they are certainly "writing their bodies," but they are doing that in ways that are bounded by and in dialogue with other discourses privileged in the university. The literal text they produce is one of many interpretations of the violence that they might write, influenced by the immediate context, and those many texts will be continually reconstrued (whether they continue to write about it or not). If as Elaine Scarry (1985) argues, pain is language destroying (19), then these students are most likely in the process of learning to use language again—or certainly in a different way.

When teachers respond to these student essays, they are responding to the body in the text, a body that is associated with emotion, vulnerability, and the student's identity. Because the body is a central subject in these kinds of personal essays, teachers ask questions of the papers they don't often ask of essays about American involvement in Nicaragua, for example, or of a literary analysis of Toni Morrison's *The Bluest Eye*. About those less personal essays, we don't ask, "Why are students writing about these issues? How should a teacher respond? How should pedagogy be changed (if at all)?" These subjects keep the body out of rational university discourse and so we don't think of asking these questions. The student essays in this study, however, challenge us to ask why we would keep the body on the margins of the academy, especially given the contemporary discussions in postmodern critical theory about the body, and why students might bring their bodies into the classroom anyway.

As I'll argue, we need to be aware that the kind of control we think we need—over students, their texts, and ourselves—comes out of anxiety about women's bodies in particular as well as fear of the consequences of unruly emotions and psyches. Our responses to these students, in fact, are more often about our images as teachers than they are about the students themselves.

An Approach to Studying Student Essays About Bodily Violence

Given the decades-long debate in composition studies about the role of the personal in writing instruction, it might seem as if we've examined the issues I have raised with considerable theoretical depth, and I'm not arguing that we have not. What I am suggesting is that we have not asked these theoretical questions of the texts we are theorizing about; we have not asked, What are these students doing in their writings about what we consider such painful subjects? How are their teachers responding? Why are some students choosing to write about these experiences? What influence might the teacher's pedagogy have on this choice? And what do our responses to these papers suggest about the assumptions we make about emotion, the personal, the private, and language?

To pursue these questions, I asked instructors, teaching assistants, and tenure-track faculty at a northeastern research university (of approximately ten thousand students, predominantly white and middle class) if they would be willing to refer students to me who had chosen to write about sexual abuse, physical abuse, or eating disorders. None of the students were asked or required to write about these subjects. I then interviewed both students and the writing faculty and conducted in-class research for almost ten weeks of a fall semester, following two students through their first-year writing course. The primary materials for this study, then, are student essays; interviews with students, teachers, campus counselors; and observations of two composition classrooms, the weekly staff meetings for teachers, and various campus activities. I received a total of twenty-five essays, twenty-three from white women between the ages of eighteen and twenty-two and two from women over forty. The research methods I used, while all qualitative, depended on the choices of my participants: ensuring students' privacy was my first concern,[2] and not everyone was willing to be interviewed or to have me observe their classroom, so each of the chapters of this book, while focused on a specific type of bodily violence, also uses a different research and interpretive method depending on the material I was able to use. Chapter 2, which explores student essays on sexual abuse, for example, uses historical research and textual analysis, in part because none of those students was able to interview with me. However, Chapter 4, which looks at essays on physical abuse, draws from classroom ethnography as well as textual analysis in large part because the student was willing to be interviewed and observed.

Chapter 1 begins by considering the criticisms of and assumptions about students who write about bodily violence, their teachers, and their pedagogical context. Frequently, it is assumed that students will only write about these subjects in expressivist classrooms, writing them as confessions or narratives with little critical reflection or framework. I unpack several of these different arguments in the work of Lester Faigley (1992), Susan Swartzlander et al. (1993), and Kathleen Pfeiffer (1993; an article written in response to Carole Deletiner's "Crossing Lines"). I look particularly at the assumptions these writers make about students, about the purposes of university writing courses, about teachers' uses of power, and about the writers' constructions of emotion in relation to these assumptions. I argue that social construction theory seems not to apply when it comes to understanding these student texts, despite the highly ideological nature of their subjects. Often the students themselves are pathologized and the *effects* of their trauma interpreted by writing teachers as destabilizing and individual, not as socially constituted and political. Frequently, teachers and theorists read these essays through psychotherapeutic discourse and romantic ideologies, regardless of whether the students' texts warrant such a reading or the teachers' pedagogies are in fact some version of expressivism.

I then offer an alternative understanding of *why* students will write about bodily violence in the writing classroom. I turn to the sociological theories of Erving Goffman (1963) and Peter Stearns (1994) to explain why students will write about such traumatic and private experiences to people they barely know. Many students who turn in their essays before they have built a relationship with their teacher may do so because in twentieth-century America strangers have become the most likely receivers of emotional expressions that are considered too threatening to share with intimates. Students who have suffered some form of bodily violence are stigmatized in our culture, and they have limited options for managing those identities (as Goffman might put it), especially when contemporary culture has defined particular emotions (anger, jealousy, guilt) as dangerous to work environments, friends, and family relationships. I argue in Chapter 1 that students are not confessing sins but are participating in one avenue offered them for normalizing their sense of identity—writing in a classroom of strangers about a stigmatizing event, illustrating their normalcy and protecting their intimates from the threat of their emotions.

In Chapter 2 I look more closely at three student essays about sexual abuse, analyzing the rhetorical choices these writers make; the selves they construct; and the discursive conventions they adopt from popular culture, their experiences with school writing, and their reading from academic texts. Having found that students write about bodily violence regardless of pedagogy, I consider these essays not from the framework of expressivist pedagogies but from those of postmodern and critical pedagogies. What would it mean for a student to historically contextualize her experience, for example? After situating these essays within a historical tradition of women writing about sexual abuse, I ask what these student texts can tell us about pedagogies that seek to liberate students or decenter their sense of identity, suggesting that the decentered identity of a sexually abused student is not the kind of identity postmodern pedagogy seems to want to engender. Some kinds of fragmented identities are considered too unstable to be in a university classroom, no matter how postmodern or ideological they are.

In Chapter 3 I illustrate how students use various textual conventions and dominant interpretations of eating disorders to control the identity they present in their essays, a persona that tries to push aside the fragmented identity their eating disorders manifest. As in Chapter 2, I use textual analysis to interpret student essays, describing the patterns I noticed in how students wrote about their experiences, but I also explore one teacher's response to a student's successive revisions of her essay on anorexia. In addition, I offer both historical context for the meaning of eating disorders and current academic arguments. Using the work of philosopher Alison Jaggar (1989), I illustrate how these students, like those in Chapter 2, are not only adopting various discourses but are beginning to build what Jaggar calls a "critical social theory" from the knowledge they are building with their affective and rational responses. At the same time, I read these essays as testimonies to the ways culture and individuals inscribe women's bodies, teasing out the intersections of power and ideology in these various writing practices.

Unlike the previous two chapters, Chapter 4 focuses on one student and the latter two-thirds of her semester in a first-year writing class. Like Chapters 2 and 3, this chapter closely analyzes the student's first course essay—about being beaten by her boyfriend—and develops a more detailed and complex picture of a student, her relationship with her teacher and classmates, and her teacher's critical pedagogy. Although this young woman does not revise her essay about physical abuse, her other course essays address physical violence in different ways—the civil unrest in Ireland and the content of rap music (particularly gang violence and treatment of women)—and her anger takes a different shape as the term progresses. Anger also unpredictably becomes part of the classroom conversations, and the instructor pushes against the students' moves to assert dominant emotion standards about anger; that is, "Don't bother me with it, don't use it to argue a point." In the process, the teacher models how anger can become part of building knowledge, constructing an argument, and becoming critical of culture, using all these processes in writing to effect social change. The young woman who is the focus of this case study comes to see anger and written expressions of anger not as egocentric self-absorption, self pity, or therapy, but as ways of seeing the world that need to be respected, listened to, and acted upon.

As I say in the Conclusion, this study builds an argument for listening—to the words of students as they make and unmake themselves; write and rewrite culture; consider and reconsider language, power, and truth. Bodily violence has been written and talked about throughout Western history, in distinctly different ways and for distinctly different purposes, even though it has also been suppressed, obscured, and used to victimize and exploit. When our students write about their experiences, they do so from a number of different perspectives that are not limited to pop-psychology or talk-show discourses. One of the most important conclusions of this study is that a writing teacher needs to begin by first being skeptical of his or her own impulses to read these student texts only through psychotherapeutic discourses—and thus to understand the teacher's role as examining the body and psyche of students in the process of examining their texts. Although I offer suggestions for how to respond to student essays on bodily violence, I do so hesitantly, wary of how much more I need to learn. These student essays have much to teach us about the paradoxes and gaps in composition theory, and my hope is that this research offers an alternative way of reading these essays that will generate future studies.

1

This Weepy World of Confessions

I remember reading Carole Deletiner's 1992 article "Crossing Lines" as soon as my *College English* issue arrived, anxious to find an alternative way of understanding these students and their texts. It was one of the first articles I'd read about students' personal and painful writing that was more essayistic than academic, that posed more questions than it answered, and that implicitly questioned many teachers' first responses to send such students to the counseling center. In it, Deletiner describes the painful issues her students write about: one writes about the effect of his parents' divorce on his sense of the world and his distrust of people, another writes about her father beating her mother, and another about being part of a bombing that killed a homeless person. "Do *I* elicit these personal revelations from students?" Deletiner asks, "Or is it something about the process of writing itself that unleashes the anger and the pain that appear in my students' writing, as well as in my own?" (813–14). As she describes her relationships with each student, Deletiner asks the same kinds of questions Jodi is asking (in Chapter 1): Am I an effective teacher if I cross the line between student and teacher? Who benefits from ignoring the feelings and histories of the students in the classroom? Should I have asked this student about her experience? What are they learning about writing?

They don't/won't/can't stop writing (and I don't want them to) and the feelings and the pain drip off the edges of their pages, only stopped by the comments I write where I tell them about my own experiences as an estranged member of a dysfunctional family, a terrified student who never spoke in four years of college, a student now grappling with whether or not I can take another day in graduate school that feels just like the unaccepting home in which I grew up. My fear, rage, and comradeship tumble out onto the margins of their papers in the comments I write to them. This makes some of my colleagues nervous. It even made one cry. (813)

If the "Comment and Response" section of *College English* is any indication, Deletiner's article seemed to make other people nervous, as well. Kathleen Pfeiffer's (1993) response, in particular, questions Deletiner's approaches and the role that pain needs to play in the writing classroom. "How does engaging in 'true confessions' help students become better writers or thinkers?" she asks (670). Pfeiffer views the writing classroom as a place to teach students how to "fluently and expressively speak the language of the university" (669), a job where teachers are not therapists, where it is misleading to create the expectation in students that professors are "comrades . . . sharing pain" (669), where "sophisticated communicative ability" (671) is not served by egocentric personal disclosures. Her final paragraph rather searingly describes the student body who writes (or, it is implied here, is encouraged to write) such essays in Deletiner's college composition course:

> Throughout [Ms. Deletiner's] essay, we see powerful influences from the cult of the victim, the ethos of the twelve-step program, the mentality of the chronically dysfunctional. Ms. Deletiner *is,* in the end, teaching her students something in the classes she describes—but it is not good writing skills. It is not effective communication. It is, in fact, just the opposite. What she teaches in this weepy world of confessions and revelations is a fundamentally egocentric sort of self-absorption. Such teeth-gnashing and soul-baring might help a student recover his or her lost inner child, but it will do little in the way of developing a sophisticated communicative ability, analytical skills, or a clear-sighted understanding of the world. The purpose of the university is to look out at the world, to wonder at what we see, to understand its meaning and purpose. None of this can be accomplished when a student is taught only to look inward and cry. (671)

Despite her assertion that we needn't choose between either personal or academic writing, that assignments "which ask students to draw together personal narrative and critical analysis elicit marvelous essays" (670), Pfeiffer figures "emotional" writing as threatening to the purpose of the university, as a "radical destruction of community and communication" (671); it seems, in fact, to be so unrelated to the real work of the university as to be laughable, worthy of caricature. Such writing is only valid (and yet still not valid at all) within the context of popular culture, in twelve-step programs, popular psychological understandings of the inner child, victimization, and dysfunction. It is difficult to read anything other than contempt for this culture in Pfeiffer's response, further emphasizing the implicit hierarchy of high and low culture, the academic and the popular, reason and emotion. The personal and the emotional are only worthy of ridicule; can only be used in egocentric, solipsistic ways; and are not subject to the same kinds of critical analysis that reason and ideas are. Teachers are obligated to keep threatening emotions at bay, to reinforce cultural dictates about how emotion can be expressed and understood. If they don't, the very foundation of university education will come undone.

As one kind of response to student essays about painful experiences, Pfeiffer's comments indicate how ideologically charged these essays are: Students and their essays on these subjects are characterized as threatening to the order and purpose of academic values as well as weak and in need of both discipline and protection. Ultimately, the teacher's power is being preserved in this discourse on emotion, the student is being disciplined into her subordinate power position, and the larger structures of power in our culture are reinscribed. As we will see shortly, this agenda is implied in some of the other work in the field that addresses these kinds of student essays, but because we haven't yet fully developed a consciousness about how writing classes educate the emotions, it is often difficult to reflect critically on a response that seems so natural.

In Pfeiffer's response, for example, she taps into a cultural conversation about "the cult of the victim" (671), a backlash against recent therapeutic approaches to sexual abuse, physical abuse, and other experiences in which an individual is victimized. Although not the only response that may feel natural to teachers, Pfeiffer's argument draws from cultural discourses that have become commonplaces, so familiar to readers that brief phrases can stand in for larger concepts and philosophical warrants. As David Bartholomae notes, a commonplace is "a culturally or institutionally authorized concept or statement that carries with it its own necessary elaboration" (1985, 137). All writers use such commonplaces, of course, but in this case I'm proposing we ask why *these* are the commonplaces a teacher might draw on to interpret a student's essay about a painful experience. What do they tell us about how emotion is constructed and who benefits from that?

At the root of Pfeiffer's argument is a belief that emotions cannot be subject to the same kind of Western rationality to which we expect other ideas to be subject; they can only be known through individual analysis, not sociocultural critiques. This is a fairly common assumption. As public a forum as the "Sally Jesse Raphael" television show is, for instance, when a guest shares a painful and private story—let's say about the incest she suffered, which has led her to accept her husband's multiple affairs—few people on the show ask how power relationships are served because a woman feels enraged at her abuser; few ask what this rage tells us about our culture, or why the audience might ridicule her because she expresses her anger on TV. I'm sure the audience would laugh if someone asked questions like these. Many cultural critics have analyzed how such talk shows function in our society, exploring some of these questions, but I want to emphasize a key point: The audience for such a show rarely asks these kinds of critical questions of the guest because they would seem unnatural, not the way most people talk about emotions or subjects we designate as personal. Emotions are not subject to academic, ideological criticism; they are protected from it. In the West, we believe that emotions are psychobiological—that is, not products of culture, but of our physiology—and so we can only understand and analyze them if we adopt self-referential explorations such as Thoreau's self-reflection or Freud's psychoanalysis. As my students might put it, questions about culture and power would seem like "some wild tangent" that only an academic would find the least bit interesting.

For years, though, anthropologists have been studying the ways different cultural groups define and express their emotions, illustrating how an emotion such as anger, for example, is defined quite differently in some cultural groups than it is in the United States, while other societies have emotions not understood in the West (Jaggar 1989, 150; Lutz and Abu-Lughod 1990, 3).[1] In Japan, a man who is angry with a friend will not do what an American might, go and talk to the friend about whatever has made him angry or even get involved in a fight. Instead, a Japanese man will avoid any confrontation and stay silent, smiling at the target of his anger (Cornelius 1996, 155). In Japan, this behavior is considered appropriate; in America, it would be considered avoidance and denial, a sure way to create a dysfunctional relationship. In each culture, anger is interpreted quite differently, shaped by social rules and values. Anthropologists have also found that some groups have emotions that do not translate to dominant Western emotionology. For instance, in an island society in the Philippines, the Ilongot, anger is only part of the emotion *liget*. To have anger (*si liget*)

> means that they are neither shy nor fearful, not unduly quiet or reserved. *Liget* points in human life to a readiness to be "different" or take offense, . . . to stubbornness and conviction, but also to the fact that one is quick-moving, youthful, active, . . . and "tied up tight" or "strong." (Rosaldo 1980, 45)

Although an emotion might have a biological expression, the social group names the physical feeling, and that name—like anger or *liget*—carries with it a host of rules for when and how and why it can be used. The meanings and uses of emotion can tell us a great deal about the social relationships in a culture: the distribution of power, gender roles, and definitions of deviance (Lutz and Abu-Lughod 1990, 11). In the West, it is less acceptable to express anger at one's father while giving his eulogy than it is to do so while visiting with friends over a beer or coffee. In addition, expressing that anger by punching someone out at a bar or beating one's spouse is less appropriate than channeling it into something like football or kickboxing.

In American discourse, anger has been gendered and talked about in terms of control—those who can control anger appropriately (through football, for example) are seen as more normal than those who can't (like those who beat their wives or kill out of jealousy and rage). Often in American culture emotions are construed as weak, dangerous, and irrational, and thus those who can transcend or control them are considered more powerful than those who cannot. In this sense, Pfeiffer has the best interests of her students in mind: She wants to give them a language of power, and that language will not allow uncontrolled emotions. An academic analysis of sexual abuse, for example, is considered more scholarly, intelligent, and appropriate for university compositions than one written from the perspective of the abused person. Same subject, different means of controlling the personal and emotional. Here emotions are intimately linked with ideology and power:

> A "paradox of will" seems consistently to attend dominating relationships—whether those of gender, race, or class—as the subordinate other is ideologically painted as weak (so as to need protection or discipline) and yet periodically as threatening to break the ideological boundary in riot or hysteria. . . . Given its definition as nature, at least in the West, emotion discourses may be one of the most likely and powerful devices by which domination proceeds. (Lutz 1990, 76)

Feminists have argued this point for years, of course: When the more powerful are trying to control the emotions of the less powerful, what is at issue is not the biological basis for the emotion ("any woman would feel this way; it's in the genes") but the cultural interpretation of it. How is this person expected to express this emotion? Why? Who benefits from that interpretation? To see emotions as biologically based, then, ignores one of the more subtle and extensive ways socialization and power works.

What does this mean for how we read student essays about bodily violence? As a field, composition has certainly explored the ways writing instruction is a form of discipline, but it has not yet fully explored its role in disciplining emotion. A few theorists, for example Lynn Worsham (1992–1993) and Richard Miller (1996), using Pierre Bourdieu, have argued that emotions are permeated with ideology—that feeling disgust or compassion when reading about someone being abused supports or critiques or complicates different power systems in our culture. Feminists have asserted this for many years, illustrating, for example, how women's anger has been renamed with such words as whining, shrillness, complaining, bitchiness, all denigrating women's anger so it can be dismissed and a woman's credibility can be undermined. It matters a great deal who gets to express which emotions, in what contexts, and for what purposes. Writing classrooms participate in shaping our language about emotion. The intense debates about the role of the personal in the teaching of writing suggest that some of us feel much is at stake in how emotion—which is linked with the personal—is disciplined.

Discourses on Emotion in Composition Studies

I will never forget the first time I cried in front of my class. I was a second-year doctoral student and one of the new teaching assistants was coming in to observe me. We were focusing on revision that week, and I had come up with a new assignment, which asked the students to (1) look at three successive drafts of some student essays and draw conclusions about what it means to revise (which they would discuss in groups) and (2) read Nancy Sommers's "Revision Strategies of Student Writers and Experienced Adult Writers" and compare the conclusions they had reached with hers. I had done this in the past with fairly good success. The students were challenged to name some revision strategies before reading a so-called authority's suggestions, and by the time they finished with Sommers's piece, they realized they had drawn similar conclusions. Not this day. Only a stalwart few wanted to talk about the article. The rest sighed heavily, their chins sinking to their palms, their eyes pretending to scan the printed text before them. I asked open-ended questions. I got nothing.

I was generally stressed that day because I had papers of my own to finish and things weren't going too well at home. I was behind on returning student papers. I was overwhelmed. I wanted—needed—this discussion to work. But it obviously wasn't, so I tried to make a joke and let them go early. Then, much to my surprise, in utter frustration, I began to cry. I was mortified. Only my family had seen this little quirk of mine, crying when I'm so angry I could explode. To do this publicly was humiliating. As my students quietly filed out, I was turned away from them, facing a window. Then one of them came up to me and said, "I don't understand what you want us to do for tomorrow—can you explain it to me?"

I learned that day how out of control I could become when I tried hard to control class discussion and to present myself as a capable, skilled teacher.

In trying so hard I actually undermined the very thing I was trying to prove. As a student said in her course evaluation, "She shouldn't cry in front of the class because it weakens her authority." I threatened the boundaries between student and teacher that day simply by crying, and my students responded by adhering to the unspoken rules about when, where, and by whom certain emotions could be expressed: Some of them squirmed; some of them completely ignored the whole scene, pretending it hadn't happened; some of them pointed out what my behavior should look like; and a small handful stayed after to ask if I was okay. Even my own shame at crying in such a public space had the effect of pushing me back onto my side of the boundaries. They wanted me to return to my professional role as teacher, to restore the power balance in our relationship; in short, they were trying to discipline me, but to all of us it felt like a natural response to inappropriate behavior.

This is the same kind of anxiety I mentioned in the Introduction, an anxiety about how an emotion is expressed and the ways it threatens the relationships of power among students and teachers—only in the case of this study it is the *students* who are making a gesture that seems inappropriate. How individuals in the field respond to this expression will vary, of course, but at the heart of the response will usually be a concern about the teacher's role and the use of power, as well as a criticism of the pedagogy that is assumed to invite such texts.

In their 1993 article in *The Chronicle of Higher Education,* Susan Swartzlander, Diana Pace, and Virginia Lee Stamler open by using sexual abuse narratives as an example of how university professors are violating their students' privacy under the auspices of teaching writing:

> Imagine a university professor asking a student to reveal in class the most intimate details of a childhood trauma like sexual or physical abuse. We would all agree that such behavior would be shockingly unprofessional. And yet, every day in college classrooms and faculty offices across the country, students receive writing assignments requiring inappropriate self-revelation. (B1)

The authors criticize the teachers who behave like "frustrated therapists" because they violate acceptable boundaries between students and teachers, potentially hurting the vulnerable students involved: "When the boundaries between professional and personal are blurred by turning personal revelation into course content, paternalism may thrive in the guise of professional guidance when the professor is male and the student female" (B1). Because those who have been abused "often have difficulty understanding appropriate limits in relationships" and "allow[ing] themselves to be emotionally vulnerable with others, course requirements that demand self-disclosure can intensify a student's feelings of abuse and powerlessness" (B1). Although acknowledging that not all personal writing needs to be foresworn, the authors emphasize that too often autobiographical writing is intrusive, shifts more control over to the teacher, and stirs up memories that students may not be prepared to deal with. Each of these concerns emerge from values familiar to the audience for this article, values that regulate the expression and use of emotion in a social situation. The explicit agenda of Swartzlander et al. is to convince teachers to change their behaviors so the system can be maintained.

It is the students' behaviors that need to be controlled, however, and one of the best ways to do this is to criticize the pedagogy that informs what teachers do. Swartzlander et al. imply that essays about subjects such as sexual abuse only occur in classrooms where teachers ask for personal writing. They assume, like many of us, that students' painful experiences will only be evoked if students are asked to write directly about themselves. I certainly did when I began this study. But this assumption suggests that a history course studying racial oppression, for example, or a women's studies course reading about domestic violence will not also recall similar memories and emotions for students, regardless of whether the students are asked specifically to write about the issues (which many of them are). If such memories and experiences only surfaced when talked about directly, then repressing memories should make the abused functional and healthy—which the authors take pains to point out is not the case. This argument is based on a belief that individuals can be emotionally and ideologically removed from ideas or abstractions, that the closer and more directly one gets to the source of the pain (a core self, perhaps?), the weaker and more uncontrollable the thoughts and emotions. However, writing teachers, it is assumed, are not trained to deal with uncontrollable emotions and ideas—which brings us back to the claim that writing instruction needs to focus on nonpersonal, cultural, academic issues, keeping the mind/body, emotion/reason split intact and the disciplines of writing and therapy in their institutional places. As Lutz and Abu-Lughod (1990) suggest about discourses on emotion, Swartzlander et al.'s argument constructs the student who is writing about something personal—or, more specifically, emotional—as both vulnerable to more powerful teachers and yet threatening to university education.

The theoretical debates in the field of composition reflect a similar contradiction, although they locate a student's vulnerability and the source of her threat quite differently than do Swartzlander et al. Students' personal and emotional writing has been central to much of the scholarly debate in the last two decades, raising concerns about how teachers use their power to shape students' identities and affect their relationship to competing ideological concerns. Asking students to write about their lives (which is assumed to be the

focus of expressivist pedagogies) is not only more appropriate in the therapist's office, it is also ideologically suspect, part of the bourgeois sentimental-
ism and individuality of which writing teachers need to be critical. Writing
about personal experiences encourages a student to discover a unified, coherent, ahistorical and acultural self, a writing task that asks the student to turn
herself into an object of analysis. So while it may seem that the teacher exer-
cises less power and control when she receives papers on personal or emotional subjects, empowering the student more, Lester Faigley (1992) argues
that the teacher is still exercising institutional power more than he or she may
realize. Writing about the self in college composition, Faigley says,

> might be viewed as part of a much larger technology of confession for the
> production of truth in Western societies—witness Foucault's description of
> the frequency of confession in legal, medical, and educational practice as
> well as in family and love relations and even in the popular media. Foucault
> argues that this production of truth is deeply embedded within relations of
> power where teachers are receivers of confessions as part of the institutional
> exercise of power. (23)

Students are then socialized into subordinate power positions when sharing a
self that is considered private, making them vulnerable to a teacher's power
and control over them, as well as to the power of the state. At the same time,
when a student is encouraged to truthfully represent her experience, the
teacher is reinforcing a liberal humanist ideal of the self, which has been the
source of oppression for many marginalized groups. This liberal humanist
self is threatening to the political project of many academics, many of whom
argue that disrupting oppression and the power relationships that create it
begins with disrupting students' beliefs in a unitary self.

Depending on which argument against expressivism one looks at, students who write about their personal lives can also be threatening to the
goals of a university education, which expects students to be able to write
critically and adopt academic conventions with their field's discourse community. Again because reason and emotion are separate from each other, the
personal and emotional are deviant modes of expression within the larger
goals of higher education.

In analyzing the discourses on emotion in composition studies here, I've
been focusing only on the *criticisms* of students' personal writing because I
most frequently hear these criticisms when I give presentations on my work
or talk informally with colleagues. As anxious as I am in these situations to
share what I've found about the textual patterns these students use or the multiple discourses they adopt, the most common assumption about these texts
is that they are solicited by teachers who use an expressivist approach. (I have

found, though, that these essays emerge as well from courses that focus on critical pedagogy or social construction theories.) This turn to pedagogy as an explanation for essays that seem inappropriate is both a way to discipline teachers and students and to turn away from the ways these essays challenge our ideological and pedagogical commitments. The ethics of autobiographical writing are not an issue because of the assignments, the pedagogy, or the course content. Rather, they are an issue because some students have experienced trauma, something that places them outside the normal functions of a university. Without the effects of oppression and marginalization, would such writing assignments cause so much anxiety? As Cinthia Gannett (1992) points out, critics

> appear to be more concerned that children might be *writing* about sexual or physical abuse, than about the abuse itself. . . . If some of the student journal entries were uncomfortable for [readers] to read, think how terrifying they must have been to write, and worse, to live. One must ask whose privacy we really protect when we deny students the right to address these topics, and whose interests it serves to maintain the traditional taboo on these subjects. (39)

Our concern with pedagogical explanations—and solutions—obscures the fact that someone was abused, as well as the cultural and historical contexts that make such abuse possible.

Pedagogical explanations, then, while important, misdirect our attention. In addition, they can obscure a contradiction within many postmodern critiques of so-called expressivist pedagogies. Let me explain. When my student Stephanie wrote her essay about her incest, it can be argued she was reinscribing a unified, liberal humanist self, focusing only on her experience, trying to write about it as honestly as she could. She wasn't critiquing gender roles or taking an academic approach to the subject. Although she was making an argument, her evidence was drawn primarily from her experience not from the published articles and essays we had been reading or from library research. However, her essay's subject was not only the abuse and her recovery but also the fragmented identity that occurred as a result of the abuse. She literally represents this by splitting herself into two characters: herself and a friend who helps her come to terms with the abuse and her self-destructive behavior. Even though Stephanie may have been searching through her writing to construct a unified identity, the self on the page is not a liberal humanist one; it is quite a postmodern self, aware that meanings shift depending on who is in control, aware that the dominant beliefs that had grounded her world before no longer apply, aware that her self has been shattered into pieces.

It is easy to ignore the postmodern nature of this self because the phrase *sexual abuse* has become one of those commonplaces that is so naturally associated with psychotherapy (or the cult of the victim, depending on your perspective) that psychotherapy becomes the dominant lens through which to interpret it. I don't want to dismiss the importance of that perspective. However, I do want to emphasize that being abused is not only a psychological trauma. Sexual abuse is a trauma created in part by cultural and historical beliefs about gender and violence: about men's control over women, about the weak and uncontrolled nature of women's bodies and emotions, about the appropriateness of using violence to solve problems. So, if a writing classroom can be a site for critiquing power relations, for contextualizing experiences and beliefs within historical discourses, then it can be a site to analyze and contextualize one's experience with bodily violence. If such abuse is only associated with psychological trauma, it is too easily separated from other legitimate discourses in a writing classroom, it is too easily assumed the writer is invested in a liberal humanist self, and it is too easy to ignore current theory on the students' experiences from sociology, feminism, or cultural studies. All of this makes me wonder whether some postmodern selves are more privileged in the writing classroom than others.

For composition, then, debates about the role of the personal and emotional in a writing classroom are debates about social control, particularly control of less powerful students. Students writing about sexual abuse are often constructed as both vulnerable and in need of protection (especially from professors) and yet threatening to the ideological purposes a writing class should support. When critics link personal writing (such as writing about bodily violence) with emotion, expressivist pedagogies, and liberal humanist ideology, they may point out how beliefs about emotion support unified and individuated selves, but they seem implicitly to reinforce the belief that emotions are outside culture, untouched by ideology, not subject to critical reflection, and able to render people vulnerable. When it comes to emotion, social construction theories seem not to apply.

In the next few chapters, I will look more closely at the selves these students are creating in their texts and how they challenge some of the assumptions most frequently made about them. To respond ethically to these students, we need to reflect first on our beliefs about them and their experiences. Until we do, we will continue to focus most of our attention on ourselves, not our students, and we will continue to see their texts through psychotherapeutic discourse and worry about the boundaries between ourselves and therapists, only seeing the students as vulnerable and unstable. These are important concerns, but they obscure the other equally important moves students are making that demand that we take them more seriously.

But Why in My Classroom?: Composing Normal Identities

Students told me a lot of surprising things during our interviews, but one recurring theme struck me: Almost every one of them had requested that their teacher treat their essay about bodily violence like any other essay in the course. Many of them wanted their drafts read by their group members and hoped to get concrete, helpful feedback about where to develop, where to clarify, what direction to go. When the student Jodi was concerned about asked Jodi to help her with her draft in this way, Jodi was surprised. She hadn't expected the student to be ready to have her experience scrutinized on the sentence level, but the student felt strongly that she wanted other people to understand her point. Why might that be a choice she would make? To write about an issue such as sexual abuse is risky at best, no matter how persuasive my earlier analysis might be. It stigmatizes the student who might otherwise pass for "normal." So why reveal such a private experience?

According to Erving Goffman (1963), all of us learn strategies for contending with our culture's dominant beliefs about what is normal, learning rhetorical skills in how to control information about ourselves that won't threaten relationships (57). As Goffman illustrates, cultural beliefs about what is "normal" and what is "stigmatized" are culturally constructed, and I use his terms with the same understanding. When an individual knows a part of her identity stigmatizes her in the eyes of others, she can try to conceal it (if it isn't visible) or she might feel compelled to disclose it to others. But most often when someone decides to tell others about a stigma—being abused, being an alcoholic—that person does so because a group has been formed around it—for example, a group for Adult Survivors of Child Sexual Abuse or Alcoholics Anonymous—one that publishes material about the issue or creates social activities designed to educate others. We could certainly interpret the growing materials about abuse and eating disorders as one stage in the "management" of these stigmatized identities (as Goffman phrases it). Because talk about these issues is so pervasive on campus, in the news, on television, in movies, and on the radio, most people have at least passing knowledge about the various theories on these subjects, and this knowledge, however contradictory it may be, has changed the ways victims and witnesses can now speak. Using the word *survivor* instead of *victim,* for example, changes an individual's subject position and offers a set of interpretations that critique dominant ways of stigmatizing abuse experiences. Survivors may then act from a sense of strength that a victim may not. Within such a context, Goffman argues, people are often persuaded they should be "above" passing, and part of this process is often disclosing how one is part of this stigmatized group (100–101) (one of the steps, for example, in twelve-step recovery programs is to tell others that one is an alcoholic or drug addict). But a person often shares this information according to a "disclosure etiquette": one "admits his [or her] own failing in a matter of fact way, supporting the assumption that those present are above such concerns while preventing them from trapping themselves into showing that they are not" (101).

When some students use the writing classroom as a place to share an experience that the dominant culture defines as outside the norm, those students are using the writing classroom as space to become fuller members of groups who share their particular stigma, adding to the body of knowledge others like them and associated with them have produced. As a disclosure, the writing constructs a well-adjusted individual who has transcended the shame of his or her difference—shame that has been imposed by those of us who believe we are normal. So, when a student chooses to write about an experience of bodily violence as a researched essay, a genre most privileged in college classrooms, that student is managing an unaccepted identity with discourses that normalize it and make it acceptable for an academic audience. In fact, as I illustrate in the following chapters, many of the students and their essays suggest that normalizing is one of their motivations.

As the vehement objections to writing about such subjects in college indicate, however, so-called normals will never really accept someone who reveals him- or herself to be deviant. Instead, Goffman asserts, the person who has divulged a "disgrace" is implicitly expected to assume a "phantom normalcy," an identity that accepts the norm but does not demand the full acceptance from normals that others like them might receive. Someone whom the culture might consider "other" must still assume the role of an acceptable identity so fully "that [she or he] can perform this self in a faultless manner to an edgy audience that is half-watching him [or her] in terms of another show" (Goffman 1963, 122). As I pointed out earlier, a young woman who has shared her experience with abuse immediately changes the relationships with her teacher and peers because she has disturbed the default assumption that everyone is normal—that is, not abused—and writes about normal subjects. To demand the same acceptance she had when her social identity was viewed as normal is to demand too much. When the stigmatized assumes the role of a well-adjusted normal (I'm cured, I'm emotionally stable, I accept myself and realize I was not to blame, I am beautiful the way I am) and thus doesn't push her acceptance too far, she ensures that

> the unfairness and pain of having to carry a stigma will never be presented to [normals]; it means that normals will not have to admit to themselves how limited their tactfulness and tolerance is; and it means that normals

can remain relatively uncontaminated by intimate contact with the stigma-tized, relatively unthreatened in their identity beliefs. (Goffman 1963, 121)

When a student writes, then, about being abused or about starving her own body, she is threatening the relationship of power in the classroom and the as-sumed identities of her audience. She is, in Goffman's terms, presenting the members of her audience with the possibility of their own wounded or un-acceptable identities, of their own stigmas that are otherwise concealed by beliefs about normal social identities and deviant ones. To repress essays about bodily violence becomes another way to maintain these dichotomies. The fact that many of the students in my study tend to claim they are "cured" or self-accepting now, and often adopt the language of academic study to rep-resent and argue for their own experience, suggests the composition class-room has become, in part, a space for composing and controlling identities that have been constructed as "unacceptable."[2]

Even So, I Really Don't Want to Deal with This . . .

Disclosing something like sexual abuse or an eating disorder in a university writing class inevitably changes the social relationships of everyone involved. Although most of the teachers in my study were supportive and encourag-ing of these students, a few of them wondered about what it was costing them emotionally. Some of them described themselves as feeling "drained," and "worn thin" after conferencing with a student who was writing about a painful, personal subject. Even when a student's readers (both teacher and peers) were sensitive and understanding in responding to her essay, many of them still felt uncomfortable, sad, or ambivalent. A few teachers who were generally burned out from teaching seventy-five to one hundred students, holding nontenured status, and earning relatively low pay said, "I'm having enough trouble deal-ing with my own life; I don't have the energy or the time to deal with my stu-dents' traumas."

I didn't realize until I started doing some reading in the field of emotion studies that what I've described is only a recent phenomenon, a perspective on emotion that began to develop in the 1920s. The "feeling rules" in American culture shifted around this time, particularly when it came to defining how one should deal with and respond to emotional intensity (such as anger, grief, jealousy). Although a frequent stereotype of a Victorian is that of a tightly laced, sour-faced, and proper man or woman, sociologist Peter Stearns (1994) suggests that Victorians didn't repress their emotions so much as divert them into "more productive" avenues. Although Victorians were not fond of ex-cesses in emotion, they believed that passionate feelings had purposes, that emotional vigor could be expressed appropriately if one had been taught how to do so: "Many a tightly dressed, respectable young man or woman could pour out his or her passion with no sense of contradiction—indeed, their physical rigors could be endured precisely because the emotional outlets seemed so much more important" (56).[3]

By the twentieth century, however, certain emotions were considered too negative and not useful at all. Emotions such as anger, fear, grief, and jealousy were now "good versus bad rather than good versus dangerous-but-useful" (96). If a person's anger made someone uncomfortable or demanded that someone else respond, then it was defined as bad and dangerous (96), both for the individual and for those around him or her. Although the twentieth century saw new freedoms in dress, sexuality, and manners, threatening emotions became the targets of a different kind of repression (95). The word "cool," Stearns suggests, conveys how twentieth-century individuals were expected to present themselves, as restrained, laid-back, and nonchalant: "Cool has become an emotional mantle, sheltering the whole personality from emotional excess" (1).

Cool was necessary because it protected other people. The concern was less about the individual's emotions and more about how those emotions might disturb others. Strong emotional expression threatened the harmony of groups (such as workers) and worked against individual control (190). In addition, emotions were beginning to be linked to bodily threats—to health problems such as heart disease and ulcers (227). If one seemed to lose control of one's temper, for example, such expression not only affected one's health, but it demonstrated an immaturity (245) and individual failing that needed "remediation" (230). It also potentially threatened job loyalty and "'more authentic' personal relationships" (246). People could vent emotions— "identify and verbalize" them—but only in particular ways that did not demand response from others (245). (Note, for example, how quickly some of us want to define assignments so students will not write about their lives, or how gratifying it is to read a list of how to's that clearly define the boundaries between teacher and therapist). If I'm focused on controlling my own emotions, the assumption went, I certainly don't want to feel obligated to respond to someone else's excess emotions. It's difficult enough to handle negative feelings within, I don't need them from without. "Thus," Stearns argues, "one could 'be oneself' only so long as one's maturity assured that one's emotions would remain in check and not bother others. . . . Good emotions blurred with bad when excess threatened" (192). And excess meant an unwanted vulnerability (230).

Instead of focusing one's emotional energy on family or friends, people were encouraged to attach themselves to objects or buy things to express strong feelings to someone else, creating "surrogate attachments to objects as a means of preventing emotional intensity among people" (274). With commercialism appropriating emotional expression, new media could keep viewers from feeling emotions by having actors portray them. "People wanted more to witness emotion than to experience it," Stearns notes. "Removal from participation, except for an anonymous shout or two, was precisely the point, for active participation would contravene the dominant emotional rules" (281) (in this sense, "The Jerry Springer Show" is about a kind of voyeurism that protects individuals from directly dealing with the pain of others). Within this context it makes sense that therapists and support groups would be appropriate outlets for emotional intensity, "elevat[ing] strangers to a position of emotional importance simply on the basis of the unavailability of sympathetic others, including friends. The bond might fill the void, but it also testified to the growing distaste for other people's intensities even at times of crisis" (247–48). Strangers became the most likely receivers of emotional intensity—with strangers there would be no fear of contaminating a relationship with intense emotions because no intimate relationship existed to be affected.

Ironically, then, the very emotion standards that have socialized us to resist stories of abuse and eating disorders have also made it more likely that students will share them with us. When I began this research, I assumed that most students, if they were going to write about bodily violence, would usually do so after they had developed a trusting, safe relationship with their teacher and their classmates. Many of the teachers I interviewed had that same assumption. I didn't expect to have students contacting me about their essays until after the first few weeks of the semester, after the students had met in conference with their instructor at least once or twice. Within a week, however, I had heard from two instructors who had students writing about bodily violence. In both cases, the students wrote about the experience before meeting with their teacher. It was their first essay draft of the semester, and their teachers were surprised. Although I found out later that students often will write about these experiences early in the term or right at the end, the teachers I talked to were as puzzled as I was by the timing. The timing of these essays didn't fit our explanations for why students choose to write about sexual abuse or eating disorders: We had assumed that the nature of our relationship with the students influenced the student's decision, but not *this* nature. What did it mean that a student would hand in an essay about this issue before any kind of trusting relationship could possibly have developed?

As I talked with students, a few of them told me they would rather their classmates know about their experience than their friends at home or their family because their words would be less dangerous within the classroom.

Parents could be protected from feeling responsible for not seeing the signs their daughter was being abused. Abusers could be protected from the law, particularly if the young woman was still sorting through her feelings for her attacker.[4] As Erving Goffman (1963) points out, the mask afforded an individual in an anonymous situation lessens the risk that a stigma will affect one's reputation and long-standing relationships (65). Intimate friends and family would not have to witness the emotional struggle, embarrassment, and profound uncertainty the young woman is going through—they would not, in short, get to see any emotional intensity that could make the receiver feel obligated or prompted to judge the young woman as immature and out of control. As one woman told me, the writer could worry less that her feelings were being analyzed by a therapist who could "see through" them.[5]

From the perspectives of both Stearns and Goffman, a student writing about bodily violence in a college course may believe she has a degree of control over what she reveals and how that information is interpreted by a reader—or, rather, how her self is constructed by others. It may, in fact, be one of the few places she believes she can have this control and where her words, her voice, will effect the least amount of damage. If a student has been used to teachers commenting only on an essay's structure, grammar, and style, and ignoring content, then that student might expect her college writing teacher to do the same (as many of my own students initially expect me to do). When you've been socialized through schooling not to expect anyone to attend to the meanings, gaps, and consequences of your essay's subject, then it is not so paradoxical that some students will insert such potentially shocking subjects into a five-paragraph theme structure. Their experience is contained, their emotions controlled and limited by the expectations of the form and the purposes of the course, and they choose what to include and what not. In fact, some of the students I interviewed could clearly articulate what they decided to leave out of their drafts and why—usually it was material they felt was "too personal" or "too psychological," sometimes material they sensed they weren't ready to work through yet.[6] And, although they felt gratified by the compassion and empathy their peers and teachers would express, some students told me explicitly they did not want "pity" or "sympathy"—they wanted their essays to be treated as any other essay in the course. Not all expressed this—some clearly wanted their draft on one of these subjects to be ungraded "expressing"—but it was fairly clear these students did not want to disrupt the principle of restrained intensity that Stearns describes, either by making their readers feel obligated to respond or by allowing themselves to express emotions that might run out of control.

Students may write about their experiences with bodily violence in part because strangers—within the impersonal nature of public spaces—have been constructed within American emotional culture as safe spaces to express emotional intensity and lack of emotional control. Although many writing teachers assume the student wants a therapeutic relationship with them, some students may be counting on a well-defined boundary between writing teacher and therapist. Students may not expect a response on the feeling level from a teacher because that would contradict the prevailing emotional standards. How teachers and students actually respond in these situations, however, is variable, and the consequences of writing about such emotionally intense experiences may indeed disrupt the emotionology Stearns describes. The fact that many writing teachers are surprised when they receive essays about intense personal experiences and concerned about how best to respond, suggests that some teachers do not perceive themselves in the role of an appropriate stranger to whom to express such feelings. Some teachers wonder if the student expects a similar exchange of personal experiences, something that often happens in developing friendships, again illustrating how the receiver of someone else's feelings worries about what it makes him or her responsible for, what it assumes he or she might do in return. And this ambiguity creates even more discomfort.

I've begun to suspect that teachers' discomfort with these subjects may speak to changes in the emotionology Stearns describes, changes influenced by the growing archives of material written by survivors of abuse and eating disorders. At the very least, students who write about these issues to strangers in the university may perceive that their emotions are of little threat there, but given the university's historical disdain for subjective, emotive discourse, these students are also challenging power relations and dominant epistemologies. As I explore in more detail in the next chapter, the emotions expressed by victims of abuse are often considered what Alison Jaggar (1989) calls "outlaw emotions," constructed by dominant culture as "conventionally unacceptable" (160), but from Jaggar's perspective part of the process of revising dominant ideologies. When students express these outlaw emotions in a college essay, the potential exists for developing a critical social theory that, I would argue, resists the emotionology that helps maintain distinctions between normals and deviants, emotionally controlled and uncontrolled.

Yeah, But When All's Said and Done, This Is Still Just Confessional Writing

The normalizing functions of a university writing classroom have been well criticized by a number of compositionists (Susan Miller [1991], Lester Faigley [1992], James Berlin [1987], and others), and I suspect this function seems even more problematic when young women who have been abused or who have eating disorders appropriate (or make explicit) this mechanism for inscribing middle-class ideologies. This situation seems more complicated by the role confession seems to play: According to Foucault (1978), the act of confession serves to maintain the separations between the normal and the deviant, requiring the deviant to confess her sins and promise to realign herself with normals, all before a silent judge who confirms the truth about the confessor's deviance (59–63). Panoptical power—power which is internalized through constant self-surveillance (1979, 228)—turns self-analysis into an instrument of maintaining power, with someone like the teacher in a dominant position to verify truth through shaming. Faigley argues that the personal nature of expressivist pedagogies—its expectations that students write about themselves truthfully and honestly—enacts this confessional relationship, producing and maintaining students' inferior status and a teacher's authority, contradicting any efforts such a teacher might believe she or he is making to "free" students (23, 129–31).

But what does confession mean in relation to students who have been victims of abuse or who suffer from eating disorders? What deviances are they confessing? Certainly in the case of abuse they have been told they are deviant, bad, dirty—the seductress Eve who deserves punishment for her uncontrollable sexuality and threat to masculine values.[7] They have internalized the shame and guilt of being stigmatized, but what have they done that they need to confess? "Many women survivors of incestuous abuse (as well as rape and other forms of abuse)," Vikki Bell (1993) argues,

> may feel guilty or in some way to blame because they inevitably move within those discourses which hold women at fault in sexual abuse. They may understand themselves through discourses which do not give them any way to articulate the abuse apart from a self-critical "how could I let that happen to me?/ why did I do such and such?" . . . But the confession of the incest survivor is not straightforwardly a confession in Foucault's sense because it is not a confession of one's own guilty deed, even if, due to societal prejudice, the survivor may feel guilty. (102)

In the case of sexual abuse, a survivor's disclosure participates in discourses of sexuality only to the degree that sexual abuse can be considered part of sexual desire. Even then, Bell points out, "it is not the speaker's sexuality that is at the forefront of discussion, but the abuser's" (103). If anything, to avoid such a disclosure, as feminists have pointed out, only protects the abuser and maintains his power over the survivor. In this case, judging an essay about physical or sexual violence as a confession contributes to maintaining those discourses that blame the victim and construct women as sexually deviant and threatening.

The term *confession*, then, is not appropriate when describing survivors who speak about their abuse. In addition, the relationship between speaker and listener, Bell suggests, is not predicated on "listening to pleasure, as are the confessions to which Foucault refers, but on listening to pain" (103). In this sense, the essays do not add to the archives on pleasure. Bell goes on to suggest that when an abused woman shares her experience with feminist workers or researchers, she is not in a power relationship where an authority can affect her in other aspects of her life (103). Although such a relation of power does exist in a classroom, I propose that the kinds of truth such a teacher might be validating—the right to be angry, the right to speak, the re-assessment of blame and guilt, and a critique of cultural systems of gender and power—function as a set of disciplinary truths, to be sure (as Bell reminds us, feminism is also a disciplinary discourse), but truths that are set *in opposition to* dominant ideologies. From this perspective, student essays about abuse function as resistance. I would be more concerned if the kinds of truth being validated were ones that reinscribed the woman's essential complicity.

It might be more appropriate to describe student essays on bodily violence as witnessing or testifying to trauma. Such trauma is both physical and discursive because by its very definition *trauma* is a violent disruption in the order and understanding of one's world—a collapse, if you will, of the barriers constructed between deviant and normal identities, dramatizing the arbitrariness of such distinctions.

> An individual is traumatized by a life-threatening event that displaces his or her preconceived notions about the world. Trauma is enacted in a liminal state, outside the bounds of "normal" human experience, and the subject is radically ungrounded. Accurate representations of trauma can never be achieved without recreating the event since, by its very definition, trauma lies beyond the bounds of "normal" conception. (Tal 1996, 15)

As I will argue in the next chapter, students who have experienced bodily violence have witnessed and suffered a deconstructive reality where signs and signifiers no longer correspond. For some, reality is a deconstructive text, their urge to testify a desire to know what cannot be fully known because it was not conceivable beforehand. In the cases of long-term abuse, when the abused knows no other reality, some might argue the trauma is less severe than when the violence is unexpected, as during war. Nonetheless, it is important to understand these essays as witnessing to a postmodern reality—a "wild subject" as Lynn Worsham (1992–1993) calls it—in which disciplinary power shatters language, reality, and self. If seen as a crisis of truth, as Shoshana Felman and Dori Laub describe testimony (1992, 6), what would it mean to attend to the truths to which these students are testifying?

2

It's Like It Never Even Happened

SITUATING STUDENT TEXTS WITHIN DISCURSIVE TRADITIONS OF WRITING ABOUT SEXUAL VIOLENCE

Dear Miss,

. . . You would not realize, I know, how many troubles I have because I try hard to be cheerful and happy. Now my heart is overflowing with grief. I have brought them to Jesus and I know he will make them right for me. I am telling you so that you may understand why I cannot be with you.

I have suffered since childhood my father's abuses. He hates me for what I am. I work for him and obeyed him as much as I can even if they are unjust. . . . [Y]et he says that I am still a slave to him. I am willing to work if he gives me my freedom to do the right thing. . . .

This last month father seemed to like me for he was very kind, but no, it didn't last long. He tried to make me sin *[emphasis added by MSPCC social worker], I wouldn't do it so he made me promise not to tell anyone, but the week before last mother found out. I told her all. How many tears were shed, I can't say. Father is very angry and hates me worse than ever. He wants revenge and he torments me in every way. . . .*

Don't you think this is hard? Cruelty cannot seem to rule me, only love can so I disobeyed him last Sunday.

. . . [He] knocked me about so that my head was in a whirl. . . . He told me he would kill me with a knife, I answered and told him I would be very glad to have him. I was ready to die, I couldn't bear it any longer. . . .

—"Grace," 16, Chinese-born American,
1920, a letter to her Sunday School teacher
(excerpted from Gordon [1988, 238–39])

*T*his excerpt from a letter Grace wrote to her Sunday School teacher is an artifact of resistance and escape. Grace was the oldest of six children in this family and her father repeatedly raped and beat her. Although her father consistently tried to isolate her, she was able to write to her Catholic Sunday School teacher and begin the process of leaving her family. Her teacher took her to the Massachusetts Society for the Prevention of Cruelty to Children [MSPCC] where her social worker tried to persuade her to return home. In spite of her father's threats and her social worker's indifference, Grace did in fact leave her family and eventually entered a seminary. Her letter, full of euphemisms about her father's sexual aggression, was a crucial rhetorical act that translated an otherwise private experience into a public issue and enabled Grace to flee her father's control and violence.

As in the texts of the other women I explore in this chapter, Grace's letter demonstrates the rhetorical and emotional skills needed to construct an identity that would be visible to the authority figures she wanted to reach, as well as an awareness of the competing discourses of truth she could use to represent her experience and argue for her escape. In the letter, we can see that Grace is caught between the sinfulness of her father's cruelty and her cultural and Christian beliefs to obey her father, searching for a way of understanding how she should respond. In the end, she sees her father's coercion and violence as sins she must resist, using the authority of her religious beliefs to reject paternal authority (Gordon 1988, 236–39). Although she embraces an ideology that reinforces the patriarchal system she wants to escape, Grace's identity as a good Catholic allows her more power to control her body than her identity as her father's daughter. In the end, the identity she constructs in this letter is the one that can be visible to her Sunday School teacher and the MSPCC and enable her to escape.

Student essays about sexual abuse differ significantly from historical texts, but both adopt popular discursive traditions not only to structure how they understand their lives and their selves but also to ensure they will be listened to. Students use their writing to sort through what has happened to them, to make sense of their suffering within the discourses available, and to argue for the choices they have made and hope others will make upon reading their essays. As I reviewed the ten student essays that focused on sexual abuse, I noticed that they all struggled with the conflicts Grace does, how to present an identity that is good, normal, capable, not deserving of the abuse (although many of them felt that they did deserve the abuse), or obligated to remain bound by its effects. As they search for explanations and alternative identities, students have to negotiate among multiple discourses: their version of events, cultural and academic interpretations of sexual abuse, the unpredictable responses of their audience, and the rhetorical moves accepted in the university. Some students are more skilled at this than others and some are more conscious of it than others, but all their texts draw on contemporary authorizing discourses (dominant and powerful discourses which offer a writer authority to speak), just as Grace's letter does, and they explore identities that might offer new ways of being in the world.

I propose that we begin to read student essays on bodily violence through the same lens we might read Grace's letter, with the same theories of language, ideology, and power that we use to read literary texts. Although they write within different time periods, within different institutional contexts, both Grace and our students are implicitly aware that it matters a good deal *how* they represent their experience and their identities to their audiences. I think teachers often assume that students will only write about their abuse using psychotherapeutic discourse or adopting the confessional and unreflective language they hear on talk shows. Although we may have read strong researched essays about child sexual abuse, we may not expect students to choose a wide range of approaches to these kinds of papers. An experience as traumatic as sexual violence seems only speakable within a classroom that has validated personal disclosure and self-reflection, an expressivist classroom where, it is believed, students are not asked to reflect on the larger contexts within which they live their lives.

Contrary to what many critics believe, the students in this study did not limit their rhetorical choices to a talk-show type confession, to a self-reflective personal essay, or to a psychotherapeutic analysis of a liberal humanist self. Nor did they all write their essays in courses in which the focus could be defined as expressivist. The students in this study wrote about bodily violence *regardless* of the kinds of assignments required in their first-year writing course, and *regardless* of whether the teacher focused on personal or academic essays or on any combination of the two.[1] Although some survivors may only feel comfortable writing about their abuse within a class focused on personal essays, they are not necessarily deterred from addressing the issue in a class focused on academic, critical, nonpersonal genres. In fact, several of the students in this study chose to write about their abuse in a researched essay, a genre traditionally considered academic and public. In addition, over half of them structured their texts to move, either implicitly or explicitly, from often hauntingly detailed or powerfully understated narratives of the abuse to analyses of how it has affected their relationships with others and themselves, as well as generalizations about what such abuse suggests to them about families, American culture, gender, and power relations. Clearly, these students are not simply looking inward and crying, but they are engaging in sophisticated analyses and critiques of the social and institutional contexts within which they live their lives.

Although I can't draw broad conclusions from my research with the ten students who wrote about sexual abuse, I can argue that their work complicates some of the assumptions often made about essays on bodily violence and the pedagogies that engender them. Too often it is assumed that someone who has been abused sexually can only write about it as a purely emotional, psychically traumatic experience, a narrative not likely to engage in academic critique in part because few if any autobiographical traditions exist for doing so. Yet students and their written texts often disrupt these too-simple dichotomies, first by the very act of writing about a private experience in a public genre, and second by doing so with both rational and emotional rhetorical practices. If this is surprising, it may be because, as Swartzlander et al. (1993) illustrate, a sexually abused self has been constructed as too emotionally vulnerable to sustain appropriate relationships with others (such as authority figures) or to engage in intellectual activity that requires a less vulnerable, more stable self. A survivor of rape or molestation, the argument might go, needs the stabilizing process of therapy to create a self capable of academic work. I don't want to dismiss the effects of trauma by questioning this assumption—as Judith Herman notes, some survivors may not be able to maintain all of their responsibilities at various stages in the recovery process (1992, 162). I do want to point out, however, that we do students a disservice to see them primarily as psychologically unstable, as ill, and as vulnerable. When we do, the abuse and the abuse survivor become knowable only through this psychotherapeutic discourse, a "strateg[y] of cultural coping" Kali' Tal calls "medicalization" (1996, 6); and, in the case of the women in this study, we are in danger of further infantalizing them, turning their victimization into an illness. As I illustrate in the following section, students writing about sexual abuse are part of a long line of women who have done so, going back to at least the twelfth century, and the texts they have all produced demonstrate an ability to appropriate discourses of power that help them not only be listened to but also change their identities, resist, and revise the discourses of violence from which they are emerging.

Imitating Academic Conventions: "Oprah," Shame, and Anger as Critical Reflection

Emily[2] was a young woman in Stephanie's class who sat in the back of the classroom, her head often in her arms on the long black table she shared with two other students. Early in the semester I began to wonder whether she was ill or simply disengaged from the class, doing as little as possible to get by. She would shuffle out of class as soon as it was over, rarely giving me a chance to talk with her. Her drafts and reading responses were rather cursory and flat, and I began to wonder why she had chosen this particular course—Writing About Female Experience—out of all that were offered. Most of the students who had selected the course were fully engaged.

Then Emily handed me her third essay with my own words staring back at me, the ones I thought I had stealthily embedded in my introduction to the readings on sexuality: "I bet most of you in this class have been sexually abused in some way. I know I have. . . ." Although I had said, "One out of four of you" instead of "most," what Emily obviously heard was, as she says in her next line, "I could write about it and Michelle would understand." She figures me as a potentially nonjudgmental listener who is willing to hear this secret, a move many of the instructors in my study read as the student's desire to have a therapeutic relationship with them.[3] In many ways, Emily's essay appears to fulfill writing teachers' fears about this situation: I was the first person she had told about the incident, and the essay narrates the abuse with minimal detail and for the apparent purpose of getting it out. In her process note to me she says,

> This paper was difficult to write because it's so personal. I had some problems being detailed because a lot of what happened has been blacked out of my memory. I'm glad to get it off of my chest. It's been bothering me this past year. As I wrote about it I discovered that the incident has affected me more than I thought. Please focus on the subject itself as opposed to the grammar.

The essay seems to be written only to me, not to a larger audience, and, as Emily says in her process note, the process of writing the piece has led her to a new understanding of its effects. Based on her note, she may not yet be aware of what purpose she wants the essay to have because she is just now beginning to compose the experience with language. Without reading further than this reflection, we might assume that Emily is still coming to terms with the meaning of the abuse and so may not be ready for the kind of critical reflection her essay needs to make it effective.

However, the structure of her paragraphs suggests that Emily is aware that an essay makes claims and then offers evidence. In the second paragraph, for example, the essay gives a one-paragraph summary of the abuse—an assertion, "I was sexually abused by my stepuncle when I was four years old and again when I was eight"—and then offers support that provides context, explaining why she ended up in such close proximity to this uncle and why she trusted him:

> When I was four my mother and I went to live with my grandma and step-grandpa for a few months. Whenever they would go out grandpa's son,

Henry, would babysit me. I knew and trusted him and thought what he was doing to me was o.k. No one had ever told me it wasn't.

She provides only the briefest of details, using euphemisms to carry the sexual content of the experience, and she begins with the innocence of the situation, the normality of having a relative watch a child. As in the other essays in this chapter, Emily is echoing a pattern to sexual abuse stories, one that usually begins with a trusting child and a caretaker in a situation where reality is supposed to follow acceptable rules. Later, of course, all those rules are shattered by the experience. As Emily narrates the events that follow, her paragraphs elaborate on the claims of the previous one, as well as on the responses of the adults she told at the time. It is clear that she is giving supporting evidence to her claims but not in the kind of detail usually seen in contemporary, published nonfiction essays on sexual abuse.

I can't really remember everything that happened; parts of it are blacked out, which is somewhat of a blessing. I remember that when mom, grandma, and grandpa left the house Henry would make me sit on his lap on the big brown chair. We would sit there and watch T.V. He would kiss me open mouthed and fondle me. He would also make me touch him in places that I shouldn't have. He never actually raped me but he might as well have.

When I was eight years old Henry came to stay with us in _____. I hadn't told my mother anything so she let him stay in my room; there was no other place for him to stay and I had twin beds in my room. One night I was afraid of the shadows in my closet so Henry got into bed with me to protect me. He started fondling me and whispering in my ear. "It's alright [sic]. It's o.k.," he told me. But it wasn't and this time I knew it.

He managed to pull my panties down and was really close to having intercourse with me. Somehow I found the strength in my eighty pound body to push him off of me. I ran from there into my mother's room; I stayed there the rest of the night. In the morning, I told my mother and her boyfriend what happened. They made immediate plans to send Henry back to _____. My brother Jim's reaction was somewhat different.

At this point, the essay shifts from explaining what happened and why and begins to explore, as Emily's clear transition suggests, her brother's response. Like the other students in this study whose essays focus on sexual abuse, Emily describes how it felt to have someone not believe her story. The meaning of the event is at issue, and, instead of directing her anger at her stepuncle for abusing her, she directs it to someone she thinks should have believed and protected her. Her brother's response seems to affect her as much as the abuse itself because it throws her sense of reality into doubt:

Jim and Henry were only a year apart and they were very good friends. When my mother told him why Henry was being sent back, Jim was very upset. "She's making it up! Henry wouldn't do a thing like that!" he argued. When he should have been big brotherly and beat the crap out of that skuzball he deserted me. My own flesh and blood turned his back on me and believed that disgusting waste of a human being. For that, I don't think I will ever forgive him.

Although the essay is relatively dispassionate (again, suggesting Emily's sense of appropriate tone in a college essay), this tone is disrupted when she expresses anger at her brother for not believing her. This anger seeps out again a phrase or two later in the essay, and, like the emotional descriptions in other students' essays, it seems to beg for a purpose in the text that hasn't yet been found. The paragraph seems unreflective, and, for many readers, the anger in this paragraph suggests that Emily is not in control of her emotions and therefore not in control of her text (a response that also suggests an anxiety that we as teachers are not in control of them). However, she turns in the next paragraph to a moment of reflection, focusing on how the event may have affected her, trying to make some meaning out of it that, not surprisingly, sounds as if she is sorting out whether to blame herself or the abuse for her sexual behavior. She shifts immediately from an angry outburst to a reflective stance that seems to step away from the emotion and control it with an interpretation she has found from watching "Oprah."

After Henry left nothing else was said about it. I didn't receive counseling, my mother and I did not discuss it; it was like it never happened. My mother didn't even stop to think about it when she found out about my not being a virgin. Doesn't she understand that I probably wouldn't have made my stupid mistakes if I didn't already feel so dirty?

I didn't really think it affected me much. I did not start analyzing it until just last year. I used to watch Oprah and hear her talk about sexual abuse; that when a woman is molested as a child she is either promiscuous or wants nothing to do with men as a teen and into adulthood. But I was different. I was totally unaffected—right?

As I look back at some of the decisions I've made, I now realize that I leaned more towards the promiscuous side. I lost my virginity at fifteen. I was drunk; I had just met the guy a few hours before and things got out of control. I still kick myself for it. It was awful. I didn't love him; I didn't even know his last name. It was painful mentally and physically. It still hurts; I feel like the biggest slut alive. Was my decision three years ago somehow related to my experiences when I was four and when I was eight?

At this point, Emily is making a move I value in my students' writing, using an outside text to help them reframe a question, resee an issue, challenge their ideas about their subject, and draw new conclusions or raise new questions. No matter what we think about a student using a talk show as an outside text, it is one of the most visible sources students have for understanding their experience within a public forum, a way of becoming part of a larger community of survivors that Goffman (1963) suggests is part of the process of "disclosing."[4] This is one of many gestures toward academic writing in Emily's text that I believe we need to recognize and encourage. It doesn't matter how well Emily may be imitating those gestures in this draft—what is important is that she is making them, demonstrating the same potential for academic writing that we would recognize in any other student essay. Even if the subject is her own experience, her reflection on that subject and the ways she attempts to frame it demonstrate her ability to engage in—to learn—the conventions of academic discourse and analysis.

This ability is also clear in her final paragraph where Emily speculates on possible solutions to the problems she now recognizes she has as a result of this experience, making an explicit move toward a purpose that turns the personal, narrative details into support for a socially directed claim.

> I think that there should be more support groups for victims of childhood molestation. Maybe if we could talk about what happened to us when we were little and shared our feelings the aftereffects would not be as dominant as they are now. Therapy can begin at any age. It's never too late to start over. Past traumas can't be changed but future ones can.

Emily's last three sentences are noticeably different from those that begin her essay: They are more general, more assertive, and more conventional. If she were writing about this experience to a friend in a letter, I doubt she would make these final gestures. Even the nonfiction narratives many survivors of sexual abuse have published in the last several years do not make these moves toward a message or a moral to the story. But Emily intuits, like many of her peers, that a personal experience has to mean something within a college essay, it has to have a point that goes beyond the self, and so she pulls from the commonplaces she is familiar with to assert some meaning. This meaning turns her experience into one of hope for change instead of despair.

If, as Lutz and others argue, "emotion discourses may be one of the most likely and powerful devices by which domination proceeds" (1990, 76), then it is imperative that we begin to read student texts like Emily's as a struggle over identity, discourse, and power, as well as a desire for what Alison Jaggar (1989) calls a "critical social theory" (160): "Critical reflection on emotion is not a self-indulgent substitute for political analysis and political action. It is itself a kind of political theory and political practice, indispensable for an adequate social theory and social transformation" (164). Emily's anger (as well as her guilt for "los[ing her] virginity at fifteen" and feeling "like the biggest slut alive") has historically been constructed by dominant culture as an "outlaw emotion" (as Jaggar would term it), a "conventionally unacceptable" emotional response that is characteristic of subordinate groups (160). Taught to feel guilt and shame for any sexual activity, especially when a woman actively seeks it, it is Emily's anger at these feelings that are outlaw and that create a space for critical reflection. When Emily begins to resee them in the light of the discourses presented on "Oprah," she is beginning to turn that anger and guilt into ways of acting both individually and socially.

Women's anger at being sexually assaulted has been dismissed, seen as a symptom of hysteria, and ridiculed as evidence women can't control their emotions; yet, in therapy and feminist theory it is often seen as the source of resistance to the pain inflicted by such violence—an emotion that, combined with a historical, psychological, sociological, and sometimes feminist perspective, can help a victim (a subject) become a survivor (a Subject). This process of healing and resistance occurs when the outlaw emotion is placed into a different context, offering an alternative interpretation of its meaning, re-educating the emotion and the sense of self and world that has been constructed by or around it. Instead of seeing students like Emily as incapable of critical reflection because of their traumatic experiences, I propose we respect their move to bring those experiences into a public and disciplinary context and find ways to encourage the critical reflection already evidenced in their texts.[5]

My reading of Emily's essay is only one among many, and I've emphasized the echoes of academic conventions in her text not only because they are so buried, but also because many of us might readily assume they aren't there. When I first responded to Emily's draft, I thought her final paragraph was too conventional and forced closure on an experience whose meaning Emily was just beginning to explore. It didn't occur to me to recognize that she was trying to make the experience fit her approximation of college writing, or to see her use of "Oprah" as a moment to encourage her to explore other ways of understanding her experience. I also couldn't have understood then what I do now, that, no matter how conventional those academic gestures and her use of "Oprah" are to me as an academic, to Emily they are ways of being more normal, in Goffman's terms, and of being a little less alone and ashamed and separate. And now, depending on what my course goals are and how ready a student might be to take a more academic approach to a traumatic experience, I might not even encourage her to develop her analytical skills in this particular draft. If she doesn't want to work on the draft as an evaluated piece of writing or if she feels uncomfortable pursuing some of her questions, I won't expect her to do so. But I would make note of her abilities and work hard not to immediately assume she is too unstable to meet the expectations of college-level writing.

In worrying about where the lines are between being a therapist and being a writing teacher, we can forget that students can bring the same kinds of writing strategies to an essay on a painful experience that they can to other essay subjects. My own fear has been that if I encourage the critical reflection I see in a draft, I will be asking the student to intellectualize her experience, to repress her emotional response, and to impose yet another way of understanding her experience that makes little room for her version of it. However, this fear is based on a belief that emotional and intellectual responses can't coexist or inform each other, that emotions are tainted by intellectual ideas. It has taken me years to learn that I don't need to intellectualize my emotions to control their seeming unruliness and unpredictability or to present an identity that has authority and power. I think it is important that we, as writing teachers, stop seeing emotion, pain, and trauma as threatening, anti-intellectual, and solipsistic, and instead begin to ask how we might, like therapists, feminist theorists, and philosophers, begin to recognize them as ways of knowing, not signs of dangerous pedagogies or teachers who are acting as therapists.

On Educating "Wild Subjects"

So, if students will write about sexual abuse in a variety of forms, if they demonstrate some facility with academic discourse, and if they write about it in a course not focused on personal writing, then how might a teacher respond to an essay such as Emily's if it's written in, for example, a postmodernist writing course? Given that emotions are shaped by culture and ideology and that they affect and are affected by power relations, then it would seem students' expressions of emotion would be considered vital to the political projects of critical and other postmodern pedagogies. Why shouldn't a student bring her battered body into her written text and learn how her experience is socially constructed, historically situated, and woven through with cultural values and power relations? In postmodern terms, her body is a text that can be deconstructed along with her identity to illustrate how bound both are by powerful ideological systems of oppression. In the process, she will be liberated from those systems (if her course focuses on critical pedagogies) or disillusioned from her faith that her experience can be a foundation for her sense of self, relationships, or world (if her course focuses on postmodern theories of language). Either way, the student will emerge from the class with a different relationship to language and self and thus to the production of texts.

Or at least in theory. What complicates the scenarios I've described is the already postmodern nature of the abuse experience itself that these students bring into the classroom. Before we can explore how to respond to a student such as Emily in a postmodern class, we need to examine what we assume about her sense of self and her experience with language and reality. In wanting to "unsettle the complacency and conceptual identities of the student," as Gregory Jay (1987, 790) argues, some postmodern pedagogies assume the students who come into a class experience their identities as centered, autonomous, and existing in a stable, knowable reality. As much as our students might generally want to believe they can achieve such a self, students who have been sexually abused have experienced a discursive trauma that renders them always already postmodern subjects, always already decentered, their identities constructed from the violence and unspeakableness of the trauma.

Here's another way of thinking about it: The essays that I studied on sexual violence all had a similar pattern in their stories in which a trusted male adult was tender and loving, enticing the child or young woman to come closer with gifts or entreaties, relying on the girl's belief that adults can be trusted to take care of and love those who are more vulnerable. Then, what begins as a trust in a stable, knowable reality is shattered when the male adult engages in sexual activity and threatens the girl into silence. If she does choose to tell someone, she is often not believed, the experience is dismissed as incidental, or the experience is handled ineffectively by otherwise unavailable parental figures. She then feels doubly betrayed and powerless, doubting whether the violence occurred at all, believing that she invited the abuse and may have secretly enjoyed it if her body responded in any way. And, in almost all the essays I received, the woman is usually alone, without friends or family or other support systems. Detached. Fragmented. Distrustful. Questioning her perceptions, her physical responses, her sense of who she is, not daring to use language to name her experience.

These are the qualities of what Lynn Worsham (1992–1993) calls a "wild subject," the kind of identity that is the goal of many postmodern pedagogies: someone who no longer has a self that can feel, creating "a kind of ultimate estrangement from or dissolution of the structures that traditionally have supported both self and world" (133). When we can assume that most of our students experience a coherent, usually middle-class, complacent identity—and I'm not sure that we can—then pedagogies that challenge this self can create alternative identities and ways of knowing that can change oppressive structures, social relationships, and their own relation to learning. But as I look at the similarities between the discursive trauma of being sexually abused and the goals of postmodern pedagogies, I have to pause and ask myself if my own postmodernism is not only ignoring the fragmentation already in my class-room but also the potentially painful effects of encouraging it.

At this point, having studied these student texts and researched these is-sues, I'm more likely to choose the kind of pedagogy theorists such as Susan Jarratt (1991) encourage, what Lynn Worsham (1992–1993) calls part of the critical pedagogies in the field that emphasize "experience as the medium through which the conditions of domination and subordination are articu-lated and resisted" (138). Instead of focusing on discourse and ideology as the sites to critique power relations (141), this kind of pedagogy works with the student's experience and "lead[s] students to see how differences emerging from their texts and discussions have more to do with those contexts than they do with an essential and unarguable individuality" (Jarratt 1991, 121). By challenging students to situate their experiences within historical and cul-tural discourses, they will, Jarratt hopes, "argue about the ethical implications of discourse on a wide range of subjects and, in so doing, come to identify their personal interests with others, understand those interests as implicated in a larger communal setting, and advance them in a public voice" (121). Al-though Jarratt may not be referring to students' emotional expressions here, she is arguing for the same kind of reflective process Jaggar suggests, moving students toward a critical social practice—a way of understanding, being, and acting in the world where one can resist discourses that cause pain and abuses of power. Part of the process, then, of recognizing the academic moves stu-dents are making can be helping them place their outlaw emotions within his-torical and ideological contexts. What might that mean for students who choose to write about sexual violence?

As I explored this question, I began to look for historical material on sexual abuse, primary texts written by survivors. I found an overwhelming amount of secondary material *about* sexual abuse—sociological studies, psy-chological theories, historical cases—which the students often found for themselves if they chose to research the subject. What was harder to find— but I think important for students to have access to—were pretwentieth-century nonfiction essays or memoirs written by those who have been abused. By looking at these primary texts as well as secondary historical analyses, a student could explore how the meaning of sexual abuse has changed over time, for example. Just as Grace does in the letter that began this chapter, the historical material that is part of a tradition of women writing about sexual abuse dramatizes the multiple authorizing discourses writers have to choose to be visible and credible. Once we can recognize those discourses in a historical text, I think we—both students and teachers—can better talk about and analyze the discourses students are using in their own texts.

For teachers, this way of reading student essays about abuse emphasizes not only the critical reflection already often evidenced in what may seem a confession, a solipsistic narrative, an enactment of collective victimhood, it also underscores the postmodern nature of student essays on abuse. For students, this historical context can offer a community of writers struggling with similar experiences, it can illustrate quite different ways of representing abuse, and it can complicate the power others may have over how the story—and the student's identity—are defined.

"Wanton and Uncivill Carridges"

I now want to consider some historical texts that are part of a long discursive tradition of writing about sexual abuse. Few students or teachers are aware that such a tradition exists, and this lack of familiarity can perpetuate students' sense of isolation and teachers' tendencies to feel placed in the role of therapist. If I had more space I would take up Foucault's (1978) call for doing a genealogy of a discourse, tracing the evolution of discourses on sexual violence and placing student texts within them, but I can only suggest that such a tradition exists. These texts belie the common belief that sexual abuse—especially incest—has been unspeakable until very recently. The 1960s and 1970s were pivotal times for women who had suffered bodily violence; feminists called for women to "break silences" about sexual violence and thereby begin to disrupt the power structures that maintained their oppression. However, for centuries prior, women and men had been addressing these issues in fiction, poetry, drama, and various forms of nonfiction (see, for example, McLennan's *Nature's Ban: Women's Incest Literature*). One critical shift that occurred with feminist reinterpretations of sexual violence was a change in the meaning of the experience: These prior texts—and the theoretical analyses of them—were challenged for the roles in which they cast women, for the powerful agendas that were being served by interpreting sexual abuse as they did, and for the role that gender and ideology played in transferring blame onto the victim. Although some of these analyses may be familiar to our students, they are all the more startling when we compare them with the historical texts and begin to understand the consequences for these women of having sexual violence and gender roles interpreted quite differently than they are now.

Very few of the early accounts of sexual abuse I could find were actually written by the abused. Several pieces of poetry and fiction take up incest as a subject, but few autobiographical texts do. Instead, stories of sexual abuse are represented in texts like legal documents and journals or memoirs and so are buried in historical libraries and archives. Those that have been published are often found in academic texts on the history of sexuality in the nineteenth century, for example, or in the domestic violence section of the library. Simply searching for these materials can be a fascinating research project.

As context for a student's own writing, historical texts illustrate what students may implicitly know about sexual violence, that the so-called truth about the experience is usually determined by those in power and can have dangerous consequences for everyone involved. Some of the earliest accounts I found of sexual abuse in America date back to the colonial period and are found primarily in court records. These documents functioned to establish a number of truths about the alleged incidents to determine if they were illegal acts: who the primary actors were, as well as their ages, marital status, race, and class status; what physical acts occurred; who witnessed the activities. These accounts are therefore quite detailed, often slowly narrating the acts of sexual violence as in the following description from a case in Middlesex County, Massachusetts, in 1660, documenting sexual intercourse between seven-year-old Elizabeth Stow and Thomas Doublet, a Native American, given by a witness, Mary How, who had been caring for Elizabeth and her baby sister when this occurred:

> Elizabeth Stow says Here comes my man & the Indian says Here is my squa. [While How was getting the baby to sleep] the Indian and Elizabeth went out to the corn field out of her hearing. He laid her down upon her backe and turned up her coats on her face & then put his finger in at the bottom of her belly and then lying upon her did with some other thing hurt her at the bottom of her belly which made her cry Oh Oh but afterward hee let her goe. . . . She [How] hath often seen & observed wanton & uncivill carridges by the aforesaid Elizabeth Stow and hath told her father who corrected her. She found signes of seed upon the childs wombe & some attempt of breaches in entering her body but not very farr. (Thompson 1986, 74)

It's important here that this testimony was not given by Elizabeth Stow nor was it used to break silence about child rape. This document was used legally to establish who the victim of this crime was, and, within colonial law, it wasn't Elizabeth. Instead, this testimony was key to deciding whether her *father* had been violated, and Mary How's visual observation and the physical signs of intercourse were the two crucial pieces of evidence. Elizabeth's version of the event, could she have articulated it at age seven, is by colonial standards irrelevant. This document only presents Mary How's perspective in which Elizabeth is only visible through How's rhetorical use of seventeenth-century truths about sexual deviance.

In this account, How authorizes her interpretation of what happened with prevailing beliefs about girls' sexuality: In describing Elizabeth's "wanton and uncivill carridges," How casts her in the role of seductress, reflecting the predominant assumption that she is sexually aware at the age of seven and has the qualities of older women—"physically and sexually vulnerable, easily aroused, quick to succumb to flattery" (Ulrich 1991, 97). A woman's complicity usually determined whether an act of intercourse was in fact "illegal," and this was largely determined by her connections to males. In cases of rape, court documents from Massachusetts suggest that "single, adult women were often perceived as willing sexual partners: the death penalty for rape applied only if the woman was married, engaged, or under the age of ten"—that is, if she were considered the property of another man (D'Emilio and Freedman 1988, 31). Elizabeth's identity—her subjectivity—is thus defined here by her relationship to patriarchal structures.

The result of defining intercourse as abusive under these conditions meant that the woman or girl was never a victim. The victim of Doublet's crime, for example, was ultimately not Elizabeth but her father. Because she is believed to be the property of her father, Doublet has violated that property and harmed Mr. Stow. This suggests the extent to which sex crimes were defined as and prosecuted according to gender and power relations. At the same time, these cases were adjudicated along the lines of race and class. Then, as now, the fact that Doublet was Native American made it even more likely he would be convicted and sentenced for this crime. In eighteenth-century Massachusetts, three of the five men actually convicted for having intercourse with girls under age ten were either Native or African American. The same was true of rape cases during this period: Although 86 percent of the men accused of rape were white, three out of the five men executed for the crime were Native or African American. The other two were white laborers (D'Emilio and Freedman 1988, 31).

During the colonial period, courtroom accounts of sexual abuse produced for the courts served to establish truths about the event that supported racial, class, and gender dominance. They established whether a threat to that dominance existed. In this way, certain sexual acts were defined as criminal. Whether gathered from witnesses or the abused themselves, these written accounts were (and still are) used to establish truths about sexuality and power. In contrast to the late eighteenth-century memoir I discuss in the next section, these court documents not only defined the legal issue of abuse and limited the role of women in the courtroom, but they effectively repressed the "subjugated knowledges" of the abused. No opportunity existed for a sufferer to do what Abigail Abbot Bailey would do two centuries later—engage prevailing discourses in a written text and interpret as well as question the prevailing discourses of her day—which would eventually lead to significant social action.

I Endeavored to Console My Afflicted Heart with My Pen

> ... I clearly saw that Mr. B. entertained the most vile intentions relative to his own daughter. Whatever difficulty attended the obtaining of legal proof, yet no remaining doubt existed in my mind, relative to the existence of his wickedness.
> —Abigail Abbot Bailey (Taves 1989, 75)

In 1792, Abigail Abbot Bailey of New Hampshire began writing a memoir about her life with an abusive and incestuous husband. She was pregnant for the fifteenth time, carrying twins, and her husband, Asa, a prominent figure in town from a family of means, had begun "courting" his sixteen-year-old daughter, Phebe. Over the course of their twenty-six-year marriage, Abigail had already forgiven Asa for an affair with one of their servants and an attempted rape of another, believing he had reformed when the sexual dalliances had stopped and he had become a political leader in town.[6] Then Asa began to pursue his daughter Phebe's affections, spending more and more time with her, appearing to ignore everyone else: "He seemed to have forgotten his age, his honor, and all decency, as well as all virtue," Abigail writes. "He would spend his time with this daughter, in telling idle stories, and foolish riddles, and singing songs to her, and sometimes before the small children" (Taves 1989, 72). Not wanting to believe her husband capable of incest, Abigail declares,

> Had such conduct appeared toward any young woman beside his own young daughter, I should have had no question what he intended: but as it now was, I was loth to indulge the least suspicion of base design. . . . All his tender affections were withdrawn from the wife of his youth, the mother of his children. My room was deserted, and left lonely . . . while this one daughter engrossed all his attention. (70–71)

To come to terms with her abandoned bed and her frightened daughter, Abigail turns to her diary and her Christian beliefs, searching for an explanation of her husband's "abominable designs" (72).

This stunning account of Abigail's struggle with her husband's violence and sexual abuse was found after her death in 1815 and was published soon

afterward with the editorial help of her Congregationalist minister. Historically, *The Memoirs of Mrs. Abigail Bailey*[7] is one of the few published narratives that deals directly with domestic abuse, one of the early texts in a tradition of writing about sexual and physical violence that few people are aware
exists. Like student essays, Bailey's memoir carefully represents her experience, framing her behavior within the belief systems of eighteenth-century
New England. As an illustration of the choices one woman makes about how
to write about sexual abuse, her memoir can become an important resource
for students as they explore ways of writing about and understanding their
own experiences.

Abigail's account is startling; it overflows with her prayers and supplica-
tions, her grief, and her anger. As in the colonial court records, *The Memoirs
of Mrs. Abigail Bailey* is a public document and Abigail uses various authorizing discourses to understand and establish several truths about herself, her
daughter, her husband, the act of incest, and God's mercy. In doing so, she
adopts the rhetorical form of the captivity narrative as well as the traditions of
conversion narratives and spiritual diaries that were a vital part of Puritan life
(Taves 1989, 10; Kagle 1986, 29–30). One of her central struggles is to gather
enough valid evidence to prosecute Asa, knowing that her own suspicions,
observations, and information from her children are not enough to prove his
crimes given his reputation in town. Abigail tries to make sense of her husband's rages, deceptions, and repentances within legal discourses of what incest means, as well as within her Congregational religious beliefs. Throughout
the text, Abigail tries to be a good Christian and a good wife and mother, but
finds herself in conflict over what this means when her husband is commit-
ting incest. Her writing leads her to assert what power she has to keep her children and herself away from Asa's violence, but it also maintains the power
structures embedded in all the discourses she engages to liberate herself and
her family—within the legal system, the patriarchal family, and religious doctrine about women. Nonetheless, it is a remarkable account of how literacy
practices can lead to resistance and change.

Throughout the period when Asa clearly has a sexual relationship with
his daughter, Abigail, pregnant with twins, is physically unable to stop him.
Abigail watches as Asa turns from a pleasant and cajoling wooer into an angry
and violent one, whipping Phebe in one instance, "without mercy . . . striking
over her head, hands, and back . . . her face and eyes" (Taves 1989, 76), at other
times with a "beach stick, large enough for the driving of a team; and with
such sternness and anger sparkling in his eyes, that his visage seemed to re-
semble an infernal" (75). While pitying Phebe for what she must be suffering, Abigail admits "a degree of resentment, that she would not, as she
ought, expose the wickedness of her father" by agreeing to tell her mother and

authorities what had been happening (76). But Abigail is well aware that Asa's "intrigues, insinuations, commands, threats, and parental influence" caused Phebe fear and shame that prevented her from speaking. We see Phebe, through her mother's eyes, trying as best she can to resist her father's advances while not disobeying him, an impossible task, and we see the very quality of the father-daughter relationship that enables incest to occur and to remain secret. Like her mother, she is suspended in the dissonance between her father's socially and religiously defined role and his actual behavior, as well as between her own defined role as an obedient daughter and the religious imperative to resist evil and temptation.

Not until one of the twins dies does Abigail find the strength to confront her husband. It is at this point that Abigail, as both sufferer and witness, has moved through critically reflecting on her outlaw emotions. Having no one else to share her emotional responses with, Abigail becomes confused and unable to name what she is experiencing; she turns to a text that helps her organize and accept these outlaw emotions and also provides a means of acting on them without deviating too much from her defined roles. In the following scene with Asa, Abigail's resolution is bolstered by her firmly held logic. She relies on neither emotion nor reason to the exclusion of the other, suggesting the extent to which her spiritual diaries have become sites for engaging her emotions with other persuasive discourses, producing a change in epistemology and action.

Abigail tells Asa what she thinks of his behavior with his daughter (he had long ago stopped sleeping in his wife's room), and, when he becomes angry—even though such anger had frightened her in the past—she tells him that "the business [she] had now taken in hand, was of too serious a nature . . . to be dismissed with a few angry words." Throughout this discussion, she attributes God's will to her resolve and the justness of her actions, authorizing her assertiveness in terms of direct revelation and biblical commandments. She says,

> I would now soon adopt measures to put a stop to his abominable wickedness and cruelties. . . . And if I did it not, I should be a partaker of his sins, and should aid in bringing down the curse of God upon our family. . . . Gladly would I have remained a kind faithful, obedient wife to him, as I had ever been. But I told Mr. B he *knew* he had violated his marriage covenant; and hence had forfeited all legal and just right and authority over me; and I should convince him that I well knew it. (Taves 1989, 77–78)

Abigail makes it very clear that she "is not in a passion" (78) but acting on "principle and . . . long and mature consideration" (78). After writing through her uncertainty and fear in her diary, she has come to a well-reasoned argument for acting independently and on behalf of her family. When Asa tries to appeal to her trust in God by offering to swear his innocence on the Bible, Abigail is undeterred, seeing clearly that "such an oath could not undo or alter real facts" (78).

As a result of Abigail's confrontation, Asa becomes appropriately scared and repentant after a while, even though he "denies the charges of incest," and he and Abigail conceive a sixteenth child. But when Abigail finds he has continued his incestuous relationship with Phebe, she finally separates from him, eventually asking for a divorce in which she gives her children to other homes and loses all her property and money (Taves 1989, 82–87).[8] Having given him every chance to reform, Abigail is finally determined to keep Asa away from her children so they will not all end up in hell. Asa's continued incestuous relationship with his daughter becomes the catalyst for Abigail's action but not because his behavior is a crime against Phebe. During the eighteenth century, incest was considered an "unnatural act," and, in Abigail's case, it is a form of adultery of the most cruel kind. Abigail, not Phebe, is therefore the victim in this story, and that is one reason we hear little of Phebe's experience (Taves 1989, 26). Abigail's story, then, highlights for contemporary readers how differently sexual abuse was defined and understood historically.

As many historians and literary critics have argued, it was common during the eighteenth and nineteenth centuries for women to assert a degree of power through Christian ideology, maintaining their roles as true women even as they boldly transgressed them. Harriet Jacobs' *Incidents in the Life of a Slave Girl* is a good example, a text where, as Houston Baker argues, Harriet is a victim of sexual violence (fatherhood under slavery connoted rape) (1984, 52). Unlike Abigail Abbot Bailey, however, Harriet critiques the power structure that enables such abuse to occur. Like Jacobs and Bailey, Grace, the young author of the letter that began this chapter, is trying to contextualize and argue for the choices she has made to leave her family and abdicate her role as caretaker and surrogate wife to her father. In writing to her Sunday School teacher, Grace situates herself within her Christian beliefs and adopts its arguments to justify her rebellion against her father.

Because Christianity has lost its efficacy as an authorizing discourse in the twentieth century, it seems easy to note the differences between Abigail's interpretation of events and a contemporary reader's interpretation, and it is this jarring contrast that emphasizes the role of discourse in shaping reality and subjectivities. If a student were to read Abigail's text, that student would encounter what the abusive experience has already taught, that reality and one's sense of self is figured by language and power. At the same time, that student would be confronted with the fact that such abuse has occurred for centuries[9] and that even in this unusual memoir the victim is silenced and almost effaced from the text. Her subjugated knowledge is part of what motivates her mother to write and to act but is not yet part of the critical dialogue that might intervene in this physical form of oppressive disciplinary power.

Abigail's position as both a sufferer of abuse and a witness to that of her daughter renders her both a disciplined subject and a subject with a degree of power to act on and for another. She locates these subjectivities within her Christian belief system, finding in its literacy practices a place to write her way into a discourse that allows her to act. In the process, Abigail constructs a self that enables her to suffer and yet still do what she can to protect herself and her children. Such a sense of wholeness, transient though it may be, is an identity that doesn't deny fragmentation and situatedness but holds them in tension with discourses that construct a unified self free from the effect of culture and history. Although the text does reinforce a number of dominant ideologies about gender, race, religion, and class, it also figures moments of resistance. In reading Abigail's narrative, a student can become a witness of another kind, watching a woman find a language for her outlaw emotions that enables her both to reflect critically on them and to act critically in a social way.

"By Speaking Out We Educate"

Outlaw emotions stand in a dialectical relation to critical social theory; at least some are necessary to develop a critical perspective on the world, but they also presuppose at least the beginnings of such a perspective.
—Alison Jaggar, "Love and Knowledge" (160)

The pedagogical problem in the era of the postmodern is to place emotion, which has been severed from meaning, at the disposal of meaning once again and thereby to produce affective investments in forms of knowledge that will lead to empowerment and emancipation.
—Lynn Worsham, "Emotion and Pedagogic Violence" (139)

A recurring theme in the student essays I received for my study is the process of sorting through conflicting notions of truth, a perspective on language and ideology that informs many critical and postmodern pedagogies. In their texts, students often weave together the voices of others who disbelieve them or who believe them but don't act to protect the child, who seek to overlay family tales of deception and abuse with dominant constructions of the normal family. Who gets to decide what happened, and why? Who decides whether an individual has in fact been abused, and on what terms? To begin to answer these questions, these student essays engage the authoritative discourses of various disciplines, from sociology, history, and the law to feminist and various psychological theories. In doing so, they begin not only to work toward some of the features valued in academic writing but also to argue for a particular way of defining their experience and themselves.

Fanny, a nontraditional student and mother of high-school-age children in an advanced writing course, centers her essay around this permeable line between truth and lies (see Appendix). She chose to write about her abuse within the context of her family, and, like Emily, never steps into the academic research about her subject or ventures to comment on the social conditions that may have allowed the abuse to occur. She told me that her daughter had recently confronted her with memories of being sexually abused, and this had prompted Fanny to begin the therapy with which she was still involved. Written in a course explicitly focused on the tradition of the personal essay, Fanny's paper engages psychotherapeutic and feminist discourses as she structures her essay around themes of revision and the handing down of traditions and stories:

"My family is charming," she begins. "Through generations on both sides of my parents' family, the apocryphal tales and myths are all about dapper, witty men, and women who were warm, talented mothers. I collected these people and the stories about them with zeal; they gave me an identity, a persona, a tradition." What becomes clear is that this charm is a facade, a deception that enabled generations of women to be abused and to be oblivious when their own daughters were being abused: "Now, I am looking at all those charming people with new eyes. Now, I know I am part of a long line of abused women, and that I, too, was both abused and was unable to see when my daughter was, in turn, abused." Arguing and illustrating that revision leads to new knowledge, Fanny carefully chooses details to reveal both the charm and the violence of her male ancestors. Her grandfather, who had a mistress and was quite rich, was a Christian Scientist who refused his wife treatment for stomach cancer: "I can hear my mother's voice as she told me this part— her father held her mother on the kitchen table, with my mother and uncle present as young children, while she died in extreme pain, screaming and weeping in front of her children. My charming grandfather did that."

The sarcasm in this last line becomes more explicit anger on the next two pages when she describes her father and her belief that he molested her.[10] Again balancing details that describe a sinister and yet compelling charm, Fanny demonstrates apparent command over the artistic shaping of the essay, which gives way to language that seems inconsistent with the rest of the paper:

I was the oldest, and the first to experience both his charm and his filth. He was rotten to the core; in fact, I don't think he had a core in the sense of

having a character, some sort of moral sense. He stole my brothers' caddying money from their dressers, he lied and lied and lied. But, by God, he
was charming . . . he fooled a lot of people. He even fooled us children into
loving him.

This anger and sense of betrayal leads into a discussion about her mother, a
woman who seemed loving and giving as well, but who "also coldly rejected
my sister and me at times when we needed her most." After she describes the
process of reconstructing the past with her siblings and discovering that her
daughter had been sexually abused, Fanny focuses on the point to which she
has been leading: that she cannot simply stop with reseeing her own family.
She must also ask how her own behavior has been shaped by that. This self-
reflection means she has to accept her own role in "not being there" for her
daughter, in recreating the same neglect and "intolerance of fuzzy thinking
and sloppy behavior." In the language of current discourse on sexual abuse,
she no longer views herself as a victim, but as both a survivor and a partici-
pant in the abuse of another.

The purpose of this essay seems to be to describe her process of revision,
arguing that when "I rebuild the past, I am beginning a process of inventing
or maybe transforming my future." Fanny very clearly borrows from therapeutic discourse about family relations, physical, sexual, and verbal abuse: remembering one's past with one's family as a way of healing past wounds, accepting both the pain and the love of one's parents, understanding that when
a survivor becomes a parent, she will need "to hold herself to such a high standard and to control both herself and her children in order to save us all from
the abuse she [has] experienced." The very assumption implicit in her last line
is consistent with most therapeutic approaches: "No amount of revision is going to influence that future if I cannot summon the courage to look behind
that curtain."

Fanny's essay constructs a view of the family in which no one person is
to blame for abusing the intimacies of familial relations, a view of the family
consistent with family systems theory. As many feminists have argued, such a
view posits a dysfunctional family against a normal one, reinscribing the
unequal exercise of power that occurs in family structures (Bell 1993, 87). Yet,
much of the physical space of Fanny's essay is devoted to discussing her male
relatives as abusive toward women, men who had economic and familial
power that allowed them to exploit women sexually and physically both in-
dide and outside the home. She calls her paternal grandfather's family a
"charming patriarchy," evoking a set of feminist arguments about gender and
violence that seem to stand in for a preexisting set of social critiques. Given
the popular currency of family systems therapy and some feminist arguments

about sexual violence, it may be that Fanny is assuming her audience will bring this knowledge to her text. Nonetheless, as a teacher, I might encourage her to reflect on the differences between these two discourses and to explore further what that might mean for her process of revision and reshaping her identity. Fanny is using these discourses, as well as the expectations of personal essays discussed in her course, to reshape the truths handed down to her about her family and abuse. She also is establishing a few truths about these things herself, using the framework of these discourses to structure an argument, to give a context for naming and expressing emotions, and to illustrate the consequent changes to her understanding of her affective relationship and responsibility to others.

Although Fanny may seem to be constructing a unified, individualized, humanist self through this writing, arriving at an inner truth, I would argue that she is engaged in the very processes valued and encouraged by most social constructionist approaches to composition. The controlling metaphor of the essay is revision, and its substance is the reconstructing of dominant familial epistemologies. She is using her own traumatic experiences and the authoritative, dominant discourses that define ways of speaking about families and abuse to critique those ways of knowing, situating herself within a sociopolitical dialectic. The fact that she does not extend this critique to ideology and power is not a consequence of her analytic approach or her self-absorbed introspection. It is a place for teachers to begin talking about what such a critique might look like and what its consequences might be (if this is a direction the teacher wants to encourage). Within a course informed by critical pedagogy, for example, a teacher might ask Fanny to further contextualize this experience historically, particularly by looking at Abigail Abbot Bailey's memoir, and reflect on how those historical materials invite her to see her own experience differently. Within a postmodern pedagogy, the teacher might point out the various discourses within which Fanny situates herself, as I have done here, asking her to pursue some of the conflicts between them and consider what other discourses she might have chosen.

Nicole: Child Sexual Abuse

When the students in my study wrote essays that integrated academic research on sexual abuse, they, too, often used the arguments and purposes constructed in this material to shape their own, and they rarely questioned or critiqued what they were reading. This sometimes uncritical stance, however, is not necessarily the result of the students' inability to analyze critically an emotional and potentially destabilizing experience—it may also be affected by the instructor's ways of challenging (or not challenging) the student to adopt this stance (regardless of whether the subject is bodily violence). Nicole, a college freshman, has written an extraordinary researched essay (see Appendix). In it, she weaves scenes and reflections on the memories she has of her uncle fondling her over a seven-year period with a broad range of outside texts and interviews, from the popular *The Courage to Heal* (Bass and Davis 1988) to psychological and sociological journal articles, to a government document and an interview with a perpetrator.

Nicole begins her essay in an unusual way for a research paper. Instead of opening with a general definition of sexual abuse or a statement about how horrible a crime it is, she describes a scene of the general sequence of events that usually occurred when "it" happened, when her uncle decided he "wanted some company." She speaks euphemistically about the abuse until the last third of the paragraph when she describes his behavior as "fondling."[11] She sets up a scene with all the features now associated with sexual abuse: a young girl is alone with an older male, usually a relative she trusts, he entices her, abuses her, then threatens her if she tells anyone, calling her a "bad, dirty girl." From this introductory scene, she then asserts that her "story is not uncommon," using this as a segue into the statistics of boys and girls who are abused by the time they are eighteen. Throughout her essay, Nicole either uses her own experience as an opening for a researched claim or uses the research to frame her own experience. Her specific details, opinions, and reflections primarily support and illustrate the research, and they rarely question or critique what she has read.

Nicole is explicit in the essay that her purpose in writing is to educate: "In order for this abuse to end our society needs to wake up. We have to work together—family, schools, and the legal system—to stop this heinous abuse against children." By the final paragraph, she reiterates this sentiment and adds, "By speaking out we educate. As Ellen Bass [and Laura Davis] stated: 'In truth itself, there is healing.'" This essay is not a conscious attempt to use writing to work through unresolved feelings, to ask for help from her readers, or to document in painful detail the emotional impact of the abuse. She presents the "truth" of her abuse as an event of the past, one that does affect her in the present, but one that does not interfere with her abilities as a research writer. Like the academic and psychologically based texts she has read, Nicole tells this truth about sexual abuse by addressing the who-what-where-when-and-how questions: why sexual abuse is underreported, what often happens if a child does tell someone, what the emotional effects are for the survivor, why some men molest children, what elements of popular culture contribute to this molestation, and what is being done legally to prosecute offenders. Given the sociological and legal rhetoric she uses to educate her readers, Nicole really has no reason to mention her own experience at all—the research she quotes carries its own authority and offers examples that could illustrate her points.

Nicole integrates her personal experience in large part because her instructor introduces the research paper by having the students write a personal essay, then an argumentative essay on the same subject without using research. After the students draft an essay from the research they have done, the instructor then asks them to combine all three drafts, resulting in a research paper that presents an argument using personal experience and outside research. Thus Nicole's choices are prompted by the specific assignment,[12] and she skillfully composes a multiple-voiced, transactional piece of writing. What is striking about her use of experiential details, however, is the way they guide the shape of the essay and equally share actual space on the page.

After opening with a generalized scene of how her uncle usually touched her, Nicole moves from general statistics and her desire for change to a specific moment when her uncle is caught. A friend has come over to play and Uncle Karl grabs her, evidently attempting to fondle her, as well. Nicole's friend screams and brings "Grammie" into the room, arousing hope in Nicole that "Karl would stop touching me forever and Grammie would kick him out for being a bad man." When Grammie accepts Karl's pledge to never do it again, she tells Nicole not to tell anyone. This scene introduces the essay's next section, which focuses on why people do not report sexual abuse.

As in the other student essays I've discussed, the issue of betrayal is a dominant theme in Nicole's essay, suggesting how much an issue it is to determine a degree of truth about where to place responsibility. It is here that she expresses indirect anger at her grandmother for not taking the incident seriously enough. She describes a day that she overheard a conversation in a restaurant that "reminded me of what happened with my grandmother." In the following description, notice the shifts in tone and discourse:

> The lady said: "I thought they were abusing their kids, but I wasn't sure so I didn't report it." I wanted to scream at her. It is much better to be overly cautious than to have an innocent child hurt. According to Gail Wyatt and Gloria Powell, in 1984, 200,000 child sexual abuse cases were unreported in nineteen states. . . .

The juxtaposition here of several discourses is fairly clear. Nicole weaves together her experience—as a sequence of events—her emotional responses to those experiences and the ways the research echoes both the events and her responses. Her text is an extended example, I would argue, of a woman situating her outlaw emotions in relation to those of others, albeit conveyed through the voices of researchers, and then beginning the process of critically reflecting on those emotions, a process that opens the way to a critical social practice.

What is also significant about this section of Nicole's essay is the way she asserts her authority as a writer and researcher. Not only does she fairly equally weave her experience and responses with outside research, she also comments on that research, positing herself as both the subject of this essay and a researcher in control of it:

> These figures don't even take into account the countless children who, *like I did,* remain silent about their abuse. According to Elizabeth Stanko only about 6 percent of women sexually abused as children ever tell the authorities and one out of five had never told anyone (25). *To me,* this shows how prevalent sexual abuse is in our society and how hard it is for children and adult survivors to tell their experiences. . . . [emphasis added]

In the rest of this section, Nicole discusses the various reasons children don't tell adults about their abuse, citing a campus Sexual Harassment and Rape Prevention Program advocate as well as a 1952 study that argued that sexual abuse had no lasting negative effects on children.

This study effectively opens up her next section, an examination of the effects of sexual abuse on children, and she returns to her grandmother's betrayal. She links this kind of silence to the conclusion many survivors draw that they are in fact the ones to blame for the abuse. Nicole then describes in euphemistic detail the way Karl would approach her and, on this particular day, the way he forced her to perform fellatio.

> It made me feel so disgusting. I still don't remember everything that I felt that day, but I do remember running to the bathroom after and gagging. I brushed my teeth repeatedly as if that would change what he'd made me do. It was that day that I promised myself never to tell anyone because everyone would think that I was a dirty, terrible girl.

At this point, readers may wonder why she feels the need to narrate this scene and her own feelings of guilt and shame. *Guilt* and *shame* should carry her meaning here, one might argue, and she should avoid letting us peer into her vulnerabilities. Yet these terms do not carry the emotional and imaginative impact of the scene, nor do they demand that the reader directly confront what it meant for this young girl to be forced to engage in oral sex. In fact, they distance her from the reality of what she has experienced. If she has made readers uncomfortable, then she has affected the sites where dominant ideologies have conditioned bodies to respond to distasteful behaviors (Bourdieu 1984). Such an emotional response on the reader's part may feel natural, but that naturalness obscures "the ways culture is present in the writer's very act of experiencing the composing process and in the reader's responses to the writer's texts" (Miller 1996, 272–73). By describing the scene, Nicole invites readers to confront their natural responses to her text, opening the way to an important process of critical reflection for them.

Nicole does not hesitate over this scene as I have, however, but instead moves into her own self-doubting questions ("I wonder if I couldn't have done anything to stop Karl") and the explanations for that self-doubt given by Bass and Davis (1988) in *The Courage to Heal*. Nicole asserts that the child is never to blame, reiterating one of the dominant assumptions that operate in current theories about sexual abuse. Throughout the rest of the essay, she calls on interviews, academic journal articles, incidents reported in the press, and specific laws being considered in other states to both create and advance her arguments. The essay is primarily informative, seeking to establish various assertions about sexual abuse with which the audience may be unfamiliar, but that people need to know if they are going to be motivated to change the conditions that produce such sexual violence.

Like other students whose essays I have read, Nicole chooses from a seemingly limited number of rhetorical purposes in writing this polyvocal essay: to render her experience and its significance into essay form, to argue for social change through education and legal reform, and to criticize the media for its role in sexualizing children. These purposes are dictated by the discourses these student writers appropriate, just as Abigail Abbot Bailey's purposes were structured by the available narrative frames of the captivity narrative, spiritual diaries, and Congregationalist Christian doctrine. By engaging these discourses, these writers restructure the meanings of their experiences, their identities, and the possibilities of socially oriented change. If the work of the student essays I've analyzed in this chapter can be considered a form of healing, however, it is one that occurs within a dialectical process, not only among the many discourses they use but also between the teacher and the student. As many students have said to me, they want as much to heal on a social level as on an individual one. This is not a healing that creates wholeness in the sense of a unified, self-authorizing whole but one that is continually in the process of accepting fragmentation, otherness, and difference.

3

"The Bruises Were Inside of Me"

WRITING THE HUNGRY BODY

My body is no longer my own. I don't recognize the bones that stick out, or the emaciated legs and arms. I stare at the world from behind sunken, dark-circled eyes and hollow cheeks, and even they are not mine. When I see those old pictures of myself with rosy cheeks and bright eyes, I feel as though I am looking at a stranger. My body belongs to my doctor. He sees it once a week, plops me on a scale, pokes and prods me, watches my body's defenses against starvation, and charts my "progress." I am not a patient. I am a case study; this week's science project.

—Laura, a student

Why Am I This Way, Why Am I That? Why Do Myself and I Constantly Spat? [1]

When I was seventeen I played the Flesh in a church play. The Devil, the World, and the Flesh were all competing with each other to tempt an adolescent male, Chris, over to the dark side. My friend Missy was drafted to play the Devil because she could sing so well, and I vaguely remember the World being cast as a man. To play my part, I donned my father's Wabash College sweatshirt, a decades-old memento from his days as an undergraduate before he was ousted for his low grades and penchant for partying. I looked sloppy, heavy, and self-indulgent, as any good Flesh would. At home my family laughed at how appropriate a choice I was for the role.

They often teased me about being a grazer, a veritable food processor, willingly enjoying ice cream, cookies, and, my favorite, fried chicken and

48

mashed potatoes. My parents would often disagree in front of me about whether I should be allowed to eat so much after basketball practice because they feared, as I found out almost fifteen years later, I would become as increasingly heavy over the years as my pediatrician warned them I might. So they monitored me.

The morning of the play I worried about whether I could perform one of my key lines without bursting into laughter as I had done during rehearsal. Chris and I are in lotus position meditating, Chris trying hard not to be tempted.

"Ummm. Ummm," Chris murmurs with his eyes closed.

"Umm. Umm. I think I hear a twinkie calling me from the freezer," I say in meditative rhythm, trying to deliver the line straight. The congregation laughs, my parents and brothers about to explode through their German Lutheran reserve. With that line, the distance between me and my character collapses. I weigh only 130 pounds at seventeen, but on that stage, in the guise of the Flesh, I am acting out what I have come to believe—that my flesh is my primary temptress (after all, as a female I am chosen for this role) and that I'm overweight. I have been dieting since junior high school, going on Weight Watchers; drinking Tab (a sugar-free soft drink); and following every diet my nutritionally minded, slender mother tries. I play basketball for the school team and climb mountains with the church Youth Group in the summers. A few years before, my father had told me I could only fly to Florida to see some family friends if I lost ten pounds. I tried desperately, not eating or eating only one small meal each day. I lost only seven pounds and was convinced I would not be able to go. Instead, my father chided me for believing him.

At seventeen, I embody a woman divided against herself (as later feminists and psychologists would define it), part of the growing number of young girls going on diets before they reach puberty. I am only beginning to hear about eating disorders, and later will read about Debbie Boone's bulimia and descent into eating dogfood. Karen Carpenter will die, and, like other teenagers at the time, I will forever remember the image of her skeletal face and the notes of her smooth, impassioned voice.

During the summer of my sophomore year of college, I work at McDonalds and eat only a hamburger or salad all day (and maybe a little ice cream at night). I lose ten pounds, have little energy, and feel like an attractive, powerful young woman for the first time in years. My parents sit me down and ask what's going on, why I'm not eating very much. I don't remember much of that conversation, but I end up changing my major first to nutrition, where I learn what I have just done to my body, and then to English. In retrospect, this conversation, my shrinking body, and my ambivalence about what to do with my life are not coincidental. Nor, I imagine, is the link between my tightly controlled body and my desire to be a writer. I begin to eat normally but with a constant Panoptical gaze watching every piece of food I put in my mouth. Like a character on a stage, I have been born into a series of discourses that have shaped my subjectivity and cause me to be ever watchful of the temptations of the flesh.

I remember the pleasure of feeling my hipbone through my jeans, of gazing at the hollow my collarbones make when I wear a tank top, and of being able to zip those one-size-too-small jeans I used to hang in my closet as a body check. It is this pleasure that is probably most difficult to understand when one reads about people's experiences with self-imposed starvation, excessive exercise, and cycles of binging and purging. As the women in my study describe their daily rituals, it is difficult to ignore the pain—of hunger, of stomach acids, of burning muscles, of dying bodies, and of desperate souls. But these extremes of self-denial and punishment can lead to a kind of pleasure in being so close to an idealized and sexualized or fetishized female form. Most clinical and social studies argue that this pleasure is also associated with the ability to control one's body and, to a certain degree, to control even its uncontrollable impulses (some researchers have suggested that starvation becomes addictive [see Katz 1985, 622–23]).[2] Yet with this pleasure comes the danger of kidney failure, for example, or angina, and, in extreme cases, death.

The paradoxical nature of eating disorders, their multiple meanings, seems inescapable in a study of this phenomenon, and I have found the paradoxes of eating disorders particularly difficult to address as I have read student essays on the subject. The young women who write about their eating disorders have inflicted or continue to inflict violence on their bodies, and when they sit in our classrooms or offices, we are face-to-face with both victim and perpetrator. A few of them have almost died. How can a teacher respond to an essay about such a complex and potentially dangerous type of self-abuse? What does it mean for the student to revisit these experiences through writing? As a researcher, I struggle to negotiate the feelings these student essays evoke for me, the memories of how pleasure is linked to pain and obsession to resistance, how a small tight body feels powerful in its emptiness and leanness, how the self in the mirror is never the self I want, even now that my own work tries to critique this body shame that seems woven as a sticky spider web.

This chapter has been the most difficult one to write. When I began to read the essays I had received about eating disorders, I realized I couldn't distinguish most of them from each other. Unlike the essays about sexual abuse in which the textual features and approaches to the subject were fairly different, the essays about eating disorders made similar arguments, followed similar organizational patterns, and rendered their writers almost indistinguish-able. The teachers I talked with confirmed that most papers on eating disorders seemed the same to the extent that they had moved into many instructors' lists of common but generic essay subjects—the death of a friend, the night we got drunk and were caught, the boyfriend story, the abortion paper. These essays on eating disorders seemed merely to reproduce what I assumed my au-dience would already know about the subject, causing me to wonder whether I had anything to say about them.

I soon dispensed with the pressure to find something unusual about these essays and began wondering what it meant that the pieces were all sim-ilar. As I explore in more detail in the pages ahead, this similarity is consistent with the characteristics of eating disorders—the desire for control, the desire to achieve an asexual body, or the need to look like a particular image of a woman. In addition, most student essays on eating disorders do not address the more dangerous consequences of the disorder, reproducing a control over the material in their texts that doesn't allow for the possibility of permanent damage to reproductive organs or to the heart, or for the probability of death. In addition, all the essays present the student's identity as an eating disordered woman in terms of how the eating disorder is defined, by whom it is defined, and what other identities it replaces; and many of them explore the student's identity as a recovered anorexic or bulimic. As with the essays on sexual abuse, the essays on eating disorders take up the subject of a postmodern identity and the effects of having so many forces struggling to define and control a woman's body and her self.

Instructors told me that anorexic and bulimic women seem to write about their bodies more frequently than do women who have been physically or sexually abused, but, like the students whose essays I presented in Chapter 2, these young women also create polyvocal texts in which they use various in-terpretive frames to piece together identities and conflicting notions of truth about their ravaged bodies and senses of self. The bodily violence anorexic and bulimic women experience may seem significantly different from that of sexual and physical abuse—and in many ways it is—but all are produced by similar kinds of power. Although some psychological studies have posited that sexual and physical abuse can be precipitous factors to eating disorders,[3] cultural theorists have focused on the role of power and violence on those connections. As Michel Foucault has argued, power works most effectively when it cannot be seen (1978, 59): with both physical and sexual violence, the fear and unpredictability of the abuse (especially within long-term, inti-mate relationships) work like Foucault's panopticon—just a gaze reinforces the possibility of the violence and teaches the woman proper and submissive attitudes, gestures, and understandings of herself as a female (Bell 1993, 68–69). As feminists argue, violence against women is not deviant behavior, but it is part of the same cultural process that creates "subservient femininity [as] the norm" (66–67).

An anorexic woman is in many ways the embodiment of this panoptical power, a woman who has internalized this violence and identity so that physical and sexual abuse are no longer necessary to accomplish the same goals. For feminists such as Sandra Bartky (1988), eating disorders are on a continuum with sexual and physical violence, all three creating a similar sense of identity for women that maintains a focus on the body as a site for control. In studying students who have written about anorexia or bulimia, then, I am considering another example of young women who, consciously or not, make the disciplinary nature of femininity manifest in an institution that has traditionally participated in reinforcing such identities.

Reading the Body, Reading the Writing

> *To have a body felt to be "feminine"—a body socially constructed through the appropriate practices—is in most cases crucial to a woman's sense of herself as female, and, since persons currently can be only as male or female, to her sense of herself as an existing individual. To possess such a body may also be essential to her sense of herself as a sexually desiring and desirable subject. Hence, any political project which aims to dismantle the machinery that turns a female body into a feminine one may well be apprehended by a woman as something that threatens her with desexualization, if not outright annihilation.*
>
> —Sandra Bartky, "Foucault, Femininity,
> and the Modernization of Patriarchal Power" (77)

When Jenn handed in an essay about her struggles with bulimia, it was after a friend from her honors composition class spent a night helping her "not give in to the temptations" of her disorder. The piece is a moving essay about her painful struggle with her body that doesn't fit any of the patterns of the other essays in this chapter. I want to begin my discussion of the student essays with Jenn's because it dramatizes what the other student essays work so hard to control and conceal: the fragmenting sense of identity and reality these women experience. Most of the essays I received that focused on eating disorders were composed after the student had sought some help, allowing the student to assume a conventional stance as a wiser, more knowledgeable writer whose disorder had been resolved. Jenn's essay was one of the few written while the student was still in the midst of the disorder, and it allowed her to powerfully render the conflicts and desires that she cannot resolve.

What is so striking about this piece is how thoroughly textualized the self and the body are, how Jenn's sense of identity is conflated with her body and shaped by nameless voices telling her what to do, how to be. Like the narrator at the end of Charlotte Perkins Gilman's "The Yellow Wallpaper," the speaker in this text is fighting "those eyes" that gaze so ominously, and yet is almost abandoned to their definitions of her and her body. And, like Gilman's narrator, the speaker portrays the doctor and the other female character, Jenn's mother, as insensitive, intrusive, and controlling. Trying to free the woman behind the paper, she entraps herself even further, and the written text illustrates postmodernism's wild subject, a decentered, socially mediated, discursive self.

THOSE EYES

They got the best of me tonight. I thought I had finally found the strength to control *them,* but I guess I was wrong.

When I came to college I told myself that I was not going to do it anymore. That I was going to be healthy. That I was going to be like everyone else. I told myself that I was stronger than *they* were. For the first two weeks I did everything I was supposed to. I put fat and calories in my stomach and kept *them* there. I worked my muscles until my muscles started to take over the room that had been occupied all of my life. But tonight I was weak.

I went to dinner and I could feel *them. They* were watching me. I have felt their stares many times before. I had been ignoring *them.* I had been strong. I was showing *them* that no one could control me. I was telling myself that I could do anything I wanted to. But, tonight *they* were looking through me. *They* were seeing inside me. *They* found a weak spot and made it grow.

No one else can see *them.* If I told anyone that *they* were there everyone would think I was crazy. *They* do not have blood running through *them. They* are not composed of bone and flesh. *They* are real only to me. *They* watch me day and night. *They* never sleep.

Sitting alone in my room with the door locked and the shades drawn I feel *them* watching me. *They* scrutinize every move I make. Telling me that I am not good enough without ever speaking a word. *They* are a part of me. A part that exists outside of my body but in my mind.

It is because of *them* that there is no curvature in my spine. Even when I am alone in my room and trying to relax my spinal cord must be straight. My head must be held high. My legs have to be crossed. When crossing my legs, the top one must never rest completely on the bottom one. Allowing this to happen causes the fat to spread sideways instead of hanging down. Legs that are crossed with all the weight resting on the bottom leg look fatter *they* tell me. You look more confident when your head is held high *they* tell me. Your spinal cord will be permanently curved if you slouch *they* tell me. The doctors all say there is not truth to what *they* say. The people at school say I play the part of a snob. I was just doing what *they* told me to.

It was always easier to do what *they* said. To think for myself and to go against *them* would take more strength than I have ever possessed in all of my eighteen years. I seriously thought *they* knew what was best for me until I lost all of my friends.

My friends said that I thought I was too good to eat lunch at their table or to hang out with my friends. I did not know how to tell my friends that I did not think that my friends were dragging me down. *They* said that *they* were the only friends that I had. I started to believe *them.* For two years I was without friends who required food and oxygen to live. That is when I first realized that *they* did not always have the right answers for life's problems. For example, purging after that bowl of ice cream did not make my crush like me. I have been battling *them* ever since. I am the only one who ever gets wounds. I am afraid that I will never get a purple badge for courage for all of the wars that I have been in. Most people will never hear of my war.

Thinking for myself was the first battle. When it was over I was covered in bruises that no one else could see. The bruises were inside of me. There were scratches in my throat and pains in my stomach. If I ever told anyone how much the bruises hurt *they* would twist the knife deeper into me. I was slowly bleeding to death inside. The doctors gave the wounds names. One was called "Bleeding Ulcers." The other one was called "Gallstones." *They* told me the wounds were punishments for trying to leave *them* behind. The wounds were punishments for trying to accept my body the way it was. *They* told me it was my fault. This is where *they* and the doctors agree, in a way.

The doctors said it was my fault I had bleeding ulcers and gallstones. It was after my mother complained that I was too young for "such things." She never did call *them* by their proper names. Sometimes I think that she was afraid if she did use the proper names it would make it real. No one else in my family had ever had "such things." The doctors told me in privacy that the doctors had to tell my mom why I had "such things" because I was a minor. I thought the doctors were going to be sympathetic. I thought the doctors understood. I asked the doctors to tell me exactly why, in their minds, I had "such things." Maybe it was a medical problem I had and not a mental one. Besides, why should my mom get a clarification and not me? It was my body, in a way. We, the doctors and I, spent the next five minutes discussing my diet. The doctor got out a little book and did the simple addition in the doctor's head.

The doctors brought my mother in the room and had her sit down. I was still lying on the table with gel on my belly and a nurse rolling something over it. The doctors did not bother to use nice words. The doctors used easy-to-understand words and bluntly state the reasons. It is my fault because I lowered my calorie intake to less than one thousand calories a day the doctors declared. "From our calculations," the doctors proclaimed, "she is currently taking in around three hundred calories a day. Some days considerably lower." I believe I eat more than that and tried to explain this, but the doctors wouldn't let me. The doctors did not understand after all. The doctors thought it was a phase I was going through. The doctors said I would grow out of it. The doctors said the only sad part about it was I was going to have lifelong reminders. The doctors prescribed some drugs that had to be taken with food. My mom said the only problem I had was that I wanted to be a size five. She agreed that it was a phase. My mom was on a diet at the time. She had no right to say anything about what size I wanted to be.

They agreed with the doctors. *They* know that it is my fault, but *they* don't have to tell my mother. There are no laws saying *they* have to tell my mother. *They* have no laws at all.

They say it is because I don't exercise enough. *They* say it is because I ate too much when I was a kid. *They* say it is because all I did while growing up was watch the television. *They* say it is my fault because I have the kind of body that if I eat I am going to be fat. *They* think I have control over that. *They* say if I were smarter I would not have "such things." *They* say if I were attractive I would not have to worry about "such things." I believe all of what *they* say. I believe that I would be able to enjoy all the rich flavors that exist in the world if I would never have to taste *them* backwards if I was not so pathetic in every way.

They control me more than I like to admit. I once thought that when I wanted *them* to go away *they* would. That was the deal in the beginning. All I had to do was say so and *they* would go away. I was wrong. Maybe I do not want *them* to go away, maybe that is the problem.

Although the pronouns "they" and "them" shift meaning throughout the essay, their initial referent is "those eyes." This evokes a nameless, dispersed panoptical power who is trying to control her body and its desires by seeing all and dispensing judgment: "*They* were looking through me. *They* were seeing inside me. . . . telling me that I am not good enough without ever speaking a word." These beings "not composed of bone and flesh" structure her body's movements, admonishing her to keep her spine straight, her legs crossed but not relaxed, her body disciplined into an image of confidence, slenderness, and health. As Sandra Bartky (1988) has argued, the female body is subjected to the state's disciplinary power differently from a male's because the female body is made more docile, subjected to ritualized practices that construct an image of femininity, implying the body is deficient and in constant need of self-surveillance (64, 72, 75, 65). As in the other essays on eating disorders, Jenn details the rituals and agonizing discipline she subjected her body to, or as indicated here was induced to subject it to, in a tone that seems to both admonish and relish how well she accomplished this control and mastery. She is both a master of these rituals and a victim of them.

For most of the essay, however, she describes herself as too weak to resist "them," implying some faith in an active, resistant self that could win this war. Who that self is does not become clear; instead, we see the selves structured by competing discourses (those eyes) as devouring and then rejecting (purging) any self that might resist. She says that "[t]hinking for myself was the first battle," yet it isn't clear what the fight was about. On the one hand, thinking for herself could mean she tried to stop heeding the voices that prompted her to purge and gave her so many "scratches in [her] throat and pains in [her] stomach." On the other hand, this could mean resisting the doctors, choosing what to do with her body despite their advice. Regardless, the speaker in this piece finds her "thinking self" attacked, blamed for the "wounds" on her body.

As is characteristic of many anorexic and bulimic women, Jenn creates an identity in this essay that is divided against itself, fragmented by the contradictory surveilling eyes that offer seemingly irreconcilable interpretations of her body, her identity, and her need to control. It is as if she has walked into a vortex of preexisting discourses that so thoroughly textualize and discipline her that she cannot sustain the fiction of a self capable of resisting. Those eyes teach her how to shape her body to convey particular messages, and a key element of that shaping is to control or get rid of "fat." The extent to which she fails in this control affects how others respond to her and how valued she is: One set of voices, most likely from popular culture, "say [the fat on her body] is because I don't exercise enough. . . . I ate too much when I was a kid. . . . [A]ll I did while growing up was watch the television. . . . I have the kind of body that if I eat I am going to be fat." If she "were smarter" or "attractive" she wouldn't have to worry about "such things." These lines illustrate the paradox of an eating disordered body: a belief that one has control over the body's hunger and production of fat, and yet that one has no control at all because the body defies such willful definitions. Jenn conflates her sense of self with this control over her body, and yet she wants desperately to separate herself from a body that turns against her.

Intersecting with this interpretation is that of the doctors, a set of explanations that Jenn laces with disdain. On the one hand, she calls the doctors' number crunching, diagnosing, and naming of her body's wounds an explanation of her "mental [problem]," but she wonders if it isn't a "medical problem." To construct it as a medical problem means her "wounds" are not "her fault" but her body's, evidence that she is victim to this unruly mass of cells. Yet all the images she describes of the doctors measuring, probing, and treating her body as an object of analysis suggests how thoroughly medicalized the process of interpretation is. Even when she thinks the "doctors were going to be sympathetic," they actually dismiss her problem as a "phase" and, from Jenn's perspective, betray her to her mother. She feels abandoned by the doctors' diagnosis, by her mother's inability to accept the reality of Jenn's body, and the willingness of both to name her body and her thoughts as if she could not. With each of these different notions of truth about her condition, Jenn responds as both a victim of their words and as a resister. Her ambivalence about the relationship between her body and her self is evinced when she says, "It was my body, in a way." Whose body is it, really? And what kind of self is this body writing?

Jenn's essay enacts her body's struggle over what it means to be a female subject in Western culture. During a night when she was fighting her desire to purge, she instead tried to render with words what Bartky (1988) might argue is endemic to all women's experiences: "Woman lives her body as seen by another, by an anonymous patriarchal Other" (72), and through the extremes of these disciplinary rituals learns to feel shame for the ultimate failure of her body and her will to achieve a docile femininity (72). Yet, any attempts by her doctors to disrupt Jenn's behaviors, to heal her, are ultimately threatening to her sense of self, initiating a sense of loss. Her identity has been structured around her abilities to control her unruly body and the space it invades, a metaphor of control and emotional cool like that expected of authors in some writing classrooms—whether the student is admonished to purge tangents, clean up grammar weaknesses, or tighten up the essay's coherence. Unlike many of the essays I received for my study, Jenn's is not neatly organized into an expository or argumentative paper. It is an essay in the tradition of Montaigne: It explores, it wanders, it circles back, and it comes to no definitive conclusions. Unlike Montaigne, however, Jenn less easily assumes a stable sense of authorial identity and essentially undoes herself.

Reading the Disordered Body

Jenn's essay is different from the others in my study in many ways, but a key difference is that it deviates from a more controlled exposition (such as a thesis or support structure, an argument form, a researched report about bulimia). We might interpret this difference as Jenn resisting her desire to control her body and self, choosing not to make her essay fit a particular academic form. Or we might read her essay as a protest against "those eyes"—the structures of femininity that have created these conflicts—a protest readers need to applaud. However, we might also argue that with her writing she is reinscribing an identity or body that is so fragile, so weak, that it cannot resist other forms of oppression such as physical or verbal abuse—that it is more submissive than reeling in protest. How we read Jenn's essay, however, largely depends on how we explain eating disorders—how they're defined, how they develop, what meaning they have for the individual and the culture. Just as what we now call sexual violence was defined quite differently less than a century ago, our contemporary understanding of an eating disorder is only a twentieth-century development. It's important to know this history so we can complicate our tendencies to pathologize these students and to help them see their experience within a historical, cultural, and ideological context.

Historically, women have controlled their appetites to the extremes of starvation since at least the medieval period, and the meanings of self-starvation have shifted over time. From the thirteenth to the sixteenth century what we now call anorexia was understood as "fundamental to the model of female holiness" (Brumberg 1988, 41) because women's bodies were associated with food—thus spirituality could be expressed through the symbolism of eating behaviors (45). Currently, as Brumberg argues, this same behavior is no longer linked to piety; it "is embedded in patterns of class, gender, and family relations established in the nineteenth century" (46) and has come to signify an individual pathology for some, an embodiment of oppressive femininity for others.

Today researchers understand anorexic and bulimic behavior through the lenses of psychology, biomedical studies, and cultural theory. Psychologically it is understood as a young woman's struggle for autonomy and individuation during adolescence; her body becomes the site for her to control her identity in the face of feeling inadequate to the challenges of adulthood and sexuality. Usually high achievers from middle- to upper-class families, these young women are often afraid of choosing wrongly from the many opportunities they have and are "in a desperate fight against feeling enslaved and exploited, not competent to lead a life of their own" (Bruch 1978, ix–x). Although some psychologists locate the disorder in oedipal or preoedipal struggles (a rejection of the mother/sexuality/fat and a desire for the father/intellect/muscle),[4] others in family systems theory identify the causes within enmeshed, overprotective, and controlling family relationships. The young woman is taught to subordinate herself to others' needs and avoid individuality, often, it is argued, having a mother who is also preoccupied with food and her body, is submissive, and is unable to separate from her daughter.[5] As Jenn's essay illustrates, key to understanding the paradoxes of an anorexic's struggle is the way she both conflates her body with her self (her identity comes from how well she masters control of it) and sees it as separate from her self (hunger is her body turning against herself and so trying to obstruct her control and identity) (Orbach 1985, 85–87).

Physically, the results of starving or binging and purging range from dehydration, esophageal sores, and abnormal body hair, to irregular heartbeats, amenorrhea, kidney failure, and death. Physicians have posited a number of theories to explain why some women risk such bodily harm, theories that point to the hypothalamus, but none of which are conclusive or explain why the disorder is more prevalent in white, middle-class young women than in other groups.[6] To better explain why the disorder affects this population more than others, cultural theorists have argued that Western ideals of femininity, particularly twentieth-century, mass-produced images of slenderness, contribute to the increasing numbers of women who exhibit eating disordered behavior (a so-called fact that is disputed on several grounds).[7] In addition, many critics argue that in the industrialized West a disdain for fat is a disdain for low socioeconomic status, suggesting that eating disorders are also produced from class and gender distinctions. From these perspectives, eating disordered women are viewed as martyrs, Debra Gimlim says, rebelling against the strictures of gendered identity and powerlessness (1994, 105). They are no longer considered pathological but victims of a patriarchal culture who are enacting a form of protest.

It might be difficult to read a starving woman as an embodiment of protest and resistance—she is, after all, inflicting self-harm and appears quite self-focused, not overtly political and socially oriented. Brumberg asserts that

> If the anorectic's food refusal is political in any way, it is a severely limited and infantile form of politics, directed primarily at parents (and self) and without any sense of allegiance to a larger collectivity. Anorectics, not known for their sisterhood, are notoriously preoccupied with the self. The effort to transform them into heroic freedom fighters is a sad commentary on how desperate people are to find in the cultural model some kind of explanatory framework, or comfort, that dignifies this confusing and complex disorder. (1988, 37)

Brumberg's point is important, particularly in emphasizing that this type of self-starvation is not *consciously* politically motivated. However, political protest need not be conscious and organized to be considered resistance and critique. Self-starvation is a physical manifestation of the discipline and control required to be "feminine" in Western culture, challenging gender constructions without the woman needing to intend such a critique. As a manifestation of the trauma of femininity, anorexia exaggerates the kind of woman which best serves androcentric and capitalist ideologies: An emaciated woman is one who is quite dependent, isolated, and often disconnected from sociopolitical life because she has been socialized to focus primarily on her body; she is so invested in feminine ideals that she cannot organize to protest in politically effective ways. Because this exaggerated form of femininity illustrates the self-immolating consequences of feminine ideals, it is a form of protest against those ideals (even while it is succumbing to them).[8]

While critics argue whether one can read historical cases of food-refusing behavior through contemporary psychological and sociological theories, it is important to emphasize that as a language associated with females, this behavior has served very different purposes and meanings over time, and contemporary interpretations reflect our cultural preoccupations and ideologies. This does not mean, as Bordo points out, that no connections can be made among these time periods (1993, 69): Significantly more females than males suffer from eating disorders, and they are concentrated in "advanced industrial societies within roughly the last hundred years" (1993, 49–50). Although not a recent phenomenon, eating and body control have come to signify what it means to be a woman in contemporary culture: "Most women are 'disordered' when it comes to issues of self-worth, self-entitlement, self-nourishment, and comfort with their own bodies" (1993, 57) because how they see themselves in the mirror (literally and figuratively) is what the culture has taught them to see. When a woman like Jenn is participating in the rituals of health and body reduction, she is confessing her deficiency as a woman: not good enough with the body she has, she needs to change it to be aligned with social norms about women's body size, and she can readily find several strategies that also promise through religious metaphors to save women from the earthly and uncontrollable bodies they inhabit (Spitzack 1990, 159–60). Without this socialized need to confess one's deviance from the norm, consumer culture could not flourish—no make up would be sold, no portable gyms, no aerobic shoes or kickboxing videos. So when a student in a writing class chooses to write about her anorexia, she is caught in a different kind of web than her fellow sufferers from the medieval period, but it is a web that has competing claims to her identity and her sense of agency.

Although in this chapter I emphasize a feminist, poststructuralist reading of these student essays, it is important to note that the biological and psychological interpretations of the disorder offer just as much insight into understanding these students and their writing. I have chosen a feminist perspective because I want to put feminist theories on the body in dialogue with student papers like Jenn's: They especially resonate with these theories, challenging postmodern tendencies to see the body as only a text that cultural discourses create. The identity described in "Those Eyes" illustrates well the fragmenting effects of such textualizing, making me wonder again about the kinds of postmodern identities some of us may value in our writing courses. Students with eating disorders physically confront us with some of the dangerous effects of a postmodern identity. At the same time, feminist theories help us to question those perspectives that may be constructing a woman purely as a victim, purely as a victimizer, or pathologically unstable and so not prepared for an academic identity.

Within some feminist frameworks, particularly those emphasizing the role of culture, ideology, and discursive practices, it matters greatly whether Jenn is understood as a passive victim of disciplinary practices of femininity or as a person enacting a protest of those rituals. To see her as passive reproduces androcentric constructions of women as malleable, controllable, or waiting to be given an identity; whereas, to see her as resisting the very gender codes that threaten to control her is to invert this historical construction. The struggle over the meanings of eating disorders has become a struggle over the meanings of women's bodies, gendered practices, the reproduction of ideology, and various forms of oppression, as well as over women's agency and possibilities for resistance. From this perspective, Jenn's essay becomes vitally important to political and cultural projects, and Jenn's writing instructor—how she responds to Jenn and her discursive representations of her experience, her emotions, and her body—carries enormous responsibility.

Whether a composition classroom can or should carry such responsibility for the ideological implications of language is an ongoing debate, and one I don't think a study like this can avoid addressing. I know I cannot sit in my office across from an emaciated or bruised young student and avoid asking myself what my responsibilities are. Although the theoretical explanations I have and will continue to use to read these students' texts and bodies may seem to remove me and other readers from the actual bodies that daily experience such pain, I hope instead they help me argue why we need to take these texts and these students seriously. In articulating their own experiences, bringing their subjugated knowledge into the public and academic space of a writing class, can these students resist the disciplines of femininity? Or are their texts simply reinforcing the discourses that have converged to create the eating disordered identity?

Textual Features: Making a Body Visible

In her historical study of the changing meanings of food-refusing behavior among young women, Joan Jacobs Brumberg (1988) describes the "typical anorexia story" she found in adolescent fiction about eating disorders:

> These stories are nearly formulaic: they emphasize family tensions and the adolescent girl's confused desire for autonomy and control, but they do not advance any particular interpretation of the cause or etiology of the disease.

The plot almost always involves an attractive (usually 5 feet 5 inches), intelligent high school girl from a successful dual-career family. The mother is apt to be a fashion designer, artist, actress, or writer; the father is a professional or self-made man. In two of the novels the central characters say they want to go to Radcliffe. (16)

The young girl starts out wanting to reduce her weight because she notices that slenderness is valued in young women, but eventually "ordinary dieting becomes transformed into a pattern of bizarre food and eating behavior that dominates the life of the central character" (17). This behavior disrupts friendships and worries her parents, and usually the mother is the one who refers the young woman to professional help. Despite their purposes of providing information and warnings, Brumberg argues, these stories stop short of depicting the graphic realities of the disorder, the "classic battle for control that absorbs so much time and energy in psychotherapeutic treatment" (16) and the painful process of uncertain recovery (17).

Similarly, student essays about eating disorders rarely seem to address the more dangerous consequences of starvation — only three of the nine essays I received mentioned developing heart problems, having blackouts, or possibly dying. Often, in fact, the writer summarized her recovery in one sentence. In general, the papers I received follow a plot line similar to that of the fictional adolescent narratives Brumberg describes. They recount

- Why the writer started either to purge or to restrict her food intake
- What prompted this decision
- What measures she took to conceal her behavior
- How this behavior alienated her from her friends and family
- What physical changes she went through and how others reacted
- How she was discovered and by whom
- How she recovered

These writers pay close, detailed attention to the particulars of their rituals (hiding Tupperware containers in a closet for vomiting) and of their bodies (visible ribs, sunken breasts and cheeks, calloused fingers). And they never fail to note how much weight they have lost.

These essays about the writer's struggles with food are often intended to be warnings for other women. The writers told me they hoped someone else might be dissuaded from succumbing to the addictive cycle of food restriction and weight loss. If the essay involves research, its purpose was often to explain the causes and effects of the disorder or to offer a cultural analysis of gender constructions and body image. Like the essays about sexual abuse, these texts all use authorizing discourses that structure what can be said about the experience and how it can be said. The most common discourses the students used to explain why anorexics or bulimics become so obsessed with food were either a psychological interpretation that argues these women desire control, associate food with emotions, have low self-esteem, and struggle to become independent from their families; or a cultural interpretation that links media images of women, the culture's attitudes toward thinness and obesity, and women's desires for these ideal bodies.

"Maybe She's Born with It": Femininity as Disordered Body

What I found most interesting about the patterns in these essays was how the writers situated themselves between two types of images, that of the model and that of the anorexic or bulimic as in the following introduction to a narrative:

> In our generation today, I feel that many females experience an eating disorder at some point in their lives. It's my belief that the reason why women are so concerned with their weight is insecurity, men, and society. Women strive too much to make themselves resemble the models they see in magazines and on television. It is believed in women's minds that being thin is what beauty is all about. Some women lose weight to either impress men or to fit in a tight dress. I think females are so obsessed with losing weight that they either starve themselves or purge after eating. These diseases are known as being anorexic or bulimic. Throughout my life I have dealt with the disease bulimia.

In this paragraph, women are either striving to be like models or are becoming anorexic or bulimic—striving to be a model often leads to an eating disorder. And, because this writer can assume her audience has heard of eating disorders before, she gives a thumbnail description of what they are—starving oneself or purging—and why they occur—insecurity, men, and society. Her experience has been made visible by the authorities (who no longer need to be named) who have made eating disordered women not just a category of identity but a group to be taken seriously. In relying on the image of a bulimic or anorexic, this writer carves a space for her own narrative and draws on a community of fellow sufferers to validate her authority as a writer.

At the same time, the eating disordered woman is primarily visible here through her association with the image of the model. As this student says, when women compare themselves to models, they inevitably find themselves deficient and then are motivated to try all kinds of weight-reducing behaviors to achieve this image. Even if women do not practice food restriction or intense exercise, they are never without an image of a model to reinforce what they have learned about being female: It means lack, deficiency, and disease. According to theorist Carole Spitzack, a woman's sense of perpetual deficiency is encouraged by the messages women hear about health and body reduction. They promise health and beauty if only a woman will buy this product or have this surgery or try this exercise machine. It reminds me of the Maybelline ads, "Maybe she's born with it. Maybe it's Maybelline." The message here is that *only* by using their products will a woman achieve the image of health and beauty that dominant culture sees as the norm. No woman is born with it. So, for a woman to be visible, she must achieve the cultural definition of health (normal) or risk invisibility as a fat/diseased/deviant woman (1990, 157).

We see this process almost every day, especially with the explosion of makeovers that are featured on daytime talk shows. On "The Maury Povich Show," for example, about a dozen men were asked which celebrity they wanted their wives or girlfriends to look like. When the women were made over to look like Pamela Sue Anderson or Cher or Doris Day, the men were thrilled. The women declared how much sexier and more beautiful they felt with these new identities, even if they were temporary. With the makeovers, the women were made more visible, more desirable, and ultimately more inadequate than the women they used to be. On Maury's next show, he was giving makeovers to women whose children thought their moms dressed too seductively, and the women were made over to look like Hillary Clinton: They wore business suits, pantyhose, neutral make-up, and one-inch block heels. With each new piece of clothing, each haircut and eyebrow wax, these women assumed a new identity, displacing the implicitly defective identity with which they came to the show.

This same process occurs for women generally: A woman's deficient identity is continually displaced in the belief that she can achieve an image of health and beauty, but the very act of having a makeover or buying a Thigh-Master simply reinforces the essential inadequacy of being a woman. The image of the model, then, depends on the image of the fat and deviant woman these students all believe they are.

Because Spitzack's argument is grounded in Foucauldian theory, she argues that confessing one's deviance from the norm—the traditional purpose of confession—is a vital part of ensuring that women are continually feeling deficient. This analysis suggests that young women who write about their eating disorders in college courses are not in fact resisting these discourses of body reduction but are continuing to participate in them. According to Spitzack,

The confessional relationship and its operations have considerable rele-vance for an understanding of women's body experience. As outsiders to dominant culture, women are represented as deviant and as persons who are held accountable for their wrongs, who must "display" their imperfec-tions. Women are often expected to testify openly to deficiencies or "sins." Further, women are promised greater self-knowledge through confessional behavior. . . . Through a speaking of one's deepest thoughts to a relational partner, a woman becomes wholly visible and known to herself and to the social body. (1990, 61)

Within this framework, these students' essays participate in the confessional nature of women's health discourses. The catalyst for the confession is the image of the model, a desire that begins the student's weight loss and cycle of violent discipline. From this perspective, these student essays are a necessary part of women's socialization; they are not a form of protest against the lim-ited and damaging choices women have.

Many of the women in this study who write about their eating disorders do chronicle their physical failings, and they describe their disease and recov-ery in the confessional terms Spitzack highlights. As I've illustrated, the figure of the model is often crucial to the writer's discussion, and these essays are usually quite focused on deviance (some, in fact, echo conversion narratives, chronicling a student's journey from disease to recovery). In these texts, how-ever, young women confess more than deficient identities; they also confess self-abuse, which additionally blames the woman for *violence* against her body. The women's feelings of inadequacy seem to logically justify this abuse at the time. However, although these essays may be part of this confessional cycle, they also illustrate women trying to understand their disorders and create selves that aren't so dependent on the figure of the model. Although Spitzack might argue that women only have these dichotomous choices, I think these students may also be trying to resist an identity that constructs them as diseased and implicitly damaged simply by virtue of being women.

If the image of the model in these student essays seems to enact this con-tinual displacement of identity, then what role does the image of the eating disordered play? What kind of identity does it allow these women to assume? Like the hysteric body of the nineteenth century, the anorexic body com-mands attention and a degree of power, and it poses the threat of the irra-tional, the disordered. It is also a body "deadened, erased, in the creation of replicability, in the 'promotion' of feminine beauty as liberation from the bodily" (Spitzack 1990, 160). The more I thought about these student essays through Spitzack's analysis, the more I wondered if the most likely kind of body to be written in the composition classroom would be the disordered one: It enacts the necessary confession of deficiency endemic to women's health discourses, describes the achievement of displaced identity, and illustrates the culturally desired female body where health and disease are interchangeable (to be like a model or healthy woman one must become anorexic/diseased). When the young women I studied wrote about their own experiences with their unruly bodies, they could do so in part because the discourses about eating disorders offer another kind of visible identity, one that further displays the diseased female body and demands to be confessed. However, these students' essays also explore and illustrate the contradictions within these discourses of femininity, demanding attention to their pain, protesting, at times, the boundedness of feminine identity, and asking what other options they might be given.

Beyond Health and Disease: Modeling a Writer's Roles

As I read these student essays, I'm struck by how the students try to fashion an identity for themselves that puts some distance between them and their disorder. They describe themselves as anorexic or bulimic, but those who consider themselves recovered are trying to develop a different relationship to this self-abusive identity. While some may shift responsibility for their disorder more toward cultural influences and only a handful to the dynamics of the family, the students generally are taking another look at how active they have been in victimizing themselves. A paradox about eating disorders is that a woman is both victim and perpetrator, both passive and active, and it seems difficult to escape the constant self-criticism and self-blame—the cycle of feeling deficient—that is embedded in the disorder. However, I began to notice how the rhetorical positions the students assume in their essays offer a different kind of agency for them than one that inflicts self-abuse. Part of what enables them to assume this kind of agency is their belief that the university is impersonal, full of strangers whose judgment of their experience shouldn't matter.

Kristen is a good example. She wrote about her anorexia in her honors composition course, first to fulfill a memoir essay assignment and then revised to fulfill a research assignment. For the first several weeks of the course, her teacher Becky had asked students to experiment with "writing in different kinds of voices": a report of an event, a collage or mosaic paper, a memoir. Interestingly, Kristen interpreted the memoir assignment as an open topic, a contrast to the assignments she had had to write earlier, even though Becky did not see it that way. Because she was asked to reflect on herself in this assignment, Kristen interpreted it as open, even though it was as restrictive as the other forms she had been asked to practice. Becky seemed to respond more positively to her paper on anorexia than her earlier pieces, so Kristen believed that writing on "her own thing" produced better writing. She said,

> When I have something like that, it's so much easier for me to write because I can just express myself. And I could have kept on writing more and more about the topic because I enjoyed it, and I think it's a lot better. Sometimes I know you need to have a focus, and you know teachers need to say, "Okay this is what I want you to do"—if you don't do that, then, everyone will just always do their own thing. But I think this was a good break, just to write what you wanted to write on. I know I work better that way, write more freely, and express myself a lot better.

Although Becky doesn't "desire or ask for a confessional type of personal writing or an autobiographical kind," she does encourage students to choose their own subjects for the assignments she gives. She believes, as Kristen does, that a different type of writing "provide[s] a kind of meaning that I couldn't impose if I were to assign the subject." Part of the agency Kristen assumes, then, is one that seems to have more control over textual production and meaning than if a teacher assigned, for instance, a critical analysis of an eating disorder. Given that the disorder itself is characterized by an intense desire to control reality and self, it is not surprising that Kristen considers this piece more effective than the others.

However, Kristen also perceives that her control over her essay is affected by her audience: She believes she can assume a less vulnerable identity and write with authority on her experience because she was writing to people she didn't know. She also believes she is writing to people whom she can assume are "more mature" than her classmates in high school. During our interview, I asked Kristen how she decided what to include and what not; she said,

> Maybe a little bit in the beginning [I left a lot out] because this is a personal essay, and I'm writing it about myself, and I thought I might have to read it in front of the class. So at first I thought, Well, maybe I shouldn't put this in, or maybe I should. But then I decided, Well, you know, just express how you feel, and don't worry about it. It's college and so other people shouldn't take offense to, not offense, but you shouldn't be embarrassed by what you say anymore. Like in high school it'd be different, you know, but you're in college now.

I asked her what was different between college and high school that would make her believe the students wouldn't be embarrassed by hearing such an essay. Kristen continued,

> I don't know, I just think in college people are just more mature. In high
> school everyone was immature and I just wouldn't want to talk about top-
> ics like that in front of a bunch of people, and people that I wasn't really
> close to. And, the guys in my class in high school were so immature, and I
> wouldn't feel comfortable talking about a topic like that with them at all.
> And like another thing, some people would want to talk about [this to]
> people they know well, but, for me, I wouldn't mind talking about it because
> I don't know these people that well that are in my class, and so it's not like
> they can really make judgments on me, or anything. It's not like I see them
> every single day, so it's different, I think.

I did not expect to hear that Kristen chose to write about her eating disorder because she *did not* feel a sense of trust and community with her peers,
nor did I expect that writing to strangers would prompt her to share even
more of her experience than she would with her casual friends. Part of her motivation here, I suspect, is a cultural pressure to *be yourself*—as she says, "you
shouldn't be embarrassed by what you say anymore." Her expectations about
college, college students, and the writing demanded that they enable her to
write about a personal struggle, about her body, as much because of the impersonal, detached nature of the university as the freedom she felt to express
something for herself. One seemed to create the opportunity for the other.

From Becky's point of view, however, Kristen may have felt comfortable
writing about her struggle with food because Becky tries to make the classroom "a good place for them to experiment."

> I think our college classes here are a safe environment for those papers, and
> it's especially safe because we are less concerned with mechanical correct-
> ness, we are less worried about modes of discourse, we are more concerned
> about a personal sense of voice and meaning, and so on.

In some ways, the very structures Kristen is relying on to write about this subject are the features of writing that Becky argues that her course tries to resist.
It may also be the case that because the expectations of an impersonal, detached discourse never really disappear from a college writing class, students
use both the features of that discourse and the freedom to ignore it as they
compose their essays.

Although Kristen believes she has a lot of freedom in how she writes about
her subject, she also relies on the impersonal, hierarchical roles that writers
create in college writing to help her be more comfortable sharing a painful
story. It doesn't really matter whether Kristen's sense of college writing is the
same as our own—what matters is that she is operating with an approximation of it that echoes features we might recognize (claim, evidence structure;
directive and commanding ethos; connection to social and cultural ideas).

In the first draft of her essay "Reality Bites," Kristen adopts a five-paragraph theme structure to tell her story and advise others how not to succumb to the same fate. In the first paragraph, she lists what she will emphasize: her frustrations with being heavy, her difficulties finding friends to "judge you on your inner being," the ridicule she suffered, and how she decided to lose weight. Each of the following paragraphs then explains one of these events and leads to a conclusion that lists advice on how to take off weight in a healthy way and accept the body one has. She casts herself as an authority on her subject because she has experienced it, and this strengthens her move to be an advice giver. Although she acknowledges some uncertainty about how fully recovered she is, Kristen constructs herself as having resolved the conflicting messages that Jenn, for example, still experiences. These choices may reflect where in fact Kristen is in her healing process, but they also reflect traditional rhetorical positions for public, university writing: an assured, assertive, nonemotional, and unified writer.

As she tries to assume this role as a writer, Kristen also assumes a reflective stance on her experience, a role implicit in the memoir genre and one that turns her body into something to be analyzed, her behavior as something to be judged. As a result, the essay focuses on the identity she struggled with throughout her anorexia, one that was precipitated by realizing her body is a signifier. In first grade, she is called "Miss Piggy," "Fatso," or "Chubby." "It was as if I had lost my real identity," she writes, an identity that hadn't accounted much for her body size as a problem. By seventh grade, she came "to the conclusion that weight really does matter to others," and, in this case, it was a boy to whom it mattered. After she asked him to go to a dance with her, this young man said he wasn't going with anyone, then decided to go with one of her "skinny" friends. She views her body as the "problem," and later in the draft this perspective is reinforced when she describes how many boys began asking her out after she went from a size fourteen to a size five. Men figure in her story primarily as admirers of slender bodies, flocking to fragile flesh as if to reward young women like Kristen for taking up less space. Her initiation into school brought a sense of bodily shame and created a dissonance between her own sense of self and what others interpreted from her corporeal self. This dissonance is at the core of women's struggles with eating disorders, Susie Orbach (1985 "Accepting") argues, perceiving the body as one's self and yet seeing the body and the self at odds. Kristen learns that her body is a text that can communicate and can be used to manage relationships she desires with both men and women. In controlling the language of that text she is able to trade body fat for attention.

Almost two years after Kristen learned that "weight really does matter to others," she decides she is going to lose weight. The decision is "an overnight transformation. . . . I woke up one morning and told myself that I was sick of being overweight, and was going to do something about it. From that day on my life changed forever." Self-motivated, determined, committed, the agent of her own destiny. She is responsible for the happiness she feels after losing so much weight, and the shock of her friends and admiration of the boys just adds to her motivation. But soon this happiness seems less secure because she fears gaining back the weight. This fear prompts her to skip meals and exercise rigorously.

As she describes this process, she compares herself to an anorexic and lists the telltale signs. In doing so, she makes a move that is common in many of the essays in my study—she uses a generic figure of the anorexic with which to compare herself, to make her struggles with eating and controlling her body's needs visible, legitimate, and worthy of attention. A body that has been reshaped to signify a woman's desirability as a sexual being has also come to signify disease and disorder, both physically and psychologically. While trying to mold herself into what she says is a media image of an attractive woman, she also molds herself into what the media, academia, and medicine have defined as the disordered body. If her starvation has made her visible as a woman, her use of the image of an anorexic has made her visible as a writer.

This image of the disordered body, in fact, is what enables her to construct a narrative about her body that fits into the crisis/resolution plot and the thesis/support structure, to see her experience and her body as a problem to be solved, to be analyzed, to be proven by its consistency with this dominant definition of women who have eating disorders. Because she can rely on these discourses to structure and give purpose to her writing and her role as a writer, she is able to build a degree of authority for giving advice to the reader. As a body, she seems able only to inscribe herself with the disciplinary discourses that define a particular image of femininity, as both a passive receiver and an active inscriber. But, as the author of this essay, she is able to become an analyst, an interpreter of that body who can also see the dangers her other self has imposed. This role, this subject position, has been defined already by these interpretive and analytical demands of a college writer (as she understands them) and by the primary role that has been constructed for those who interpret the disordered body.

Identity Matters

Not surprisingly, this stance is further strengthened when Kristen adopts the role of researcher, integrating academic research and interviews with friends into her earlier draft and assuming a distanced, rather dispassionate tone. Her first line begins, "Anorexia nervosa is an eating disorder that afflicts one in every two hundred and fifty girls between the ages of sixteen and eighteen," and she uses this paragraph to define the disease and its causes, listing "family problems, childhood sexual abuse, and alcoholism" as "triggers." However, she chooses to emphasize that the "major factor in many cases is a lack of self-identity (Chernin 1981, 15)," a theme that resonates throughout her essay.

> Many escape this emptiness by becoming anorexic. Having an eating disorder puts you in control of your body and your actions. You are able to control the amount of food you put into your mouth at all times. For people who are weak, with a poor self-esteem, this is a self-image booster.

Equating identity with something that can fill one up or leave one feeling empty, Kristen adopts metaphors often associated with food and eating to describe "poor self-esteem," implying that one emptiness can be filled by another literal emptiness. To escape the void of identity, the body needs to be controlled and able to exist without substance. Even in her pose as an objective researcher describing and defining a subject, Kristen unconsciously illustrates the paradoxes and irrationalities of an eating disordered subjectivity.

Kristen doesn't mention the issue of identity again until the third page when she begins using her own experience as an illustration of what sociologists and psychologists say about anorexia. She restates her claim from her first draft that she became anorexic:

> Three years ago I became anorexic. It began with me wanting to lose weight. As a child, I was ridiculed by many because of my size and was often referred to a[s] "Miss Piggy," "Fatso," or "Chubby." I was a fairly secure child with self-confidence until the comments arose. At this point, it was as if I had lost my real identity. From that point on, my weight was of concern, and I was uncomfortable with my self-image, but it was a while before I actually had the stamina to change it. I knew at this point that weight really did matter to others, no matter what your personality was like.

In her first draft, the ideas in this paragraph are described in more detail, and Kristen expresses how painful it was to be called names and later be rejected by a boy with whom she wanted to go to a dance. These responses are deleted from the researched essay, and very few descriptions of physical or emotional pain or suffering are added. What emotions she does express—guilt and her desire to be thin—are all directed at herself and what she should be responsible for; little, if any, anger is expressed in this essay, at least none that is directed at others. This is emphasized more in the passive construction of the line, "my weight loss was of concern," displacing the agents who were concerned and thus their role in her weight loss.[9] Instead, her textual voice is matter-of-fact and calm, comparing the ways her behaviors and concerns paralleled those of the average anorexic.

Her text, like her anorexic body, tries to control her emotions. After establishing in great detail her identity as an anorexic, Kristen asserts in her final paragraph that "[t]oday, I have finally come to terms with my real identity." She is now "living a healthy lifestyle," but she is not "completely cured." Yet, it's hard to know how she understands this "real identity" to be different from the one she describes earlier. It could be one that has accepted that her body has a particular shape, which may not be as thin as a model's; or one that understands that she is anorexic and will always struggle with food and body image (much as an alcoholic will always struggle). Given Spitzack's (1990) argument, Kristen is certainly caught between the "healthy woman" who can now become visible and the requirement that she continually confess her deficient identity. Having confessed, tried the cure, she is now healthy but still deficient; her identity is repeatedly being displaced.

Even while Kristen is imitating the controlled voice of a researcher, she also subordinates outside sources to her own experience, something many students generally struggle with. Interestingly, as she is about to use a claim about anorexia from a text, she first narrates her own experience, but with much more detail than she included in her earlier essay, and then she concludes, somewhat awkwardly, with the assertion from her reading:

> The fear of gaining back my weight caused me a few problems my sophomore year. I began skipping meals and exercising profusely in order to lose more weight. I started to become anorexic. Every single day I woke up to the realization that I was not eating but was losing weight. The weight was easy to lose. With enough willpower I could control my urge to eat. Besides, even though I was constantly getting hunger pains throughout the day, it was locked into my mind that I was full. That was the reason my stomach was upset all the time. One of the three areas of misinterpreted psychological functioning in anorexics is inaccuracy in the way hunger is experienced (Bruch 1978, x).

In the next part of this paragraph, Kristen uses the only sensual details in the essay to describe her desire for and pleasure in eating a cookie:

> With anorexics, the mind takes over complete control of the body, and anything "bad" that they eat, they get punished for. One time after school, after not eating anything all day, I gave in to my longing for something sweet. The culprit: a peanut butter cookie. Initially, it tasted heavenly. Each bite tasted like a million dollars. After I had eaten, though, I felt like a fat slob. It was as if I had gained back twenty pounds. The fat felt like it was swelling up on my body and I felt extreme guilt for it. Major problems characteristic of

most anorexics are disturbances in the body image, in the way that they see themselves (Bruch 1978, 85).

Neither of the points she makes appear in Kristen's earlier draft, suggesting that her research has prompted her to notice her behavior in new ways, to see it as significant and part of a larger pattern. Like the students described in Chapter 2, Kristen is demonstrating her ability to use outside texts to critically reflect on her own experience, not stay mired in self-absorption as many might fear. In both drafts, Kristen imitates her understanding of the qualities of academic writing to turn her personal struggle into a public discussion that critiques larger social structures.

"Wow, You Know, You're Not Alone and Other People Go Through This, Too."

> I think I've improved on the first one, . . . not having to talk about myself any-more. I'm talking about what others have gone through, like some of my friends went through, and I'm also giving information from books, too, about the topic. So I think this is a definite improvement. . . . I just go deeper into it. . . . Basically what I knew in the first paper was just what I went through, but now I know more from what I've read, and from other people, too.
>
> —Kristen, "Reality Bites"

In her first draft, before she researched the issue, Kristen blames her struggle with body image on "society" or, more specifically, on media images of women:

> Society makes us self-conscious of our bodies. We are programmed to believe that skinny is beautiful and fat is ugly. This is what leads many to anorexia nervosa and bulimia. Models in magazines supposedly have the "perfect shape." We all strive to get this form, but who is to say what this so-called shape is.

She does not analyze or question this interpretation until she begins to research the disorder, and her use of this research offers her alternative discourses for analyzing what she has done to herself. She primarily relies on psychological understandings of the disorder in this revision, and, in the process of reading Kim Chernin and Hilde Bruch, two prominent figures in eating disorder studies, she finds herself part of a community she didn't know existed:

> I could totally relate to like a lot of the stuff [Kim Chernin] had [said], and it helped a lot with the paper. I want to read the whole book sometime 'cause it just was really interesting. It was like, Wow, you know, you're not alone and other people go through this, too.

The research material functions in some ways as a mirror, reflecting back Kristen's experience, but in a way that changes the experience. The body she sees in this "textual mirror" *is* an anorexic one, not the "fat" body she perceives in her glass mirror. Her readings and discussions with friends who have suffered with anorexia create a textual community that enables Kristen to resee herself and understand how her actions affect others. As Chernin says of her own experience reading Friedan,

> [O]n reflection, I find that there was a book, written by a woman, that helped me greatly during a difficult summer in my early twenties. As it happens, it was not a book about women and food. It did not come right out and tell me that an eating disorder was a serious form of identity crisis. But it scattered seeds, it turned my thinking in a particular direction, it set me dreaming and musing as I made my way through its pages. Reading it changed me in ways I would not then have been able to specify. But that is the way with reading. It gets in under the skin, and there, in darkness, it begins to prepare the work of fully conscious understanding. At the time, one reads and loses oneself in the reading and forgets to look up when the telephone rings, and one is transformed beyond one's wildest hopes and imaginings by this act of slipping into the aching silences of oneself, brought there by another woman's words. (1981, 15–16)

As I argued in Chapter 2, one strategy for responding to student essays such as Kristen's is to introduce them to the writing tradition they are becoming a part of, the community of people who are sufferers and analysts, writing from within the disorder and from without. In adding this third text to their writing process, we further encourage the academic identity they are developing that offers them mastery over a text other than their body, a mastery that is less self-destructive and less life-threatening.

Plenty of studies demonstrate that women with eating disorders tend to be self-absorbed and unaware of how they affect others, but Kristen, like the other students whose essays I studied, wants her writing to have a public impact. She agreed to talk with me, in fact, because she saw my research as an extension of her own project.

> It was a subject that I knew I could write about and I knew that I could maybe help others even though I didn't know if anyone else was going through it in the class or anything. . . . It's just a good topic to inform others about the dangers. It's something I liked writing about. I like helping others, and I don't want others to go through what I had to go through.
>
> And, this didn't occur to me until after I wrote the paper, but, there is a certain girl in my class that—I really don't think she's anorexic, because I've seen her eat before, and I've seen her at the dining hall or whatever—but

she looks so anorexic. I mean, she's just skin and bones, and there's not a piece of meat on her body. And so after it occurred to me, I thought, Wow. I don't know if we are going to read them in class or anything, but I thought it might be good just for her to read.

Then in the process of writing her two essays, Kristen's desire to reach other women begins to evolve into a reflection on how she participates in the discourses that have turned her against herself. Beyond all the information she has gathered about anorexia, she has learned that her words have consequences and can shape other women's consciousnesses:

There's one girl on my floor—she's a big girl—and she has a face problem and everything, but it doesn't bother her. At all. And she tells me, "Sometimes I'll hear you talk and stuff and I wonder if I should worry about myself." And I tell her, "Don't ever say that. I wish I could be like you, I wish I could just be happy with myself, you know? and not have anything bother me, or the way I look, or the way my face looks, or anything." But that's not gonna happen, so I tell her, "Don't ever change because of me. I won't talk about my body, or anything, or about being disappointed in myself anymore around you, because that's wonderful that you're so happy with yourself."

So, even though I've learned also not to always be so focused on what I look like, [I've also learned] not to always express [my criticisms of my body] to other people, because some people that aren't self-conscious could become self-conscious over it just because you are concerned about it. And there are a lot of people that are a lot bigger than you, and that are a lot worse off than you, and so, you know, you have to take that into [account].

Even though Kristen still feels bound by the cultural discourses about women's bodies, she is beginning to see herself within a larger context and understand the consequences of how she shapes her identity. Many students struggle to make this move, regardless of their essay's subject, but we may not perceive Kristen's efforts because we too readily assume her anorexia predisposes her to myopia.

Kristen's first essay—about becoming anorexic—is more self-focused than socially oriented, appropriating and changing a five-paragraph-theme and thesis-support structure to describe why and how she came to starve herself. She re-presents and re-members her body through this generic textual form, believing she is "just expressing herself." When she is asked to revise this essay into a researched paper, she finds that she cannot simply insert information as she first anticipated (as she thought she could just revise her body by cutting and pasting). Instead, her reading causes her to re-envision some aspects of her experience and thus to represent them differently, finding them more significant because she has situated them in a public discourse. In turn, the five-paragraph-theme structure breaks down, she blends academic claims with the specific experiences of herself and her friends, blending public and private discourses, and she is prompted to change her behavior toward others, especially other women. Kristen's essay becomes a medium for change on the level of the particular.

"I Don't Feel I'm Capable or Entitled to Drive Through the Middle of This": Responding to Kristen's Essays

When Becky came to talk with me about Kristen's essays, she had recently returned from a trip home for her mother's funeral. At one point, I asked Becky what connections she saw between students' development as writers and their choice to write about bodily violence. She responded,

> I can't prove it, but I think it helps their development as writers. I think that they have to work through a stiffness or an awkwardness in a lot of cases—in just trying to get this down on paper, . . . but once it is expressed and there's a text they can look at, or a manuscript, then they have taken a little control over it and given it some language which makes it not part of their body and soul so much, but also something else that they can handle. And it gives us a way to talk about something so that they know, for instance, that they're not alone with it, that it's something they can share, that an instructor can reflect on and say, "Yes, these things happened. Something like this may have happened to me or someone I know," and I think that's a valuable use of language.
>
> I told my students, for instance, about journal writing after my mother died. I said that it was very important to me when I was going through this funeral business to sometimes just [write to myself] when I felt very alone, for myself in a journal. I think that it's the same thing for them, I think that they may be feeling some pain, undoubtedly they are, and . . . I would like them to know that writing as a vehicle for expression is there for them, is available.

Becky then did not feel compelled to discourage Kristen from writing about her anorexia; she believes such texts encourage students to use writing both to sort through feelings for themselves and to learn that they are part of a community of others who have had similar experiences. The way her course was structured, to introduce students to different roles that writers play (which Becky calls "different voices"), seemed to encourage Kristen to use her writing in these ways. The challenge for Becky, however, was how she should respond to Kristen's drafts. Believing in theory that writing about her anorexia would help Kristen's development as a writer enabled Becky to respond as a listener and as a witness, but she wasn't sure how to respond as a writing teacher in the university.

From Becky's perspective, the first draft of Kristen's essay was rather short and "not a real reminiscence sort of paper. . . . It wasn't very evocative, it was clear she didn't have any hesitation in writing about it, but . . . there wasn't a lot of depth in it or a lot of feeling in it at that point." Although she didn't describe herself as uncomfortable with an essay on anorexia, she said she did feel cautious about the kinds of questions she asked Kristen.

> I remember asking her some questions about some paragraphs to try to get her to talk more about what came out of this. I wasn't evaluating the paper for her, but I wanted her to fill in more—for example, . . . I wanted to get a sense of what understanding she had of various kinds of social or cultural influences that might have affected her. She said that it had been caused because she had been too fat as a child, that she had eaten too much as a child for instance, and everyone told her that her baby weight would go away and it never did. . . . That seemed to be the limit of her understanding at that point, and so, I wanted to test that, I wanted to get a sense of where she was with that, of whether she saw that there were other issues.
>
> And there's another illustration—after she first began to diet bigtime, went back to school in the fall, noticeably thinner, she had a comment that—I can't remember the exact words—that the men were really attending to her, and I asked her probably a couple of things about [it], just to see where her understanding was of that, too, because I really wanted to know. I wanted to place her in relationship to how sophisticated her understanding was of this. And one other thing she said was she had some friends who seemed to be [anorexic or bulimic], and one or two had revealed to her that they were having eating disorders. She had a friend who had been sent to a treatment center or hospital or something out of state and [this young woman] was ejected from this facility because she wouldn't eat. And Kristen said, "That doesn't seem right."
>
> So, . . . I had the sense that she didn't have a very mature understanding of this, that even though her mother had, as she reported in the first paper, . . . gone to the doctor with her, what I was reading didn't seem to me as psychologically mature as some of the things that I have read about the disorder. So . . . I didn't want to impose that on her. I didn't want to give her a take on this disorder that I had, but at the same time, I kind of wanted to

reflect that, as a piece of writing, it was not as thoughtfully developed as it could have been. I don't know if I was successful at that or not.

Becky's concerns sounded familiar to me because I had often read student essays about eating disorders through similar lenses. The maturity and depth that Becky wants depends on Kristen's familiarity with feminist and psychotherapeutic discourses in part because those are the frameworks with which Becky—and I—are most familiar.

Interestingly, Becky believes she would be imposing an interpretation if she prompted Kristen to pursue some of these discourses, but, as she explained later in our talk, she wouldn't feel that way about a student who is writing about his faith in Biblical authenticity. She calls this a problem for her as a critical reader.

> What I do find a problem for me as a critical reader of such a paper is, for example, if we were writing about a subject that was not a disorder. For instance, I have a student who is writing about the authenticity of the gospels in the New Testament, and I pursued that logic right down to the period and comma, you know. I was able to talk with him very pointedly about the reasoning that he was using. But I am reluctant to take this young woman and say to her, "Look you haven't written about your parents. You've written about the parents of your friends, and the role that families can play in causing these disorders," but now I feel that as a writing instructor I want to or I'm uncomfortable—I feel I need to pull back. I don't feel that I'm capable or entitled to drive through the middle of [this]. I can present her with the question of causes, I can problematize by saying, "Gee, is childhood eating the only cause?" and she can answer, "No, families can be a cause," and she can write that, but I don't feel able to go beyond that at this point and say to her, "What about your mom? Where's your mom in this paper?" "Well, my mom took me to the doctor because my mom could see that I didn't have my period." "Oh, she was the heroine, then, your mom?" You know? So I don't feel comfortable to do that.
>
> It seems to me that if she were to bring it up, if she were even to write in here, "I notice that I haven't written anything about my parents, or my mom did nothing to disturb me" or something, then I might be able to ask about it. But the absence of her mother makes me feel that it's private territory. It's possible that for me to—the first word that comes to mind is "pry"—might be more emotional stuff or psychological stuff than—I don't know therapeutic discourse—than I can impose on her as her English teacher. I feel a line and . . . I guess I think that this is an issue of her stability, and that she should be able to extend it to me and I should then be able

to respond to it, but I don't think that I should take a stance that would challenge her.

Although the psychological theories that have explained eating disorders are
as "rational and logical" as those that have questioned the authenticity of biblical texts, Becky suggests here that one is more potentially destabilizing than
the other. I've certainly watched several of my students in other courses become just as ambivalent and unsettled by challenges to their religious beliefs
as I have students who respond this way about their anorexia. But because one
is about a body, and the body is linked to emotion and psychology, it seems
to have a more dramatic impact than the other. Both subjects, however, affect
gender relations, power structures, and identity, and Becky's response, like
many of ours, suggests how disrupting a student's body can be to a discourse
community that doesn't allow bodies into its rhetorical space.

What Becky does do, however, is share her own struggles with similar issues, disrupting the power imbalance between her and Kristen and opening
an opportunity for connecting as women, not simply student and teacher. At
the same time, she sets aside her power to compel Kristen to make connections between her experience and various interpretive frames. She respects
Kristen's choice to keep private what she chooses, distancing herself from the
potential role as receiver of a confession, exerciser of disciplinary power. Although she does have knowledge of a particular set of truths about Kristen's
violence to her body, she chooses not to assert those. When Kristen revises her
first essay into a research paper, she begins to think about some of the issues
Becky wanted to introduce, but Becky allows her to choose those with which
she will engage. In doing so, she further reinforces the perception of control
Kristen has over her material, something Kristen might need at this point. It
can never be easy to decide what kinds of challenges to offer students such as
Kristen, especially if we believe eating disorders can be as academic a subject
as any other and worthy of the same kinds of contextualizing and analysis.

Our struggles with these bodies are rooted within American beliefs
about the dangers of emotional excess. This excess has been associated with
immaturity, loss of control, and a particular kind of emotional deviance, which
is strikingly similar to the qualities associated with eating disordered women.
An anorexic body also carries the stigma of intense, uncontrolled feelings and
conflict—America's preoccupation with emotional cool. The feelings this
body and self want to purge, however, are the very kinds of outlaw emotions
that feminists believe can drive critical challenges to discourses of femininity
and power. As teachers, we might consider ways to encourage students like
Kristen and Jenn to express these emotions in their writing and then connect them—in a critically reflective way—to the values and practices those

emotions may critique. The literature available on eating disorders may be one avenue, but, as with sexual abuse essays, I think we need to offer students texts written by those who have suffered these ravages on the body and invite them to compare the ways their stories are represented and the ways the writers critique the forces that made such self-abuse possible.

Instead of seeing these women as diseased (confirming the "truth" of their confession) and thereby continuing the displacement of identity that Spitzack (1990) describes, why not ask where else they may exercise their desire for mastery and identity? Or how they explain the meaning of their survival? Their texts demand a different kind of attention than their bodies do—as teachers, we need to guard against always seeing them as pathological or deficient—and I think their efforts to try on the multiple perspectives on eating disorders are an effort to assume identities different from the diseased ones **they** believe they have.

4

"Sometimes I Just Want to Beat the Shit Out of You!"

ANGER AND THE MAKING OF
KNOWLEDGE IN A WRITING CLASSROOM

[W]hen I read it I cried. I was home reading them. There have actually been a few times in conferences where I've lost it because I feel so [much] . . . which is probably part of the reason why I'm nervous about anything that connects to therapy, because I don't have enough self-control, I think, in those situations to be a good person for that, you know? . . . I have this huge sense of compassion for other people's problems and I tend not to be able to get that across—I'm kind of a control freak and I don't like to be out of control in that way. Especially early in the semester, it makes me very nervous.

—Katherine, instructor

On August 30, 1994, eighteen-year-old Ann handed her Freshman English instructor, Katherine, her response to the first writing assignment of the year: Write an essay about something that has affected the person you are today. Ann had not met with Katherine in conference yet; in fact, the class had only met a few times. The writing she handed in described the night of Ann's junior prom when her boyfriend became so angry with her that he tackled her, punching her in the lower back as she hit the ground. As Ann describes him, her boyfriend tried to manipulate her into staying with him by threatening suicide, later telling her "that it didn't matter if he turned out to be a wife batterer, that [she] wouldn't stay with him long enough to see it happen anyway." After the attack, Ann became anorexic, losing over thirty pounds, exercising twice a day.

81

By the time Ann was able to meet with me her essay about being assaulted was several weeks behind her. I was surprised to find that she had not talked with Katherine about this writing. Because Ann was the first student I would interview for my study, I was still under the impression that teachers and students often developed trusting relationships, usually in conference, before a student would write about something so personal. I also found it hard to return an essay like this without talking to the student, which suggests, I suppose, my sense that written words are more impersonal than spoken ones, or that I had a different kind of responsibility to a student who was writing about such issues. The first time we met, I didn't expect to find Ann just finishing her first graded essay of the term, a research paper about the Irish Republican Army (a subject she had always been interested in, she told me, especially because she had relatives there and wanted to visit sometime). Usually, first-year writing courses at this university assigned research projects during the last third of the semester, but not Katherine's.

Instead, Katherine wanted to orient students immediately to thinking about writing and knowledge as contextualized, never solely individual, constructed from multiple sources. Katherine had emphasized that she would be grading these papers based on how well students managed the balance of "what other people think [(interviews)], what they think, and what is the be all and end all of the printed word" (material from the library). Ann had interviewed a reporter from *The Boston Globe* who had been covering the ceasefire in Ireland, as well as a student in her dorm who had been living there, so she talked with me about how her interest in Irish politics had grown as a result of doing the paper. I discovered that, later in the semester, this focus on subjects of oppression and violence would reappear in Ann's writing, sometimes fueled by an anger that belied her rather calm and hesitant demeanor.

When Katherine contacted me to say she and Ann were willing to become part of my research, she told me she was continually surprised that a student would write about something like physical abuse so early in the semester. Yet, Ann was not the only freshman to do so that fall. The other two students (from different course sections, with different instructors) who wrote about being abused by their boyfriends also wrote about it within the first two weeks of the term, before they had had time or opportunity to get to know their teachers or peers.[1] Contrary to what some of the instructors assumed, these particular students were not sharing personal traumas because they had enough classroom interaction to determine their audience was safe or trustworthy. Because it is so unpredictable whether and when a student might write about such an experience, I was unable to observe Ann's class *before* she wrote this piece. By sitting in on her class after she wrote the essay, I had hoped to learn more about the context within which Ann was writing, about her relationships with Katherine and her classmates, and about her development as a writer given what I later learned was a long history of verbal and occasional physical abuse, low self-esteem, and a long-term struggle with her weight. One thing is for sure—Ann's experience in Katherine's Freshman English course will do more than surprise those who believe expressivist pedagogies—as opposed to epistemic, postmodern, or critical pedagogies—encourage, evoke, or subtly coerce students to write about these painful experiences.

Writing as Emotional Cool: Choosing When to Disclose

With only three essays about physical abuse to study, I cannot make many claims about the patterns I noticed in how the students wrote about the issue, but I do want to look closely at the ways Ann controls *what* she shares with her readers and how she tries to approximate a version of college writing in her essay. The assignment prompt that led to this essay invited her to write about herself, but Ann could have chosen any other event in her life besides this one. So why is this the moment she chose?

> As I sat in my first session of Freshman English class earlier on this clear fall day wondering what I could write about that has affected the person I am today but that wasn't so personal I'd have a crisis writing about [it], and was still a significant event, I had kind of a difficult time. Finally, I decided to write about a point in my life when I wasn't very happy with the person I was and how I managed to make it through that hard time.
>
> Things really started to go downhill for me after I had been dating the same guy for two years. I found myself always grouchy, I felt very unattractive, I just had a very low self-esteem in general. I feel bad saying that it was my boyfriend's fault, but he certainly didn't do me any favors. We began not to get along very well together, and he always seemed to have a way with turning everything on me; I just felt like I could never seem to do anything right no matter what I did.
>
> The worst time we had was our prom night. We had a wonderful time at the prom itself, I had a great time even though I had a bad cold that night. Afterward, we went out for a walk on the golf course by his house. The night was chilly and I was feeling exhausted; it was getting late. I asked him if he could bring me home, but he took this request to mean that I couldn't stand

Do you think a lot of young women in our culture go through this? You poor thing.

to be with him. When he couldn't accept that I just felt rotten and wanted to go home, he grew very frustrated. I felt so bad because I really did have a good time, and I didn't want the evening to end with him so upset. Raging, he thundered out into the damp spring evening air:

"Sometimes I just want to beat the shit out of you!"

I couldn't believe that someone I was so close to and trusted for two years could say that to me. I was so scared. All I could think about was the time I watched my father hit my mother when I was younger. I felt just as helpless as I did on that night. I knew I had no way to defend myself. I asked my boyfriend to just take me home, so we got into the car and he sped along the [town] roads not saying a word. Suddenly he wheeled into a vacant lot and told me to get out and walk home. When I refused, he got out and started to walk toward his house. I found two nickels in his change cup and began to walk to a pay phone so that I could call my mother to pick me up. I hadn't gone very far when I heard the footfalls of my boyfriend sprinting after me. I had just begun to turn around when he plowed me into the ground, prom dress and all. Not only had he ran me over full force, but he drove his fist into my back while he was at it. I was so scared all I could do was stay there, face in the dirt for a moment. I couldn't get over that this was happening to me. I had always heard that the people often trusted the most are the ones that do these kind[s] of things, but I never thought something like that could happen to me.

When I got up, I was so mad. How could someone so significant to me betray me like that? I screamed at him to take me home, that I never wanted to see him again, and how could he do something like that. He got all upset saying that he didn't mean to and then began to make threats that he would hurt himself, maybe kill himself if I left him. Eventually I agreed to see him the next day so that we could talk.

The next day went well until he denied that he punched me in the back. Even after I showed him where his knuckles bruised me, he denied it. After that, he got all upset saying that it didn't matter if he turned out to be a wife batterer, that I wouldn't stay with him long enough to see it happen anyway.

For months after that he made me feel so guilty for pushing him out of my life. I began to lose weight very rapidly, first four pounds, then nine pounds, twenty-three pounds, and at last thirty-four pounds. My feet and hands were always purple and I could never feel them. I was exercising excessively. One day I went to work out at the gym with a male friend from school and I passed out on him. Another friend came up to me to tell me that she knew what I was going through, because she was being treated for

This is so scary, Ann

her anorexia. This was when I realized that something was potentially seriously wrong.

Things started looking up for me when I started seeing someone else. I began to see the guy I went to the gym with that time I passed out. I felt really awkward at first. He made me feel like I was fun to be with, smart, and pretty. This man treated me with respect. I felt awkward at first because I didn't believe I deserved to be treated so well. Finally, I am beginning to gain self-confidence and self-respect. I am finally coming to understand what people mean when they say you have to respect yourself before you can learn to respect others. This insight to self-respect has been a major factor in defining the person I am today.

You are very brave and very wise to realize all that you have at this point in your life. . . .

And it has to come from you, yourself. I think most women go through experiences like this. That is why it is so important to write and talk about it. . . . Be careful [here] too because it can be a hard, stressful adjustment here. Just know that you're not alone. . . .

Although this is not the most graphic essay I have received about physical abuse, Ann's piece is chilling in the minimal details she uses to describe the event. Her first paragraph, in fact, might lead a reader to think she will *not* be talking about something painful and traumatic: We see her searching for something that "wasn't so personal I'd have a crisis writing about [it]." She uses generic language to assert what the significance of this time was "when I wasn't very happy with the person I was and how I managed to make it through that hard time." This paragraph could be the prelude to a story about her disappointments as an athlete, for example, or her adolescent struggles with lying—we do not expect her to go on and tell us about her boyfriend beating her, her father beating her mother, or her struggles with anorexia. The fact that she does go on to tell a story about abuse causes me to wonder what other moments in her life she had to choose from that made this one the least traumatic to write about.

From Ann's perspective, this event is something that won't cause her to lose emotional control when she writes about it, and the meaning she has drawn from it meets the criteria for the assignment. But these are not the only indications that she is carefully choosing what to disclose. She also uses euphemisms to contain the experience and the anger she feels: "a point in my life when I wasn't very happy with the person I was," "I managed to make it through that hard time," and "things really started to go downhill." As conventional phrases, these words direct readers (and Ann) away from the painful details even as they fulfill an expected move in college writing to begin generally and then move to a specific instance. Even the words she uses to describe her emotions—being grouchy, having low self-esteem, feeling unattractive—minimize the anger she feels and casts it into phrases that will be familiar to her audience. It seems an understatement to say she felt "grouchy" while dating a young man who tried to control her with suicide threats, isolation, jealousy, and guilt. Even to call his behavior a betrayal is euphemistic. Although she told me during an interview that as she wrote she became increasingly angry, the only direct, explicit anger she expresses in the text comes after he has tackled her. Otherwise, we see it buried in words such as "grouchy" and embodied in the self-punishment of starvation and excessive exercise.

The euphemisms Ann uses are also what David Bartholomae might call *commonplaces,* conventional phrases that represent shared or common-sense beliefs (1985, 137): "I had always heard that the people often trusted the most are the ones that do these kind[s] of things"; when the young woman implied Ann had anorexia, "I realized that something was potentially seriously wrong"; and "I am finally coming to understand what people mean when they say you have to respect yourself before you can learn to respect others." She works from popular knowledge about abuse, anorexia, and self-esteem and self-respect, not from psychotherapeutic discourse, academic knowledge, or legal discourse. These commonplaces function in this essay in two important but quite different ways: They give her a language for understanding and representing this experience, both to herself and her reader, making it possible for her to write about pain to an audience while seeing herself as strong, confident, and active. In addition, the commonplaces become heuristic, helping her make significance out of the event as she reflects on a younger self: her boyfriend's need to control her explains why he beat her; her own feelings of guilt about their relationship explains her struggle with anorexia; and her new friends who respect her explain why she now respects herself and is able to stop both the abuse and the anorexia.

By adopting a crisis-resolution structure similar to the one Kristen uses (see Chapter 3), Ann is able to contain her story within an accepted form that is required by the assignment, ending with an explicit moral or lesson for the reader. Using no details to describe how things started to "look up," Ann both protects herself and maintains her emotional cool as she writes about her boyfriend's psychological manipulation and physical violence. The generalities she uses help her accomplish this control. Although her language sometimes betrays this image, Ann constructs herself as active, self-preserving, willing to pull herself out of dangerous situations (whether it's the violence or the anorexia), even as she feels scared, helpless, and guilty.

Although Ann does actively seek ways to protect herself during the assault and eventually separates from this young man, she not surprisingly still constructs herself as responsible for what happened. Her anorexia suggests how she has internalized the messages from her boyfriend and father that she is so awful she needs to be controlled with violence.[2] But it is her anorexia that she focuses on as the "something" that "was potentially seriously wrong," not her boyfriend's abuse. Ann displaces her emotions about her boyfriend's behavior onto her eating disorder, directing them at herself for her own self-abuse. In fact, the essay's main focus—to discuss a time when she "wasn't very happy with the person [she] was"—is not about her boyfriend's violence. It is about the effects of the abuse on her sense of self and on her body. Ultimately, when we reach the end of the essay, we implicitly learn that she perceives herself as the one who needed to change and to be held accountable for what happened: She learned to have self-respect and confidence after she left her boyfriend and began seeing a man who treated her with love and compassion. In fact, she begins and ends with a male figure, both of whom have a profound impact on her sense of self, and the reader is left wondering who has the most control over the person she wants to be.

This shift away from the violence as a problem is reflected in the grammar of her sentences, as well: There are points where her boyfriend has no agency, and Ann casts herself in the object position; for example, "I had always heard that the *people* often trusted the most are the ones that do these kind[s] of *things,* but I never thought something like that could happen *to me*" (emphasis added). In the first half of this sentence, Ann generalizes the perpetrator of violence by saying "people" are doing "things," and she is absent from the sentence as the person who is the target of these "things." In the second clause, the victimizer is completely missing and Ann is in the passive position. Grammatically, she doesn't cast herself as a victim of physical abuse but of a nameless act that has been drained of all its violence.[3]

When Ann writes about her boyfriend as a jealous, narcissistic, and manipulative young man, she is reflecting theories about family violence that argue that abusers are pathologically disposed to violence when triggered by a conflict, like Ann's desire to go home instead of continue to stay on the date. Not surprisingly, her essay doesn't explore explanations that look to the family system or to gender relations, explanations that might help Ann shift the blame away from herself and onto the larger social structures that make this violence possible. Katherine doesn't suggest that Ann pursue any of these angles, either, but one strategy for response might be to encourage Ann to research why her boyfriend responds with violence instead of understanding. In Chapter 2, I suggested that students might contextualize their sexual abuse essays by looking at the historical documents written by survivors, and Ann too might benefit from reading Abigail Abbot Bailey's memoir.[4] She might also put her experience in dialogue with other sociological, psychological, and feminist perspectives.[5]

Ann might be interested in learning how the dynamics of physical abuse have been interpreted over the last thirty years (although dating violence is theorized a little differently[6]). In the 1960s, psychological theory emphasized a wife's masochism as a trigger for domestic violence (O'Leary 1993, 12), but current theories argue that an abuser has predictive behaviors, that violence is a learned behavior, and that it is related to the dynamics of relationships (O'Leary 1993, 24).[7] Feminists argue that domestic violence is not about individual pathology, but about the power relationships set up in a capitalist and patriarchal culture (Brown 1990, 4).[8] Although this is not the only strategy for revision that I might suggest for Ann, I believe she might find outside texts that help her reshape her sense of self and culpability, texts that raise questions about her own theories that have emerged from her experience.[9]

Ann's own sense of herself and her responsibility is constructed in the process of writing about her experiences, given the frames she uses to resee the past. She began, in fact, to make the connections between the prom night, the verbal abuse, and her weight loss in the process of writing this piece, and her anger grew as she wrote. When she looked back on it after four weeks, she was ready to revise her portrait of her boyfriend to focus more on his culpability, shifting her anger away from herself and onto her abuser. This essay, then, while loosely fitting generic constructions of college essays, functions for Ann as a witnessing, as a place to reinterpret her experience, and as a space for her to revise her own sense of agency and her ability to protect herself.

In writing this essay, she told me, she could "think of the words [she] really wanted to use—when you're talking with someone else, you're wondering what they're thinking." Her writing becomes a way for her to revise the identity of the younger self in the essay, controlling what gets revealed and who gets to read it. Her peers, in fact, did not read this piece, and, despite her belief that "it was important to be able to say it," she told me that she would not want them to read it. Although she was confused about why she did not want to share this essay, it suggested how vulnerable she felt, especially if she was still sorting through the significance of what happened. Katherine may have been an appropriate stranger to disclose to, but not her peers.

Alternative Realities: What's Not Said

Another reason to keep this experience private might have been Ann's keen sense that words could be dangerous and frightening. She rarely spoke in class, and during our interviews she seemed shy and hesitant, a demeanor that became increasingly more at odds with the persona I read in some of her later writings. Her verbal silence corresponded with being voiceless in an alcoholic and sometimes abusive family. The only allusion Ann makes in her essay to her family is the line "All I could think about was the time I watched my father hit my mother when I was younger. I felt just as helpless as I did on that night." She feels powerless as a witness and now as a victim. The two scenes blend with the line, "I knew I had no way to defend myself," the past and present coexisting, her father and boyfriend one.

Being in college—being in Katherine's classroom—is an escape from the chaotic and unpredictable family Ann grew up in, but her body language and her speech suggest the degrees to which she has not escaped the residual effects of that environment. Although wanting to be strong, confident, and assertive—and demonstrating these qualities in her writing—she also seemed fearful and uncertain at times. Because Ann spoke softly and sometimes hesitantly, I had to fight my urge to fill up the silences while we sat and talked in my office. As she began talking about her family, particularly her father and her younger sister, she gradually explained why she was so glad to be living in the dorms with her best friend, away from her family.

> My father is very abusive. He's an alcoholic. He's drunk probably every day and he tells my sister and I how fat we are and stuff. And then he saw I was losing all that weight and he told me I have all these problems and stuff, but nobody took the time to notice my sister. She's lost probably twenty pounds. She's as tall as I am [about 5′ 7″]—she was down to ninety pounds, she hadn't had her period in a long time, and he still calls her fat. And those hair elastics hang loose on her wrists. It's awful. She's getting some help now, but he'll still call her "fatty" and all this.

As we talked about her sister, Ann's voice lowered almost to a whisper—she was glad to get out of the house and feels she is doing better as a result, but she is afraid for her mom and sister. Ann was frustrated that her mother had not taken her sister Mary to the local clinic earlier after she learned that Mary, sixteen, had only had five menstrual periods. Her mom finally took Mary to the clinic not because of the weight loss, Ann said, but because of her period, and Ann couldn't understand why her mom didn't seem alarmed by the rapid and severe changes in Mary's weight.

Wanting to support her mother, not criticize her, Ann seemed torn by her protective impulses and her desire to go to college and escape her father.

> [I]t's just helped me a lot to get out of there, but I don't know. Sometimes I feel like I'm sinking back into that now and then, but, you know, I can see how, what happened before. . . . I have mixed feelings about [getting out of

the house] because I'm afraid to leave my mother and sister alone with my father, but I'm glad cause he was just so obnoxious. For instance, [my dad] says if he catches [my new boyfriend] around the house it's going to cost my mom a hundred dollars each time, cause [my dad] saw him with a hole in his shirt.

Ann's essay provides only a glimpse of how manipulative and abusive her father is and how that has affected Ann's sense of herself. The needs of the women in this family do not seem to matter, and Ann has probably learned that lesson well. So erratic and dominating is Ann's father that he now wants her to get back together with the boyfriend who beat her. She talked of wishing she had a "good father" like some of her friends, a father who "would be around for sports or whatever, just come to see [her play soccer]." "If he ever comes," she said, "you know he'll show up drunk for his friends." On the night her boyfriend attacked her, her father was angry and said, "How could somebody push you down?" When he said that, Ann told me, "I was so mad at him. It was like, take a look at yourself. He's so crummy to my mother about. . . . I don't know, I guess it makes me appreciate her more, I think, so I try to be a lot nicer to her, I guess, because nobody else is." Ann could have offered more details in her essay about her experience instead of using all the vague and euphemistic phrases she does, but it is important that she does not. The more I learned about Ann's family, the more I understood that what I might otherwise see as a student writing too vaguely was this student's attempt to control painful material.

The Dangers of Intimacy: Constructing the University Writing Classroom

In writing this essay, Ann is enacting a kind of care for herself, reassessing her strength, allowing herself some anger about the abuse, and constructing herself as healed. She did not want Katherine to respond with pity, she told me because "I'm not sorry it happened, really. I mean, it was a hard time, but I learned a lot from it." She wants to maintain her identity as someone who is now in control of her feelings and recovered from whatever trauma she might have suffered, projecting a self consistent with the culture's emotionology— she is cool, in control, "above passing." Katherine is a safe audience because she is a stranger and she is not connected to anyone Ann knows who might use Ann's experience against her. This was not the case, however, in high school, where she had an English teacher who asked students to write about an experience much as Katherine did. Ann deliberately chose not to "write about something like that" in this teacher's class because she "felt that teacher was so nosy." He knew her father, she said, and "the class was so small and [she'd] see him everywhere."

While keeping her family situation and her relationship with her boyfriend private could be interpreted as a kind of collusion with the abusers, I think Ann was keeping silent to protect herself, not giving this knowledge to a man she could not trust. (This suggests, too, that Ann may be transferring her relationship with her mother onto Katherine, seeing her femaleness as safe and empathetic.) In high school, her writing would not necessarily control this painful part of her identity as it might in college because her representation of it could be in dispute—the two male authority figures in her life, her teacher and her father, wield more power than she to define the truth of her experience. At the same time, whether Ann is aware of this, the power of the state could intervene if her teacher reported her abuse (in her state, elementary and secondary teachers are required by law to report knowledge of physical or sexual abuse). In college, however, Ann's writing instructor has no legal obligation to report what she hears from students, so Ann may have less to fear that Katherine will pathologize her.

Interestingly, Katherine made this point as well when she was talking about her own experiences in high school, particularly with therapy. Like Ann, Katherine encountered an authority figure whom she did not trust, and she asserts that college may seem a safer place for students because they perceive everyone as equal adults—both students and instructors. Katherine said,

> I know what happened to me when therapy was tried on me at seventeen— I perceived the therapist as my parents' ally when he's telling me that everything that's going on in the house is my fault and blah, blah, blah. I'm sure that's not what he said, but that's how I perceived it at the time. And that was not what I needed. [For students who] come to college, [where they are presented with] the first opportunity to have the freedom to pursue yourself as an adult, on equal footing with an adult, I come along at the perfect time. I'm enough of an authority that I can still teach the class, but I'm also acceptable enough that they can let it out to me and feel like it's okay. . . . Usually in therapy or guidance counselor situations, they could report back to your parents. They know I'm not going to call their parents, they know I'm not. I don't even know where they live, for God's sake, how am I going to [tell their parents]?

For students who want to write about personal and painful experiences, then, a college classroom affords them the anonymity they may need to break their silence in a way they believe they can control, composing part of their identities, protecting the feelings of others who might be hurt or can hurt them, and shielding themselves from further victimization.

This is not to say that a college writing course does not have the potential to revictimize these students—I believe that is a very real possibility, particularly if the teacher is insensitive; is uniformed about the sociological, psychological, and historical understandings of these issues; and is unaware of his or her own countertransference (that is, responding to the student's experiences as if they were the teacher's own, projecting the teacher's issues onto the student). In addition, students are not on equal footing with their professors, no matter how respectful and decentered their approaches are, and it is quite possible that students, especially those who have been abused, may not fully realize the potential for professors to abuse their power. Some psychologists argue that survivors of physical or sexual abuse often don't have the ability to distinguish what is appropriate and safe to disclose because the very abuse is their primary education in transgressing boundaries.[10] However, others assert that the unconscious will not bring to consciousness something it is unable to manage.[11] We need to be aware of these concerns when students write about abuse; yet, I think we also need to recognize that students who have been abused may also have some protective strategies like Ann seems to, and college can be a place where one's words will not hurt parents, where protective agencies are not called on, or where one might find more empathetic listeners.

Some of the students I talked with assumed that with college professors they would not be subjected to the kind of scrutiny and judgment they feared from a therapist. When students express their beliefs that counselors will "see right through them," they are certainly voicing a concern about losing control, but they are also conceiving of language as a rather immutable, static, and transparent medium. Words should represent their experience without ambiguity, leaving no space for interpretation or for anyone to use their words against them. I often wonder if that is why many students complain that English teachers analyze texts "to death"—if students think of themselves as writers, and writers' words are subject to such play and metaphorical, psychological interpretation, then how much control do writers actually have over their writing? The writers I have talked to for this study want to control their writing, their subject, their identity, and I suspect this is a particularly strong desire for students who have experienced language as shifting signifiers that are used to deny their own lived or perceived experience. It is important to believe there exists a place where language can mean what the writer intends it to, without dispute.

Course Context: Writing Is Critical Thinking

Figuring the Personal

"We had a staff meeting Tuesday," Katherine is telling me, "about what do you do with dumb papers, papers that have no point, the fun-in-the-sun, vacation-in-Florida type papers. I didn't even go to the meeting because I rarely get those, and I think doing [what I do] sets the tone right from the beginning. It sets that high standard up, and they pick those more serious things to write about. But that wouldn't explain why [an essay about physical abuse] would come up in necessarily any class."

We have been talking about why students might write about bodily violence in a writing class, and Katherine seems to be saying that the subject of Ann's essay would not be unusual within the context of her course. But that is not because she focuses on personal narrative, something she emphasizes to me often. She clearly sees herself as quite different from a number of other instructors on the staff, and throughout our conversations she reiterated such distinctions. Although the staff has tried many times to come to some consensus about the common features of their courses, the qualities that constitute an effective essay, and the purposes of the first year writing course (especially in relation to the writing demands in other university courses), the group always seems to resist such attempts to define the program. Katherine says herself that she gets "as nervous as all the other instructors do about 'Let's define the course.'" She sees the diversity in approaches—and the relative freedom teaching assistants and instructors have—as one of the strengths of the program. However, in defining a pedagogy, no teacher at this university can avoid engaging with what Goffman might call the program's *social identity:* its associations with personal narrative, expressivism, and conference-based teaching. It doesn't really matter whether this admittedly nebulous construct of the program's writing courses is true—it has become a type that no one can ignore when talking about what they do and why. In describing what she expects of her students, Katherine defines it against her own understanding of this construct, the way personal narrative becomes an end in itself, an indulgence in a kind of selfishness and disconnection from community, and a way to avoid thinking about the more difficult and significant issues that affect our culture.

> I do try to get them to use narrative, personal narrative to talk about how and why they feel about things, but I tend not to do a lot of personal narrative, and that might be another thing that sets me apart from all those people who might. I don't know, without bringing my personal feelings

about personal narrative into it, I think that it tends to be easier for people to do that, and I guess I try to push them to the next level right away, you know, use your personal experiences to talk about something, don't just talk about your personal experience . . . which maybe isn't fair, maybe other people would argue with that, whether or not that works.

Katherine's classroom practice and our further discussions of the personal indicate that she thinks it is appropriate to bring the personal into the writing classroom when students are ready to think of it as always already situated within culture. The issue is not the personal; rather, the issue is how the personal can easily reproduce a belief that individuality is about escaping culture and one's responsibility to community.

As we talked, Katherine associated personal narrative with both therapy and what she believed was the selfishness of American myths of individuality. She suggested that for her to emphasize the personal in her class was to validate an ideology, a teaching role, and a perspective on writing that contradicted her values. In the extended excerpt that follows, Katherine explains (1) why she sees that personal narrative can so easily evoke a therapeutic relationship (because the significance of the event is primarily important to the writer's sense of self, not to an audience), (2) how she tries to avoid such a dynamic, and (3) why she teaches writing as something that mediates the author's identity within the context of culture and community. She continually refers to her own experiences as sources for her claims, implicitly illustrating the thinking processes she hopes to emphasize in her class.

> I don't want to be a therapist, and I find that when it's just personal narrative, that's what tends to happen. You're just kind of talking about what that issue is in their life, rather than talking about how that connects to other people and other issues, which I'm much more comfortable talking about. . . .
>
> I think that there's a place for that, there are a lot of other places for that, one. Two, I don't think I'm qualified to do it, and three, I think that the writers I really admire, always always always take it to that next level. Alice Walker never just tells you some personal narrative, or Annie Dillard, any of the people [whom I admire]. And I'm trying to challenge [my students] to aspire to that with their writing, and if I get a personal narrative I say to them very clearly right from the beginning, "Do you want to work on this as an essay, or is this just something you need to write?" I mean I don't defer to them and cut them off, but usually by just asking that question they will say, "Yes, I want to work on this" or "No, I just needed to write this." . . . I don't want to be perceived as somebody who has that responsibility, to figure that out for them. I don't feel comfortable doing that. And I think I

got treated that way by people sometimes when I was younger who I don't think knew what they were doing, and I don't like the idea that that ever happened to me. . . .

Michelle: Feeling violated?

Katherine: Well, yeah. I mean, when I was in high school, . . . I had a very bad initiation into the world of therapy for myself and it's not to say that it doesn't work for other people, but I think there's a really fine line in this relationship with students and writing, for writing to fall by the wayside and that therapy thing to start going. And it's just not something that I feel comfortable with. And I don't think it's fair to [students]—I think it sets up a sort of false sense of what is really important in the class, which to me is being able to write and articulate your feelings and your views to other people in such a way that they'd want to hear them and not just talking about something that happened to you. I also was in groups in school where, like in a 501 class, all the papers were just sort of personal narrative, and I always remember feeling really disappointed when I got to the end that that's all it was—why did you tell me this? And that feeling has hung on, in my own workshopping experiences from these classes, and I almost dreaded it because I knew I was going to read another person's story.

Although Katherine is certainly equating the personal with the therapeutic here (or with the opportunity for the therapeutic), her classroom practices suggest the issue is more a rhetorical one: Personal narratives have been constructed, she might argue, as writings where there is no audience or purpose beyond the self, and effective writing is that which engages an audience beyond the self by situating one's ideas and experiences within a community's shared stories, values, and compelling issues.

Such focus on the self is one of the values Katherine believes she is trying to undo when she teaches her writing class:

I'll be really frank with you, too. The other thing that I have trouble with is, I think that we live in an extremely selfish, self-centered culture. I think that in some ways, you know, completely validating the personal narrative all the time, it's selfishness, you're not being asked to think about how that relates to other people, you're not being asked to think about an audience, you're not being asked to think about how you make this connect to everything, which I think can be as healing. I think the people I know who have benefitted from therapy, my husband among them, did things when there was a group of people and they suddenly have this awareness that there are more people than just me, or suddenly felt that there are other people who need to know this is what happened to me. . . .

[I]t's sad because we miss out on so many opportunities to be able to bond and fix things and feel like we're okay and connect, not to mention the whole realm of stories and creativity and all these other things that are learned and passed down when you live where community is valued, that we miss out on. . . . [This individuality is] just endemic in this culture, it's such a huge part of the American identity or the myth of being an American. . . . I mean, if you're about individuality, then why don't you start letting people think about, you know, beyond this sort of mythic idea of it and what that means?

One of the ways Katherine addressed this cultural attitude in Ann's class was by asking students to consider how they would define themselves as a generation, especially in terms of historical changes and shared popular culture. She gives them readings from newspapers, magazines, and fiction that try to delineate the characteristics of Generation X, and these readings often provoke heated debates. But Katherine also asks them to place their generation, however they come to define it, in relation to those of the past several decades. In this class, she had them view a documentary film, *Atomic Café* and read Tim O'Brien's *The Things They Carried*, for example, so they would understand the historical and cultural events that seemed to define the 1950s and 1960s. Then she visually represents the ways she wants them to view themselves by drawing a series of concentric circles on the board, each representing the larger communities by which an individual is shaped: the innermost one labeled "self," the next "inner voice," then "family and friends," "town, community," "state, country," "global," and, finally, "UNIVERSAL—art, music, literature, poetry, emotion, human."[12]

As Katherine describes her philosophies about the personal, individuality, and writing, she argues for their functions in containing excess emotionality. This rhetorical philosophy creates a buffer for her between Ann's emotions and those emotions that Ann's story evokes in Katherine. This philosophy protects both women from the threat Katherine perceives emotional pain can pose to relationships and psyches. At the same time, asking students to see themselves in relation to culture mitigates the opportunities to pathologize individuals because it focuses on systemic influences, making it more likely, Katherine believes, that individual circumstances can change as the result of political critique and action. A sociopolitical rhetoric is arguably more therapeutic here than the rhetoric of psychoanalysis and therapy.

Katherine does not avoid emotional intensity in her class, however. The kinds of emotions she *wants* to arouse are those she believes will motivate students to challenge the status quo, to reflect critically on what seems natural and normal, to construct the links among the concentric circles she refers to. She does this by occasionally creating conflict or discomfort for her predominantly white, middle-class students, particularly through the readings she gives and the questions she poses during discussions (which I will illustrate more specifically in a class discussion in a later section). In doing so, she pushes against these students' desire to avoid emotional intensity (especially conflict) and directs that intensity *away* from their relationships to each other and *toward* political ideas and action. As Stearns (1994) might suggest, uncomfortable and threatening emotions are reeducated to find another object that doesn't affect other people.

However, the very contextualizing that redirects emotions like anger, resistance, frustration, and passionate commitment to ideas and that buffers Katherine from students' emotional intensity makes her emotionally exhausted. It takes so much emotional energy to enact the political change she believes in that she equates teaching with being a soldier:

> My sort of personal, political convictions about [myths of individuality] come up, I think, again and again and again in the way that I teach. For me, that classroom is like a battlefield about life and death to try to get even one person to think about something that [he or she] might not have thought of before. Because I don't see it happening other places in the world, and that's why I get so exhausted because I feel like I'm fighting this big war.

Because she sees students' resistances to her pedagogy as middle-class denial, it seems "quite a wall to have to scale."

> The fact that I feel that way about it sometimes makes me feel like I'm not the right person to do this because I put so much weight, I mean, this dominates my life, this is all I think about, and everything I hear is potentially something I could use in class. And at one level I think, wow, that must make me a really good teacher, and at another level I think, that's why I'm going to burn out in a few years. So the question then becomes, you know, is that kind of the thing that's going to block us from ever having this equality?

In conceiving of individuals as agents who, motivated by emotion, critical thinking, and action, can change the communities we live in, Katherine negotiates an American emotionology that uses metaphors of control and dangerous excess to interpret emotion. If she can't control her frustration, she seems to suggest here, she should not be teaching.

Our conversation about possibly burning out led her to question the appropriateness of bringing in her ideological commitments. In one of her comments, in fact, she questions whether to see her political agenda as similar to the inappropriate agenda behind sexual harassment—implying that her subjective values are a lack of emotional control equal to the misuse or abuse of power targeted at women's bodies.

> Should people even be bringing—I mean am I as bad as Don Silva [a professor who was recently accused of sexual harassment]? Am I bringing some political agenda into the classroom that's inappropriate, you know, or is there some boundary between trying to create an environment where people figure that stuff out for themselves without critical thinking, and kind of implementing something that isn't appropriate maybe?

Katherine is asking here how dangerous her political agenda is, and in what ways. While it certainly functions as discipline, like any ideology, it's curious she would link it to discourses that have disciplined sexuality and gender, particularly the bodies and identities of women. She walks a tough line here, as any of us do who are committed to social change through our teaching, and Katherine points out the very real danger of using our power to coerce students' beliefs in ways they may find abusive. For Ann, Katherine worked this balance well, but for other students, Katherine's use of authority may have prompted them to keep a silence Katherine would find disturbing.

Knowing Her Knowledge

Although our conversation began by critically reflecting on the purposes of the personal narrative in a college course, it wound its way to a similar reflection on the appropriateness of acknowledging one's ideological commitments and how they motivate a teacher and inform that teacher's pedagogy. Katherine seems to always be enacting the kind of critical thinking she wants to encourage in her students, a kind of thinking that reminds me of Ann Berthoff's reflective, philosopher-teacher, thinking about thinking, "seek[ing] to know [her] knowledge" (1981, vi). Her own education, conversations with the staff (especially a few of the instructors she respects a great deal), and her own reading are constantly in dialogue, prompting her to question her theories and seek ways to bring theory into practice.

Of the many ways to categorize writing pedagogies in the field of composition, it would be difficult to choose the one in which Katherine might feel most comfortable. She emphasizes writing as a process, using many of the strategies associated with the early process movement—in-class freewriting, brainstorming, exploratory writing; successive drafting and revising based both on readers' responses and on the evolving meanings of the text for the writer; and small-group workshops and reading-response groups. She emphasizes an epistemic philosophy, informed by the work of Gary Lindberg, Ann Berthoff, and Paulo Freire, and her ideological commitments, as I've illustrated in this chapter, echo some of the priorities of critical pedagogies (like those of Freire and Henry Giroux). At the same time, she focuses on issues of craft by studying the work of essayists such as Annie Dillard and Alice Walker and asking students to practice developing scenes and details that evoke sensory responses. "I focus everything from the perspective of a writer, and I say, 'This is what writers do, they take charge of language, they don't let language rule them.'" Although critical thinking is the main focus of the course, Katherine also works to develop the student's *voice*, a term that has become like the scarlet letter in the field, a moral infraction that indicates one endorses liberal humanist ideology but that shifts meaning for whomever is interpreting it. Katherine wants students to "have a sense of their own voice, and to say things in their own unique way, [and to know that] their own unique perspective on the world is valid." If, as Berlin argues, "it is this commitment to an epistemology that locates all truth within a personal construct arising from one's unique selfhood that prevents . . . expressionists from becoming genuinely epistemic in their approach" (1987, 153), then Katherine's pedagogy may be more expressivist than epistemic.

However, as I've tried to illustrate, Katherine's philosophies about identity are more complex than the binary oppositions Berlin and others tend to make between locating truth within a stable sense of self outside of culture and locating it in the competing discourses that structure reality and identity, the self being a series of discourses. Goffman's distinctions between social and personal identity seem particularly useful here (1963, 57, 64). Katherine might argue that students adopt dominant social identities that emphasize an individualism that is self-focused, disconnected from culture, and likely (in her mind) to maintain a status quo that allows particular kinds of oppressions to occur. This kind of social identity in America has been overlaid onto personal identity so that distinctive attributes become signs of this kind of individualism. For example, in a class discussion about rap music, students asserted that an artist's lyrics may reflect his or her own experience—Boogie Down Productions describes two brothers who have three pair of pants between them, for example—but that doesn't mean that experience can be generalized as reflective of a larger culture—in this case, of the poverty that can lead to drug dealing for ghetto blacks. What Katherine hopes to do, I would argue, is to disconnect this association between what she calls students' unique voices and perspectives (personal identity) from this social identity (egocentric individualism) by prompting students to consider who benefits from these identity beliefs. She wants to reconnect personal identity to a social identity where an individual is perceived as part of communities and cultural stories, all of which have the power to challenge dominant ideologies. Even as she resists the social and personal identity beliefs many of her more privileged students bring with them to class, beliefs that give them agency without ethical responsibility, Katherine also tries to work against student identities (a particular kind of social identity) that render them passive subjects in an academic environment, as well as in American corporate culture.

"She's More Like a Knowledgeable Friend than a Professor"[13]: Authority and Agency

During the first class I observed, Katherine led a discussion about what it means to claim an education. The students had finished their research papers, turning in what will be their first graded essay, and Katherine asked them what it was like to choose their own research subject, to develop their own opinion, and to gather both library materials and interviews. Before they begin choosing their own subjects for the rest of the semester (writing a concept paper or discovery draft one week and an essay draft the next, sharing their work with their writing partner), Katherine wanted them to reflect on what this research process can teach them about writing. A few of the students expressed concern that they did not have many guidelines to follow as they might have in other courses. "What does following guidelines do to prepare you as a citizen in a democracy?" she asked. The students stared blankly, remaining quiet.

"Is it learning to think for yourself?" The students still say nothing.

"There is in my opinion—and being a person who teaches writing, is a writer, and worships George Orwell—a lot of danger in only learning to follow guidelines, and there is a lot of value in learning how to set your own guidelines and becoming an independent thinker. And a large part of our course, as we're moving from a research project that challenged you to do this, will be about this aspect of critical thinking that infuses writer's work. Most writers are writing about something they have thought critically about. Part of that is going to be your job in this class." Katherine then wrote on the board a series of opposites that she says represents her view of students, teachers, and education in general:

- claim versus receive
- scholar versus student
- earn versus deserve
- responsibility versus blame

As the class discussed how each of these binaries is different and what each implies about education, Katherine challenged them to look at the ways the school publications (catalogs, guidebooks, etc.) use these words, what they imply for their own learning and for other aspects of their lives (like our expectations of government), and thus how these words shape our attitudes toward ourselves and others. She explains that she does not see students as blank slates or empty vessels but as people with much knowledge to bring to class to combine with her own and that of other students.

Throughout the conversation she and the students both joke and offer serious comments, and it is obvious that many of the students are ready to take her up on challenging guidelines when they point out, for example, that an illustration she used was faulty or when they ask whether class is a "cynical fest." Katherine is not ruffled by comments that resist what she is trying to emphasize. She respects the students' different opinions, listens to them, connects what everyone is saying, asserts her own opinion. Although this particular class remains relatively quiet throughout the semester, very few students seem to feel pressured to believe Katherine's own politics—the role she demands they assume in class, that of a scholar who claims an education and takes responsibility for him- or herself, is nonnegotiable, but the beliefs, ideas, and values the students choose to pursue are respected and discussed within a context where the speaker or writer will be held accountable to others for what those ideas imply and engender.

The first few weeks of Katherine's course, then, are structured to immerse students immediately in positions of agency and responsibility. I can only imagine what it was like for Ann, who was so silent and seemed not to have models of women's authority, to be in class where a woman like Katherine had such a strong presence and personality, who was able to encourage multiple perspectives on ideas and respect those who disagreed with her. In modeling a woman who can both strongly assert her own opinions and not feel diminished or criticized when someone disagrees with her, Katherine offered Ann at least one alternative to a female identity constructed around submissiveness, silence, and self-distrust. She also encouraged all her students to assert their opinions, to question authority, to have confidence in what they wanted and believed while also questioning those beliefs. Ann's writing reflected more confidence and conviction as the semester progressed. This conviction is particularly evident in a response she wrote to a class discussion about rap music. In arguing that rap musicians deserve to be listened to because they write out of their lived experience, Ann expresses more anger than she did in her first essay and challenges what was said in class in a way she might never have done verbally.

Who Wants to Listen to All that Hatred?: Ex(er)cising Anger

Although Ann's anger about this discussion of rap music was only expressed in writing, the other students' frustrations or annoyance seethed below the surface of the discussion. As I turn to this discussion Katherine's class had about rap music, I will focus on the ways anger was constructed, expressed, and managed by both Katherine and the students. Within the emotionology of American culture, anger has been constructed as one of the more dangerous emotions, particularly in the workplace. Stearns (1994) argues that, although adherence to these standards varied, anger in the Victorian period moved from being simultaneously controlled and properly focused to something to "manage and avoid" (120). Interpreted as immaturity, a sign of an unresolved childhood experience, "[s]ignificant expression of one of the negative emotions—as opposed to mere ventilation—now became the symptom of individual fault, demanding no particular response except (should the onlooker be so inclined) a patronizing tolerance" (135). Efforts to conceal anger, to act as if it did not exist, became particularly extensive in the United States (239). Although women were instructed in the Victorian period to control their anger, Stearns (1994) argues that by the twentieth century, "[n]egative emotions were now too devastating to form part of either masculine or feminine identity" (134). It is debatable whether restraints against anger are equally distributed across gender lines (as some of the students here might illustrate), but Stearns reiterates arguments others have made that the expression of anger has been individualized and pathologized to such an extent that witnesses can dismiss the social and political implications of it. What Stearns adds to these arguments is the historical understanding of how this change occurred and how such restraint and avoidance serves capitalist ideologies.[14] To study the ways anger is expressed and contained within a writing classroom, in both the texts students write and the discussions they engage, is to study the rhetorical and epistemological roles of emotional intensity and the way power is negotiated in a particular site in the university.

Katherine is leaning against the table at the front of the room, the large chalkboard behind her, the students still in their small groups but turned toward her in their seats. It is after 4:30 on a warm October afternoon. The groups have just finished workshopping two of their classmates' essays, one about graduation, the other about rap music, and Katherine turns their attention to the second. It argues that rap is unfairly criticized and needs to be understood as part of African-American culture.

"What's going on in the second one? Is this a subject that you want to hear about?" Katherine asks.

"It's not talked about a lot," Tara says.

"What part of it is not talked about a lot?" Katherine responds.

"How they're trying to express themselves in their music," Tara says, "a lot of people don't realize that."

From the corner Craig says, "I don't listen to rap personally, but reading [Lisa's essay] was actually educational for me."

Paul, who is sitting in front of me, agrees with Tara, "It's not talked about a lot—it's easy just to say, like, how bad it is from a distance, but this writer does a good job, I think, of showing how they're saying, what they're actually saying, and how they're trying to deal with it and stuff. I think that's why it's not talked about a lot because it's easier, you hear a lot of people say they don't like it, so they don't have to talk about it."

"Right," Katherine says to Paul, "and if you think about the issues that the artists and this writer are talking about, what are the reasons why we don't like to talk about those things?"

"They're negative," Mike says.

"It's happening, one," Katherine says, restating what someone else has said as Mike spoke. "It's negative, two. We don't want to deal with it, three. We might have to change something about—"

Katie interrupts: "I see it as just the opposite, though."

"Okay, go ahead."

"I think it is talked about and I think oftentimes it's talked about too much. I feel—"

"Where?" Katherine says quickly.

"If you just, like, listen to people, it's like . . . I was annoyed," Katie says, searching for words. "I . . . I was just annoyed by it because I mean, I think it's talked about enough to the point like where you get sick of hearing it. I don't know, I'm just tired of it."

"Okay. What do the rest of you think?"

Erik speaks without raising his hand. "I like how she used a lot of different lyrics and examples from different kinds of rap music to kind of back up her points." He sidesteps Katherine's question, avoiding the explosiveness of Katie's comments and maintaining the good emotional feel of the class. But I suspect he is also responding to Katie's classroom identity: According to most of her classmates, Katie shuts many of them down, making generalizations that are not open to dispute. When she speaks, some of them roll their eyes, others shut themselves down. Katherine works hard in this discussion to challenge Katie's comments, and eventually other students begin challenging her as well. The discussion that evolves does not surprise me—in this northeast-ern state, few of the mostly middle-class, white students have had their racial beliefs challenged, and this is reflected in their often offensive comments about rap musicians.

"What do you think about what Katie said?" Katherine asks Erik.

"I don't think it's talked about that much."

"I don't understand where it's—" Tara begins, turning to Katie, "Where is it talked about?"

"Well, you hear people say how Ice T was in the killing fields—I don't think he knows what the killing fields were. That was in Vietnam. I think that people use things to, like, personify things that just, I don't know."

"I'd just be really curious to know where this gets talked about," Kather-ine continues.

"That's what I was going to say," Josh says. He too usually speaks his un-popular opinions during discussions. "If you ever—I mean I'm not saying I necessarily agree with you—but if you ever watch MTV, every other news segment says, 'violence, stop the violence,' and they always have a big segment on it. I mean, if you look for it, it does get talked about quite a bit. I'm not say-ing it gets talked about too much, but I don't really think that there's a lack of information about it, this type of thing."

"If you listen to, like, the news and stuff like that," Katie says, "and how rappers have been arrested for violent crimes. . . ."

"Okay—" Katherine says.

Katie interrupts: ". . . and also other people have been arrested for vio-lent crimes other than just rappers, I'm not necessarily stereotyping rappers."

"Okay, so the subject of rap music gets talked about a lot maybe in the media," Katherine says, "because I know when 2 Live Crew happened it was big news, like censorship and all these other issues got talked about. But I think part of what Lisa's paper was attempting to do was to say, Look at what they're talking about, and those are the *things* that we *don't* want to talk about. Like at a higher level above this we can say, Oh, rap music, whatever, gets talked about—I know MTV has MTV Yo Raps and all these cheesy programs, but I guess what I'm thinking about when you say that," she looks at Lisa, "what I hear you saying is, we don't talk enough about what the issues are that the rap music is about—if you're saying that we do," referring to Katie, "I'm not sure that I agree with, I don't think the issues that they're putting forth get talked about enough. That's my opinion."

Admirably undaunted, Katie responds, "How can you say that, like, that 'You should have killed me last year,' how can you say that's an issue? I just—"

"That's written for the issue," Lisa, the writer says. "He's saying, 'Fuck the police, fuck—' Everything he says is against society. Obviously, he has a problem with it."

"And the problem should be addressed," Tara adds.

"Like slavery," Paul begins, "I mean way back way back when, like, basically they're brought up in that kind of environment. It kind of trails on into the future."

"I think what you're raising is important for the fact that obviously we're going to disagree about it," Katherine says, "and it explains a lot about what goes on in our culture. My opinion is we don't talk about racism nearly enough, and we don't listen to other people's points of view about racism, which is part of what I think rap music represents."

"I think talking about it only goes so far," Katie disagrees. "I think you need to do something instead." I am struck by how steadfastly Katie asserts her disagreements with Katherine, even interrupting her.

"Well, that's what rappers are doing, they're saying, Look this is where I live, this is what happens to me, this is what my experience is about," Katherine responds. As they talk, several hands go up and students who are usually silent make comments. The discussion turns to how reliable rap lyrics can be if the rappers no longer live in the city. If an artist has made it in bourgeois terms, then his credibility is in question, as well as the credibility of his message. So, the most vocal students in class have challenged Lisa's argument by asserting (1) they hear about it too much (automatically lessening the importance of the messages) and (2) they can't trust rappers are telling the truth. Then Becky returns to Katie's last point that "you can talk about it all you want, but it's what you do about it."

"Okay, so my next question then," Katherine says, "if talking about it isn't enough, is getting your message out, though, and writing something about it, be it a song lyric or an essay, doing something?"

As students respond to this question, they shift the argument to questions of pathos, how appropriate and effective it is to express anger and frustration, to describe poverty, ghetto life, drugs, and gangs. Becky says, "I think it's important to make the public more aware of their problems, but I think that—I don't really listen to rap music—but I think that it could be done in a more positive way, you know, maybe they could say things in a better way—they're catching your attention, I think that's mainly what they do, but, you know, repeating 'Fuck the police' and blah, blah, blah. They could say something much better. I don't want to listen to music that's like that." For a text to be effective, it needs to maintain the standards of emotionology and only generate good emotions in a reader. A writer's intense (and therefore dangerous) emotions need to be private and well-controlled, not unleashed to stir up negative emotions in the reader. In this case, though, as Katherine later points out, this rhetoric of control is particularly important for whites to assert about minorities. In demanding that minorities adhere to these emotion standards, whites can sever the *values* represented in rapper's anger and hatred from those emotions: Rage is no longer about poverty and racism, it's about immaturity, loss of control, and offensiveness.

Craig comments that rappers use the language they do "for effect, they do it to tick people off, to get the publicity more than to get their message across." Evoking negative emotions, again, is manipulative, self-serving, and exploitative. To violate emotion rules to make a buck is even more reason why listeners do not need to attend seriously to a rapper's expression. The issue is no longer about being oversaturated with how oppressed African Americans are or about how real their experiences are; it's about emotional control and manipulation. It is about the listener's discomfort instead of the speaker's lived experience. But Katherine wants to show the students how racially motivated these arguments are.

"Okay," Katherine says, "you know who I think of instantly after what you just explained? Can you guess who I think of? Kurt Cobain. I have this message, it is very important for me to say something and make a statement with my music, which is 'Fuck society' basically, if you listen to his music—fuck materialism, fuck America, I'm sick of it, right? That's Cobain's—Nirvana's message—right? Sort of, basically, yes, no?" Katherine uses a musician to whom these students can relate and whose work is similar to that of rappers. If the messages are the same, she seems to imply, then why do people laud Cobain and not rappers? She continues, "Couldn't do it. You can't do it. It's too overwhelming, and the expectation on him and his group was to sell out. If you want to make money and be famous in America, you have to sell out. And he walked this really fine line. . . . It is incredibly hard in this culture to make a statement for something and stand up for something. And so all these attempts that get made by people need to be looked at, things that go against the status quo need to be looked at and not necessarily be just written off as a way to make money or whatever. Now that's not to say that there aren't people who don't cash in on that in any movement. But I instantly think of him and how hard it must have been to try to do the things he believed in in the face of the system, the market, right? Does that make sense?" Instead of seeing intense, negative emotions as purely sensational and exploitative, Katherine proposes that an artist like Cobain (whom she assumes these students like) discovered that the values attached to those emotions would be coopted by commercialism. When the ideas an emotion represents challenge dominant values, they are made safer by being sensationalized.

Katie disagrees with Katherine that Cobain believed in the values his lyrics expressed, but Katherine reemphasizes her point that music artists struggle to get their messages out without selling out. Then she calls the students' attention to how "nervous [we get] about the subject of racism" and start falling into stereotypes. Katie asserts that Lisa's essay created these stereotypes, but Katherine quickly returns to the question of expressing anger and what it demands of listeners and readers.

"But are we pretty open to listening to other ways people tell things," Katherine asks, "or do we need people to be that angry before we listen?" Some of the students work hard to maintain that anger is not necessary, that it's too offensive to be productive and they should not have to be subjected to it. Not one student acknowledges his or her own angry responses during this discussion, or the way Katie dismissed Lisa's essay as "annoying" (a negative emotion, arguably, that she expects the class to take seriously as an indication of the essay's effectiveness. How useful is an "annoying" essay?). As privileged white students, many I assume from middle-class backgrounds, they have no need to understand black experience and anger, and I am not surprised by this turn in the conversation. I wonder what the silent students are thinking, how well the thirteen who are talking reflect the diversity of opinion in the class as a whole.

Andrew says, "Well, Bob Marley did a pretty good job."

"Bob Marley did a pretty good job, no doubt about it," Katherine responds. "But most of the people that listen to Bob Marley were ready to hear it. It's not the same kind of assault tactic—it's a different approach."

"I like Bob Marley's approach better," Alison says, who has been quiet up to this point. "I don't know, like (inaudible) is a lot better than 'fuck this, fuck that.'"

"It's easier to listen to," Tara agrees.

"And he's representing an African culture more in the sense of how they were," Andrew continues.

"Well, he's also not American—it makes a big difference," Katherine says. "He's from Jamaica. It's a completely different culture from being in America."

"Yeah, that's true. . . ," Andrew says.

"It's a lot easier to listen to," Tara repeats. "It's not as angry, and I think that's a lot easier to—"

"What's wrong with anger?" Katherine persists.

"Well, some of his songs are angry, but he just doesn't yell about it," Andrew comments. "He sings about them sad."

"Anger is magnetizing," Paul says. "It makes you angry listening to it. A prime example, you go to a comedy show to laugh, I mean you don't go to a comedy show to be angry, so you listen to something." Plato would be proud.

Katherine comments that she finds the messages in rap music, expressed in anger, more "honest" than some of the pop 1980s tunes that were becoming popular again.

"I think that anger is good in a sense because when you're angry enough you'll actually do something, so it promotes action," Becky says, "but I think that in so many rap songs that I have heard, I think they overkill it, you know, because, who wants to listen to all that hatred in this society?"

When the period ends, Katherine encourages the students to write a concept paper on these questions of race, anger, and rap music, and she compliments them on the liveliness of the discussion. She is quite pleased with how many people spoke, how many people seemed to open up when they saw Katie unable to specifically defend her generalizations. This class, she tells me, will lead well into her plans for next week when she will introduce her visual of concentric circles. At this point, she says, the students can only see rap music as an isolated and offensive phenomenon, not as a product of other social forces whose meanings depend on context. In the next few weeks, she will augment this metaphor with the introduction to Sonia Maasik and Jack Solomon's anthology *Signs of Life in the USA*, a piece that describes semiotic thinking, and the students will have read a number of texts about the historical events that shaped each generation from the 1950s to the present. The students will not, however, have their racial beliefs challenged in the ways Katherine values; her own comments during the conversation will be the only counterarguments they will hear unless the students choose to pursue the subject for themselves.

Ann did not speak during this class discussion, and the response essay she wrote later describes how furious she became as more students argued why the messages and situatedness of rap music could be ignored. As I have tried to emphasize, the subtext of this discussion was emotional control—who has to change their negative emotions and why. The students who spoke clearly wanted to read essays with positive messages—they even criticized the graduation essay for not being positive enough. As readers, they did not want their own negative feelings stirred up; socialized to be preoccupied with containing their own unruly emotions, they don't want someone else's to interfere. So, assuming their feelings are natural responses, and it's natural not to want to have negative ones, they can dismiss the political messages in rap music without being accused of being racist. Rap is about individuals who are a little off the mark, not able to stay in control, and many of the students in this class discussion effectively argued to silence these artists on the basis of violating emotion rules.

Much more is going on in this conversation than this negotiation of emotional expression, of course, but I want to highlight how this discourse on emotion works to sustain particular relations of power—here based on race, gender, and class. For a student such as Ann who has been silenced in so many ways, this conversation could have reinforced her shame, self-recrimination, and silence. But I think the combination of Ann's own anger, Lisa's essay, and Katherine's responses during this discussion all provided sites of resistance. In her response to the class, Ann wrote, "I was just so glad when I read Lisa's essay to see that other people (white people) see how critical these issues are in today's society." She aligns herself with Lisa against the majority of people who spoke in class, and I suspect Katherine's support of Lisa's paper reinforced her resolve. What Katherine did during this conversation was to challenge the students' a priori assumptions that negative emotions were signs of ineffective art—she argued that anger had a place in written expression and tried to confront the racial prejudices obscured by their feeling rules. In doing so, she tried to redefine anger not as an individual pathology or immaturity but as a justified response to social oppressions.

Within the larger context of Ann's classmates, Ann's response to Lisa's essay and the class discussion is not unusual in the way an intense emotion is an equal part of the process of knowledge building and writing in Katherine's course. Many of the students responded with indignation and frustration to a Kent State documentary, Tim O'Brien's novel (*The Things They Carried*), and the readings on Generation X. What I do think *is* significant about Ann's response is that, as a young woman whose sense of identity and being in the world has been shaped by violence, verbal abuse, and severe bodily discipline, she was being offered a rhetorical model that does not ask her to suppress her anger (or see it as contaminating reason) or continue to be submissive and subjected.

"Making Everyone Breathe a Little More Shallowly": Ann's Response

> *Although our emotions are epistemologically indispensable, they are not epistemologically indisputable. Like all our faculties, they may be misleading, and their data, like all data, are always subject to reinterpretation and revision. Because emotions are not presocial, physiological responses to unequivocal situations, they are open to challenge on various grounds. They may be dishonest or self-deceptive, they may incorporate inaccurate or partial perceptions, or they may be constituted by oppressive values. Accepting the indispensability of appropriate emotions to knowledge means no more (and no less) than that discordant emotions should be attended to seriously and respectfully rather than condemned, ignored, discounted, or suppressed.*
>
> —Alison Jaggar, "Love and Knowledge" (163)

"The class totally disillusioned me," Ann told me. "I didn't expect that at all." She had just given me her response paper and began talking about it before I'd had a chance to read it. "I talked to a couple of people outside the class and they were like, 'What are you talking about?' and they said that they agreed with the girl in the class that was saying 'Oh, we hear way too much about this stuff.' I don't know. So I just, well, I talked to Katherine about it in the meeting and she said she couldn't believe it either, so she just doesn't mention it cause it sets her off so much." It made sense to me that a quiet student like Ann would take the opportunity of an informal response assignment to express her anger and arguments (see Appendix). Although she would not be sharing this with anyone except Katherine, Ann works in this piece to establish her credibility by asserting how much she used to believe what some people in class do about rap music:

> I guess you could go so far as to say that I used to be one of those people Lisa discusses in her paper that thought that all rap was about the degradation of women and that it placed little value on human life until my best friend made me listen to her "mixes" and I realized that not all of the music really was that bad.

Interestingly, what prompted her to reassess what many believe condones violence against women were women rappers such as Queen Latifa who "sings to women, telling them to demand the respect they deserve. 'You ain't a bitch or a ho,' she explains. I think it was this song that told me to wake up, that there was more to rap than disrespectful sex and violence, there are serious social issues addressed in rap music." As someone who has fought for her own self-respect, Ann is willing to listen to someone else whose message counters the misogynist ones women hear daily. She also appreciates another woman who is willing to call attention to the voices of people who are suffering.

Two things are significant about Ann's response as it compares to her first piece about being assaulted: First, although she does have a paragraph in which she makes more conventional assertions about the cultural changes that could be made to better the lives of African Americans, very little of this response explicitly accommodates to whomever she conceives her audience to be. Unlike her first essays, this response is directly addressed to her classmates. Her opening paragraphs attempt to understand where her classmates might be coming from, but much of the essay focuses on her emotional response as it argues against students such as Katie. In this sense, it is more assertive, the narrator less concerned about taking care of her reader's feelings and avoiding conflict:

> [W]hen it came time for the class to discuss the essay, I was absolutely stunned when that girl, the same one who complains about everything, said

that she thought that the essay was "annoying." First of all, what kind of a person has the nerve to say that she thinks her classmate's paper is annoying and, secondly, how can anyone say that they're sick of hearing about this subject constantly? Maybe I live a sheltered life or something, but I really can't identify with her complaint. I really don't think that we hear enough about this stuff. I think that society has got a major problem on its hands about the quality of life for minorities that must be addressed and isn't.

When people began to back up the "annoying" girl (I forget her name, I'll call her Sue) by saying that information on this topic is everywhere—MTV, etc.—I was amazed. I suppose it is basically true that I never watch TV, but I find it really hard to believe that these issues are addressed everywhere.

Because Katherine was the only one who read this piece, Ann is still not directly confronting the people with whom she disagrees and for whom she feels such anger. But the anger is palpable here in a way it isn't in her earlier essay, and it becomes intertwined with her argument.

Secondly, this response is also significant because Ann questions her classmates' efforts to keep anger linked to deviance and severed from conditions of oppression. By analogy, she is arguing to have her own anger (at her father, her boyfriend) *mean* something beyond immaturity, selfishness, and irrationality. And, like Katherine, she questions a listener's right to be deaf to victims of poverty, racism, and societal abuse. She writes,

I was overcome by pure frustration. I knew I should have said something in class and wanted to, but I was past frustration. I was mad. I'm not sure why I got so angry, but I even had the little tremors and hot cheeks of true anger. People in the class, not all but a lot, were the same "Chris" that Lisa wrote about who generalized all rap as just being about killing and sex. This is true of the typical gangster rap, but this conveys a message to the listener that this is an issue that must be changed. Sure I understand when many people said that they didn't want to listen to this kind of music because it is so negative, but, for goodness' sake, at least hear and be aware of what is going on! I want people to hear the words and to say that no one should have to live like that, that something must be done. I don't want them to tune themselves out and say that we hear too much about this problem. Obviously we don't hear about it enough when conditions in the ghetto persist, even worsen as they do.

Ann is also talking indirectly about the conditions of her own life here, but the issue of racial oppression may be less threatening for her to address. At issue are the reasons for listening. Later in the piece she asserts, "the more we don't listen to these messages either because they 'don't apply to us' or we just plain don't like to hear it, the more we contribute to the problems." Here she directly implicates her readers (her classmates) in racism in a way she cannot implicate her father or her boyfriend in sexism—she is beginning to elaborate on the societal forces, supported by individuals, that produce the possibility for ghetto life in a way she has not yet done for her own experience. She is beginning to distinguish anger that is about power (and violence) from anger that is about trauma and oppression.

"I Just Seem to See Everything in a Different Way Now"

I want you to feel what I felt. I want you to know why story-truth is truer than happening-truth.
—Tim O'Brien, *The Things They Carried* (203)

What I have just described—a change in Ann's sense of confidence and authority as a writer, her challenges to emotion rules—she herself described with an example of how she would now think about a Vietnam veteran differently as a result of Katherine's course. The semester affected "the way I think about things," she told me—Katherine's emphasis on individuality within the context of community, on the practice of semiotics as a mode of critical thinking, on the dialectical relationship among rhetoric, emotion, ideology, and lived experience.

> I look at [things] broader, and try to, well, in a more analytical way, see things differently. Like after we read that book [*The Things They Carried*], I saw a guy in a movie store and his hat said, "I'm a Vietnam Vet." Before I read that book I would have said, you know, "Well, what do you want, a medal or something?" And after I read the book, I'm wondering, does he need to talk about this? And I'm planning on interviewing him. I want to see what he has to say about it. So I'll never think about a Vietnam Vet the same ever again.
>
> I used to think the war movies, it was their way of getting off, "Oh, yeah, I killed people," but now it's not, I really don't think that way at all anymore. . . . I thought they were all for glorifying the soldier, but I think maybe it's their way of having someone else understand what they've been through.

Instead of feeling resentment when a Vietnam veteran signifies his or her suffering, instead of pathologizing the veteran as dominant culture has, Ann now wants to listen. O'Brien's book affected the way Ann thought about emotion and bodily violence—it influenced what Kali' Tal (1996) describes as her "personal myths" (Goffman's concept of personal identity) in such a way that it changed her intellectual and affective relationship to victims of violence. As a testimony to the unreality of war, to its fragmenting of coherence and order, O'Brien's novel dramatized the urgency of witnessing to trauma. This witnessing—through writing—is an attempt to enter that old order again, to reconcile what O'Brien's character believed about himself, about life, and about war with the truth of trauma—itself unspeakable. "*Re*-telling the war in a memoir or describing it in a novel," Tal says, "does not merely involve the development of alternative national myths through the manipulation of plot and literary technique but the necessary rebuilding of shattered *personal* myths" (1996, 117). Speaking and writing about traumatic violence can be a way of reassembling an identity that allows one to be seen and heard by those who have *not* suffered, who represent the original state of innocence that preceded the violence. Although Ann may not yet see the connections between her experience and that of the veteran (or that there are significant differences),[15] she has been introduced to writing and speaking about the unspeakable as healing, especially within relationships.

In writing to more fully understand his experience, O'Brien also demonstrated what Katherine meant by semiotic thinking, and thus her belief that a sociopolitical rhetoric can be healing and socially transformative. He critiqued war and violence by placing the meanings of soldiers' language, of the things they carried, their actions, all within the context of war, culture, and identity—but, as Ann pointed out, he did so by combining critical thinking and emotions. This further reinforced a reeducation of emotions Ann was immersed in through Katherine's course in which the feelings someone expressed—anger, resistance, or fear—were interpreted as connected to the person's values and lived experience and part of developing a critical social theory.

This is not to say, of course, that Katherine treated all emotional expressions equally. She was uncomfortable with those expressed in a personal essay where the writer focused on only him- or herself and ignored the reader's need for mutual significance. She tried to avoid essay subjects that reinforced dominant emotionology, which is exactly my point. For Ann, this approach provided a context and *opportunity* for her to consider—through the experiences of others—her own experiences of being physically and verbally abused as part of a larger system of power. An opportunity. At the same time, Katherine's pedagogy invited Ann to consider her anger as legitimate and critical to her resistance. In Ann's own words,

> [I]t's made me want to think more about exactly what is right, and how we should feel about something. And how it's important to talk about things. I think a lot of time in our society people do feel shut down and they don't want to say anything. And I think it's important to say things.

Listening

Traumatic events destroy the sustaining bonds between individual and community. Those who have survived learn that their sense of self, of worth, of humanity, depends upon a feeling of connection to others. The solidarity of a group provides the strongest protection against terror and despair, and the strongest antidote to traumatic experience. Trauma isolates; the group re-creates a sense of belonging. Trauma shames and stigmatizes; the group bears witness and affirms. Trauma dehumanizes the victim; the group restores her humanity.
—Judith Herman, *Trauma and Recovery*, 214

When I began my preliminary research on women writing about sexual abuse, I tried to locate three of my former students from the course Writing About Female Experience, hoping to get permission to study their work. It had been over a year since the course ended, and the university had no address for one young woman (who had been raped by a stepuncle), but directed me to both Stephanie (from the Introduction) and Emily (from Chapter 2). Stephanie was just finishing her senior year and hoping to study in Russia soon. Emily, however, had moved back to her home city in the southern part of the state and transferred to a local college, working part time to support herself. I was surprised and pleased that she was still in school—she had been so silent in class, seemed so disengaged, that I wasn't sure she really wanted to be there. I had thought it significant that, after writing about being abused by her stepuncle, she raised her head off her desk during class and began participating in discussions, but I wasn't sure how that might transfer to her college experience in general.

When I talked with Emily, though, she told me that writing her essay was the beginning of a process that prompted her to transfer and then start attending group therapy for sexual abuse survivors. In the letter she wrote me later, she included a short piece she had written, possibly for publication, that narrates her experience of being selected for jury duty to try a man who had allegedly raped a ten-year-old girl. In this piece, a lawyer asks her if she has ever had a crime committed against her, and she considers what he could mean by "crime." Being slapped by a friend when they were children? Being french-kissed as a child by her teenage stepuncle? Having a rock break her window? Having her stepuncle force her to perform fellatio? Her money missing from her purse? A crime? she keeps asking. "No," she finally answers. The fact that she uses this irony to dramatize her point suggests her own double consciousness and captures with skillful understatement the powerlessness women can reexperience in the courtroom when sexual violation is not considered a crime. Her anger is palpable, her narrative voice more assured than in the writings for my course. The point of the essay reminded me of Susan Glaspell's "A Jury of Her Peers"—Mrs. Hale and Mrs. Peters recognize their shared experiences are valid knowledge for understanding why Minnie Wright killed her husband, but that knowledge is not acknowledged in a courtroom. I was surprised at the differences between the narrator Emily created in the first essay I saw and in this one. If I had not contacted her after my course, I most likely would not have been privileged to see these differences. I also would not know that now, almost ten years after our course, Emily would be pursuing her master's degree in English and teaching first-year writing as a teaching assistant. The silent young woman in the back of my classroom whom I feared would not make it through her undergraduate years is now immersed in the study and teaching of language.

Throughout this study, I have tried to keep Emily in mind and the point she emphasizes for me that we can't know what happens to our students after they leave our classes. We can't know when they turn in a piece about being abused or having an eating disorder where that writing and thinking might take them. Nor can we know if they have written about it before. A couple of students came to talk with me who had not only written about their eating disorders their freshman year, they had written about them in high school and then later in other courses. One student, in fact, was writing her honors thesis based on an essay she had written in a sophomore nonfiction writing course. In that earlier essay, she had proposed that, instead of studying only the damaging effects of eating disorders, researchers begin to study what positive, hopeful meanings anorexic women may have made from their experiences. Graduating with a major in biology and a minor in nutrition, this young woman plans to become a physician's assistant and hopes to touch the lives of other women like her. I had many more students come to me in the years since I began this study to share essays they had written in literature and women's studies courses in which they used their own experiences with bodily violence to research and analyze texts such as Dorothy Allison's *Bastard Out of Carolina*. I've also heard from teachers about men who write about their struggles with body image and eating (frequently wrestlers) and a few who write about their experiences with violence, men who aren't represented in this project. As limited as my study is, I found that students will write about these experiences in various courses and often use them to interrogate an academic theory, for instance, to analyze an artistic rendering, or to experiment with genres of creative nonfiction. A student's first-year writing course is only one of many in the university experience, and it is humbling to discover that students don't just choose nurturing writing courses as places to disclose. Much more is going on than many of us expect.

In this study, I have been trying to build an argument for listening—for attending to the words and voices of students as they make and unmake themselves; write and rewrite culture; and consider and reconsider language, power, and truth. Essays on bodily violence do not appear in writing classrooms only because Rikki Lake, *The National Enquirer*, and group therapy have made such experiences sensational, good voyeuristic fodder, or signs of pathology. To associate all writing about bodily violence with pop psychology and a "cult of the victim," as Kathleen Pfeiffer (1993) might do, is like arguing that any expression of feminist ideas means one is a "radical, man-hating, lesbian" feminist—as many of our students do. As I have illustrated, bodily violence has been written and talked about throughout Western history, in distinctly different ways and for distinctly different purposes, even though it has also been suppressed, obscured, and used to victimize and exploit. When our students write about their experiences they do so from a number of different discourses that are not limited to pop psychology or talk-show discourses. One of the most important things I've learned from reading these students' essays and talking with them is that a writing teacher needs to begin by first being skeptical of his or her own impulses to read these texts only through psychotherapeutic or psychoanalytic discourses. A writing teacher must understand his or her role as examining the body and psyche of students in the process of examining their texts.

The teacher must also attend to the polyphony of discourses students use to represent their experiences, possibly building on the critical strategies they already exercise there. The subjects of abuse and eating disorders have been politicized in both popular and academic contexts, so when a student engages one of these discourses, that student is presenting the possibility of critical reflection and sociopolitical analysis. The essays in this study also raise questions about the argument that personal and painful subjects can only be written about in egocentric and self-absorbed ways, or that these writers are too emotionally unstable to write academically at all. In fact, many of the students I worked with came from honors freshman English courses or did quite well academically. Frequently, they work from their outlaw emotions to question who has named the truths of their experiences and told them why and how they should feel, developing what Jaggar (1989) calls "a critical social theory" in the process. Their emotions disrupt their texts at times, demonstrating, as Abigail Abbot Bailey did, that emotions—and writing—can allow the strength and critical reflection necessary for resistance. In joining emotion and reason dialectically, the personal and the academic, the private and public (even in the simple act of writing about bodily violence in a university), these students challenge power relations and, in some cases, the emotion rules that organize American culture. Critical pedagogies such as Katherine's can be part of the process of encouraging all students to use and understand knowledge and language as sustained by these dialectical relationships, recovering a place in rhetoric and epistemology for emotion as biological, cultural, and critically reflective. To see these students only as egocentric, psychologically unstable, or reenacting America's obsession with victims, is to elide the rhetorical, social, and sometimes critical strategies they use in an effort to be visible, normal, and heard.

I was most surprised to learn how many students seemed to desire the normalizing functions of college writing. Particularly for those who write anonymously, early in the semester, college seems to be a safer place to write about experiences that have decentered their sense of identity and reality. Denigrated as women and as victims of abuse or self-inflicted starvation, these students attempt to manage those marginalized identities within a public institution known historically for its emphasis on objective, reasoned discourse, unified authorial identities, and the relatively inconsequential writing within a first-year composition course. Freshman English may seem like a good place to try to *pass* or to be above passing—to be healthy, in control, intelligent, not affected by the rhythms and chaos of bodies that seem to have betrayed them.

In assuming these identities, they can still be adhering to standards for emotional cool in American culture, yet also be safely expressing intense emotions because professors and classmates are strangers who will not be hurt or disillusioned to the same degree friends and family may be. The phantom acceptance proffered by the university community may be easier to manage than that of their intimates.

In negotiating their identities, students balance a dialogic relationship between the student's desired identity and her audience's projection or construction of it, Foucault's sense of being both an active Subject and yet a passive one. It is especially important, I think, for women who have suffered bodily violence to believe a unified, normal self is possible through writing in an academic context. They have a place to practice the centered and controlled sense of identity that projects (and commands) authority—or at least it has for men. The discourses these women can appropriate to represent and understand their experiences are ones that might make the experiences visible to an audience they want to reach (regardless of whether its members are fellow sufferers) garnering attention through rhetorical argument, lyrical essays, or academic research. However, because these experiences are constructed by culture as painful and emotional, even threatening to relationships and the work of the academy, these students challenge the dichotomies that produce the very possibility of having a centered, controlled, cool identity when they write about bodily violence in a public discourse, within a public, rational space. Their subjects confront readers with aspects of their own painful identities and thus with the arbitrariness of the distinctions between normal and deviant, healthy and diseased, and mature and immature. In so doing, these subjects challenge the unequal power relationship between teacher and student that is partly maintained by fearing sentimentality (perhaps now represented as a fear of psychotherapy).

Within composition studies, some readers have responded quite strongly to what is understood as a violation of feeling rules that these essays represent. These discourses on emotions illustrate an anxiety about the unruly bodies and emotions of (mostly female) students once constructed as amenable to the discipline of mechanical correctness. Often, however, arguments about such personal writing now try to regulate students' texts/bodies by linking the personal with the emotional, the emotional with middle-class ideology, and that ideology with oppressive systems of power that teachers need to instruct students to resist. The opportunity for these oppressions are partly rooted in beliefs that universal, coherent identities and values are possible and desirable—thus students need to have their identities decentered. A good place for a writing teacher to start decentering this privileged identity seems to be the contemporary manifestations of Puritan self-analysis of which these essays are perceived to be a part. I have been arguing that these theories often assume emotion as presocial, psychobiological, and weak (in that they make students more vulnerable and in need of protection), but the student texts in this study also suggest what many feminists have asserted about postmodern theory—the identities that can be safely decentered are those of white, heterosexual, middle-class males. They may have less to lose than females in being fragmented, textualized, unauthorized, their bodies written on.

Although I am skeptical about the pedagogical projects that seem, as Lynn Worsham (1992–1993) suggests, like a kind of "wilding," I think it is important for students who write about bodily violence in a college composition course to be offered multiple perspectives on their experiences, to see them as socially constituted, not isolated and therefore deviant. Academic theories have quite different interpretations of the meanings of sexual or physical abuse and eating disorders—multiple mirrors, in a sense, to see oneself refracted through—but so too do fiction, essays, poetry, drama, and film. Two recent collections that gather women's writings from various historical periods and genres are *Nature's Ban: Women's Incest Literature* (McLennan 1996)[1] and *Eight Lessons in Love: A Domestic Violence Reader* (Spilka 1992); other texts have also been published that represent contemporary writing. Abigail Abbot Bailey's memoir is a powerful reminder that sexual and physical violence is not just a recent phenomenon nor is it restricted to families of low economic status. When students can engage with another text on their subject, the focus in the student-teacher relationship can shift away from teachers' fears about being therapists and back to the student's writing and learning. In the process, students can be taken seriously as writers, not dismissed as narcissists.

I took a risk in 1990 when I taught Emily's course, a risk that the power imbalance between my students and me might allow me to unwittingly revictimize them, render them more vulnerable to state disciplinary power in the act of confessing their experiences. Although I did not conceive of my role that way then, I am not comfortable casting myself as an authority figure whose power can only be used negatively to victimize. Of course, that's possible, and as a feminist I feel strongly that we need to be vigilant about those possibilities. But even Foucault (1978) argues that power is also productive in positive ways. Compassion, humility, and a respect for students are not necessarily guises for oppressive power—to argue so casts all human behavior in dichotomously pessimistic, oppressive, and exploitative terms, a view of ideology that Foucault might argue is still situated in *juridico-discursive models* (romantic models in which the individual can still throw off the power of the state).[2] Wouldn't it be more productive to turn the field's preoccupation with its own self-analysis, its own subjectivity, to the cultural systems that produced this violence for these students in the first place?

So How *Do* I Respond?

I have tried to offer a way of reading student essays about bodily violence that makes them visible within the conversations about writing instruction that dominate the field right now, and that means I haven't considered a number of angles that may seem obvious to many of my readers. I've only begun an inquiry that I hope will raise more questions and lead to even more thoughtful, serious, and respectful studies on students who write about painful, personal experiences. At this point, I'd like to offer some closure and make a few suggestions about how we might respond to student essays about bodily violence. I do so hesitantly. Whenever I speak to groups of writing teachers about my work, I qualify my talk with my belief that the moment we set ourselves up as experts on these issues is the moment we are in danger of victimizing these students again. We don't ultimately have control over what happens with our students, but we do have responsibilities for being aware of what might happen and how our beliefs about students and the subjects they write about influence a student's writing and learning.

I will start by sharing what students told me about how they wanted their teachers to respond. When I asked them, I most frequently heard, "I just wanted to know she had heard me, that she was listening. I didn't want her to be a therapist or anything; I wanted to work on the essay so this wouldn't happen to other people." Being heard. Listening. Becoming visible to someone else who won't victimize them. Listening may seem like a rather simple request, but it means we must understand our own fears about these subjects and our own judgments, and we must work not to transfer them onto the student. One of the teachers in this program told me that she works in a men's prison with rapists and abusers because she wants to keep in touch with the part of herself that is capable of those same acts and vulnerable to being a victim of them. Any one of us can be in these students' positions. Violence and self-abuse are not the province of the pathological and abnormal—when we acknowledge that we are all capable of victimizing and potentially becoming victims of violence, we dismantle the binaries that set us up as more normal than the physically abused student sitting in our office, that create our fears that students want us to be therapists to cure their problems. When we don't acknowledge this commonality, we are in danger of trying to control the unruly bodies and emotions we fear in ourselves by controlling our students and their texts in potentially harmful ways (countertransference, in psychological terms). If we want to be ethical about the ways we respond to these essays, then we need to do what many of us ask our students to do: reflect critically on where our responses are coming from and who is benefiting from the dichotomies we set up between the healthy teacher and the ill student, situate them historically and culturally, and assume responsibility for the responses we offer.

When a student is sitting in our office waiting for the conference to begin, we need to be aware of whether we can respond in a way that respects her and her experience. If our own painful experiences with trauma or struggles with food are triggered by the student's work and we aren't sure the student's needs will remain our focus, then it might be best to tell the student we may not be a good audience for her essay. I would applaud her courage, share with her how it affected me, offer a few essays she might read that could offer context, and suggest other readers who might be more helpful. I would not tell the student her essay doesn't meet the course requirements or is something I'm not equipped to deal with. Both of those responses shames the student for inappropriate behavior and may reinforce her fears about being silenced. If my own issues are interfering with my desire to help this student learn, then I need to respect the student enough to tell her I'm not the best reader for her work.

I always keep the numbers of local counselors nearby so I can seek advice in how to respond to a student while still maintaining the student's confidentiality. Because teachers are authority figures and violence is often perpetrated by those who believe they have more power, students may easily transfer their anger and fear or their desire to be loved and accepted onto us. Although Ann Murphy (1989) has insightfully pointed out that writing teachers are too overworked to add one more skill to their lists, I suggest that writing programs invite counselors to talk with their faculty about how to deal with transference and countertransference issues. Boston College, for example, has ongoing meetings between staff and counselors to help teachers explore how and why they might best respond to students with different needs. My own suggestions, then, need to be considered in relation to the knowledge of therapists about the psychodynamics of relationships and trauma.

Once we have thoughtfully reflected on what our responses tell us about ourselves and our teaching, what might we do next for that student who is sitting in our office? To answer this, I will focus my discussion around an essay I received as a part of this study. The student wrote this draft after an in-class prompt, which asked her to slow down a moment of time, using as much detail as possible. As an example, the teacher read a paragraph about a boy who is being hit by his father, and this triggered a memory for Stacie. She tries to use narrative to dramatize her boyfriend's assault on her in her dorm room and create a self whose courage and strength hasn't been beaten out of her.

I usually ask my students how they would like me to respond to their drafts, no matter what the subject, and I use their comments as a guide, balancing what I hope to teach them with what they'd like their essay to achieve. I think this reflective question is particularly important with essays like Stacie's: Is this an essay she wants evaluated in her portfolio at the end of the semester? What kinds of comments would she like from me? Where does she see the essay taking her? How does she see it connecting to the other things we've been doing in class? I believe it important for any student to have some control over the direction of his or her text, and this is especially true for students who have suffered abuse. Psychologist Judith Herman notes that the "first principle of recovery is the empowerment of the survivor. She must be the author and arbiter of her own recovery. Others may offer advice, support, assistance, affection, and care, but not cure" (1992, 133). Although Herman's language may strike a postmodern audience as romantic, these students have had control and power taken from them, rendering them ambivalent at best about their own agency and abilities. To not be part of revictimizing them, I think we need to encourage their self-direction while helping them meet the expectations of the course. As I explore with a student her options for working on her essay, I consider with her what she might like to do if, for example, a member of her workshop group is dismissive, if she finds the draft too difficult to revise within the expectations of the course, if memories become too overwhelming. While we need to avoid pathologizing these students, we need to be aware of the possible effects this writing may have on them and explore with students the various choices they have about what happens next.

On the back of Stacie's draft, she has answered some reflective questions that her teacher has posed, which suggest to me she does want this essay graded and she would like specific feedback on the structure, grammar, and meaning of the piece.

> My largest question was, do I really want to read this out loud to a group of people? The writing came very easily because I have a lot of emotion on this subject. If I had written this paper on my own outside of *this* class it would have been more like a story of the entire event—not a detailed description. I would have hated the story. I really like this paper and believe it has a lot of potential. Should I have the beginning piece in there (my peer group said I should)? Structure, wording, grammar, stuff that's awkward or doesn't fit. Is the ending ok? I sorta like it—I'm not sure. Reading this paper to my peer group turned out to be really good. They gave me a lot of good ideas and feedback—more than I thought.

In the essay that follows, I've included her teacher Janet's responses and reproduced all the idiosyncrasies of the original draft (it is important to consider what Janet chooses to comment on). Because Stacie has written this essay in a course focused on essay writing, not in a course focused on critical pedagogy or academic discourse, her teacher's comments do not emphasize contextualizing the experience or pursuing research. As a reflective essay, the piece is supposed to render meaning to an event, and Janet has asked students to experiment with the narrative strategies they've been practicing in class.

In the background Ferris Bueller buggies so carefree above the dancing crowd as he lip-syncs to "Twist and Shout," valentine scrapes are scattered all over the green rug. Everyone is doing their own thing, some wrapped up being dutiful to their long distance boyfriend's and others dealing with their parents desperate attempts to regain control of their daughters lives by phone. I sit on the soft brown couch with the harsh florescent light of my computer screen giving me a headache. I stare into the screen *This is another issue you seem to be grappling with. . . .* looking for an answer to my question? What will people think if I write about my boyfriend beating me up? Will people think I'm a weak individual who lets herself get pushed around? Will they think I'm just looking for sympathy or attention? These feelings of anger, frustration along with thousands questions fly around in my head and can't escape, they can't seem to find that same hole that my sophomore chemistry class lectures escaped out of. I believe that I'll have to write about the whole incident and then maybe the unwanted feelings can escape out of that hole also. *Let's talk about where you want to begin and what you want to focus the piece.*

The three chairs looked so small and personal compared to the vastness of the court room. The chair closest to the wall looked the most appealing. I didn't want to be close to him. I was afraid of any emotion I might have, would I miss, hate or feel sorry for him? A bead of sweat fell from my arm pit down to my torso. I snapped myself straight up and walked to that far chair with a stride that showed everybody I was strong. Without any effort on my part Jane, my SHAARP advocate, took the middle seat as if she read my mind and felt my nervousness. Jane was protecting me. Once in the wooden chair, I rolled back my shoulders and slid in to the rear of the chair to straighten out my back and make me appear taller and stronger. I *Can you show this through her actions rather than tell us?* placed my elbows on the arms of the chair and crossed my legs. I was ready for battle. The flash of a decorated uniform caught my eye. A policeman walked into the room with my ex-boyfriend and his lawyer in tow. An *explain. . . .*

upsweep of strength came over me as I looked into his lifeless, weak eyes. There is no sign of confidence in his bodily movements; I only grew stronger.

Did the judge even say good morning or introduce himself? Al I knew was that the Judge was wearing hideous suspenders. The shinny black plastic glistened with the reflection form the over head florescent lights. The lights only enhanced

I thought they were red!

the fact that the suspenders were not leather but cheap synthetic material. I always assumed that judges would own a respectable pair of suspenders, I guess that's no the case in _____. *This fixation with the judges suspenders distracted me from looking over at Him as everyone shuffled around.*

"The lawyer barked . . . "

His barking lawyer behind me told the judge that he wasn't going to contest the restraining order. I wasn't relieved to hear this; I wanted to read to my statement to everyone in those chambers and show them exactly what he did to me. My main goal was to embarrassing him and proving how sick he is was.

good

His nervousness flashed like a blinking neon sign. I made sure I didn't even twitch even the slightest bit because then I would appear strong compared to him. I could see his hands moving and twisting about in each other. They looked helpless and afraid a complete contrast to how they looked when they were delivering blows to my head.

Good line to show that his strength was over-powering.

I started to panic because there was no possible way out. There was absolutely nothing I could. I was so helpless; the orange belt in Karate and the self defense course did me no good. I couldn't get myself out of this one. There was hard pinching around my upper arms and could feel his fingers digging into my skin. There was no competing against his strength, he threw me back onto my bed. Yes, I said my bed, in my room.

Describe items?

Everything in that room was mine, it was my personal space and I had no control over in it anymore. Shocks of anger and defeat ran through my body enraging me. I couldn't believe that he was doing this to me, he was holding me captive, he was denying me my every right. I filled with ter-

How can you be more specific in your explanation to give the reader a real sense of your physical reaction?

ror. My bed that had brought me many peaceful sleeps as a child, no longer felt comforting as I landed on it. I couldn't crawl into it and forget about what was happening to me. My body automatically jumped up and continued fighting for itself. My face was soaking with tears and my hysterical voice cracked as I choked on the mixture of mucus and snot running down my throat. My arms flailed and the rest of my body convlused with frustration. In a tantrum I pleaded for him to leave. It was as if he didn't see me right there in front of him so scared and crying. My eyes caught a glimpse of the phone and a rush of relieve washed over me, I would simply call my friends down the hall and they would come unlock my door and dispose of him. The cord was ripped out of the jack as soon as my desperate hands raced after the phone.

I imagined life going about it's business all around me, people collectively piecing together something edible in Stilling's din-ing hall or smiling to themselves as they re-

Your contrast of the events surrounding your experi-ence works well.

member how sweet their boyfriend was last weekend. Nobody knew what was happening to me, nobody could help me. Right now I was supposed to be sitting a dusty lecture hall, my stomach twisting its self into knots about my math ability, not about this. My whole body was in shock; why is he do-ing this to me? Why is he trapping me in here? The furry and anger was about to explode in a scream for help but I was embarrassed. I was embar-rassed to scream. I wanted help but I didn't want them all to know what my boyfriend was doing to me. As soon as my body was flung against the futon and my arms wrenched, the embarrassment flooded out of my body, I did-n't give a shit what people thought, I screamed out loud for help. I could picture someone opening my door and grabbing him by the arms, dragging him into the hall, I didn't know what would happen after that, all I wanted was him out of my room. This scream would most definitely catch someone attention.

Develop sense of time passing?

My first scream didn't do me justice, my self consciousness still had the reins, but the second I belt out from the bottom my stomach, nothing held it back. Nobody was coming to my rescue. My body jumped up and down, thinking it was the only thing it could do at this point. It was as if the jump-ing would show him how afraid I was. A salty mixture of sweat and tears covered me. Another lump of mucus caught it's self in my throat and I started to cough and choke but it didn't stop me from begging him to leave.

Not mentioning him seems to take away the respon-sibility. Let's talk about nominalizations.

The punches finally came. I was thrown onto the bed. His hand slammed up against my mouth to block my loud gushing screams. I crawled into the fetal position, my knees to my chest. His tight hand moved from my mouth and spread over my face, it twisted and wrenched my flesh. I saw into his eyes, they looked like he was trying to kill and enemy. A surge of hate rushing into his arms clenching his fists. At first, the punches were neatly defined and aimed. One to my upper forehead, another to the side of my skull, another nearer the top of my head but as they continued he became sloppy. He flailed on top of me, hitting or punching me here and there, with no rhyme or reason. Maybe he looked down at me and decided he had enough or maybe he realized what he had done. In the police report it said he had a scratch on his cheek so maybe I fought him off, I can't remember.

Brutal specifics. These make the incident vivid.

What if you began with this line?

> *Stacie—You have shared a very intense, disturbing experience in a powerful first draft. I'd like to talk about the beginning and the ending to see what about this experience you want to emphasize. I think you're a brave woman not only to write about this, but also to share it, and I think those in your group appreciated that. You have an eye for detail and description that I'd like to see you develop, and a willingness to find the necessary shape or structure of the piece. I look forward to talking with you about this. I also want to thank you for your strong voice in the classroom.*

Janet's comments emphasize a couple of things beyond the writing principles of using vivid detail and writing in active voice. They respect Stacie's desire to bring the reader into the experience and to recreate her fear, to show her belief that this couldn't happen to her, to dramatize how her belief in a normal reality is shattered with each blow to her body. They recognize Stacie's ability to use comparison effectively to show the insightful perspective she has on the event. They also point out how Stacie is still perceiving herself as a victim and relieving her boyfriend of responsibility by using the passive voice when describing his violence. Pointing out how the phrase "The punches finally came" maintains her boyfriend's control over her is a powerful way to teach that nominalizations and passive voice are not just rules of style but are language conventions that reflect power relationships that affect us on the level of the physical.

During our interview, Stacie told me she saw this piece as quite different from the text she had to produce for the legal system: In both, she is telling her side of the story, but in her essay she is making the reader experience it with her, seeing how scared she was and how much she believed this would never happen to her. Like the other students in my study, Stacie wants other women to be warned by her essay, even as she knows she is writing it to make sense of the experience—and her role—for herself. She clearly is still uncertain about how people will respond to her story, but her details render a moving account of how violent, unexpected, and brutal the attack was, and how Stacie tried to prove her strength again by using the legal system to punish her boyfriend.

Janet could have directed Stacie to other essays that have dealt with women and violence and invited Stacie to study how the writers chose to render their experiences and achieve their purposes. She could have encouraged Stacie to research dating violence and create a segmented or collage essay, which alternates Stacie's experience with insights she's gathered from other sources. She might point out to Stacie the discourses she is using to understand her experience and have her explore the implications of those or propose alternatives that might shift Stacie's perspective (for example, the violence, while it seemed to come out of nowhere, has roots in any number of psychological issues or gender biases). She could have encouraged Stacie to write about the issue in multiple genres, representing the experience through essay, academic argument, historical research, or cultural analysis, for example, each of which will offer Stacie a different identity as a writer and a different relationship to both the abuse and the self she perceived being abused. The comments Janet did offer prompted Stacie to reorder the draft and sharpen the focus, creating a more effective essay that achieved what both Stacie and Janet wanted for her writing in the course.

As feminists and psychotherapists have emphasized for years, telling one's story can be an act of reconstructing an identity, laying claim to one version of events, and rebuilding connection and trust with others. Often students who have suffered some form of bodily violence are isolated, not connected to forms of community because they perceive themselves as too damaged, too odd, too misunderstood. For many abuse survivors, the perpetrator tries to claim all rights to the story, forcing the victim to keep silent, to lie, or to question her responses and perceptions. As Maya Angelou has so powerfully rendered in *I Know Why the Caged Bird Sings*, being sexually abused can mean losing one's voice, one's language, one's sense of self. However, for the students in this study willing to share their work with their peers, the essays become ways to build community, to reach out to others, and to control how they represent their experience rather than allowing someone else to control it.

One step in recovering from trauma, Herman (1992) notes, is rebuilding social ties through sharing one's story with others. As the survivor comes to see that she is not alone in her experience, that others will listen to her story without judgment of her, "[s]omething in herself that the victim believes to be irretrievably destroyed—faith, decency, courage—is reawakened. . . . [T]he survivor recognizes and reclaims a lost part of herself" (214). Herman also notes, this kind of healing most often occurs in group therapy sessions, a more public venue for sharing one's story than one-on-one therapy, but it is still a somewhat private one. However, to move into a public forum beyond such a group—to share one's story with others (in a college class, for example) who have not necessarily experienced the same trauma—often occurs toward the end of the healing process when the survivor has learned how to respond without fear and self-hatred to the telling of her story. In therapy, that story may come haltingly, with few details or little of what we might recognize as narrative form, and, depending on how traumatic the experience, a therapist needs to guide the individual in learning new ways of responding to what has happened. Writing teachers are not trained to reeducate the emotions in this way, but we are trained to see the possibilities for multiple perspectives, the dynamics of power and gender in both language and relationships, and the ways identity is shaped by all of this. We are also trained in helping students build community, no matter how conflicted that community may become. When a survivor of trauma begins building social connections, she may then try to find a meaning to her own suffering by doing what many of the students in this book do, turning it into a motivation for social action (Herman 1992, 207). In the process, "a survivor of trauma is restore[d] her humanity" (Herman 1992, 214).

Writing teachers don't need to be therapists to renew humanity in our classrooms, and we don't need to reinforce the violence that has destroyed someone else's humanity by banning that person's story from the classroom or rallying around our roles as gatekeepers of the rational class. These students have much to teach us if we would only listen to what they're saying.

Appendix

REVISION

Fanny

My family is charming. Through generations on both sides of my parents' family, the apocryphal tales and myths are all about dapper, witty men, and women who were warm, talented mothers. I collected these people and the stories about them with zeal; they gave me an identity, a persona, a tradition. The marbled box with a brass latch which contained all the faded photos of many of these relatives came to me after my mother's death. When my children were small, their favorite amusement when confined to bed with a cold was to sort these dog-eared pictures and listen to my stories about each of them. My brothers and sister and I will once a year or so talk about finally putting all these faded relics into an album. We actually started an album when we were children; it was one of those square hard-covered books with black construction paper pages, held together with grosgrain ribbon. We had a little cellophane envelope full of corners. I remember sitting in my twin bed, with Vicks Vapo-rub on my chest, wrapped in one of my father's old cashmere mufflers, endlessly sorting and arranging these pictures, sticking them carefully into the album. My mother told me the same tales that I later told to my children.

I am telling you some of those stories, to give you some sense of the charm, the beguiling charm of some of my ancestors. I don't know for sure if all these stories are literally true, but that doesn't matter much any more; their impact has been just as great whether or not they are "true." Now that I know more truth, I am also trying to find a place for these stories. They deserve some honor; the women especially deserve great honor. The women may not have always behaved with honor, but they were doing the best they could to survive, to survive with humor, hard work, and love for their children. Now I am looking at all those charming people with new eyes. Now I know I am part of a long line of abused women, and that I, too, was both abused and was unable to see when my daughter was, in turn, abused.

My grandfather on my mother's side was a man I never met, nor was he ever discussed in my presence except once or twice when I was perhaps four or five. All I remember was the voices of my parents, whispering very loudly (you know those tones) in the living room after we were supposedly asleep. Apparently, that grandfather had written to my mother asking to see us. My mother absolutely refused to listen to my father's argument that they should let the past go, that he deserved to know his grandchildren, and that he must be harmless now. My mother was beyond reason of this sort, and absolutely would not allow a response to her father's request. I think I must have asked her about this overheard conversation, because I can think of no other way I could have learned about this man. She told me then, and in little bits more as I grew up, that my grandfather was very rich, kept a mistress, and was extremely handsome. He gave my mother and her brother all the best, they had cooks and maids, and the family lived in great style in Oak Park, Illinois. He was also a Christian Scientist. When my grandmother became ill with stomach cancer, he would not allow her medical attention. Now telling this part of the story, I can hear my mother's voice as she told me this—her father held her mother on the kitchen table, with my mother and uncle present as young children, while she died in extreme pain, screaming and weeping in front of her children. My charming grandfather did that.

Another brief story about that grandfather: when I was about twelve, long after he had died, I was rummaging about in the garage on a hot summer afternoon and came upon a box of papers. Examining these papers (how did I know that this was wrong?) I found a marriage certificate for a marriage between my mother and man named Bird. Again I asked my mother about her past. She spoke to me about raiding another's papers and respect for her privacy, but she must have known how important it was to answer my questions. Maybe she was finally able to talk about this man and why she had married him. Mr. Bird was apparently much older when she met him, a successful lawyer. He met her and married her when she was only sixteen, shortly after her mother's death. He eloped with her to New York where they were married in a civil ceremony. When my grandfather found out that she had run away from his house and married one of his business acquaintances, he sent private detectives to New York. They took my mother into custody, and returned to Milwaukee with her. There she was locked into her room and her father had the marriage annulled. Although my mother went on to complete college and later marry my father, she never forgave her father for this action. She never forgave him for anything he did to her.

On my father's side, the charming patriarchy is just as evident. I never met that grandfather either, but I knew my grandmother quite well. This grandfather, whose pictures were still extant in the family collection, was, indeed, very good looking with a high, smooth forehead, bright eyes with wrinkles at the corners, a straight nose, and a smiling mouth. You just knew that he would swoop you up into his arms and talk to you as an adult. He too made a lot of money, although he was more of an arriviste (second generation German) than my mother's father. He designed and sold men's clothing, and he was twice elected Commodore of the Milwaukee Yacht Club. According to myth, he too collected mistresses and was an excellent poker player. He too was an absent father, as we say these days. My mother once told me that he beat his wife with his malacca walking stick. I have no way of knowing if that story is true, but I do know that it was part of the whispered history about this grandfather.

My father was the youngest of five, late arriving, and protected by the older children and his mother from both the brutality of his father and from any other harsh realities. He grew up as the adored, pampered, and indulged. But he inherited the vicious amoral part from his father. He also inherited the fabled charm; my father could tell a story like no-one else. He was witty, well-read, and talented. He taught me how to do many different household crafts, from painting a window sash properly to building the perfect fire. He never learned how to make a living, however, and spent much of our childhood escaping my mother's anger with the perfect martini and the perfect excuse. I believe he molested me when I was very young, and that, in a totally perverted way, he doted on me. I was the oldest, and the first to experience both his charm and his filth. He was rotten to the core; in fact, I don't think he had a core in the sense of having a character, some sort of moral sense. He stole my brothers' caddying money from their dressers, he lied and lied and lied. But, by god, he was charming. He could present himself in the best possible light, and he fooled a lot of people. He even fooled us children into loving him; I spent a long time persuading myself that he loved us, but now I am able to see that love which allows what he allowed himself is not love by any decent definition.

My mother has been sainted since her death about fifteen years ago, but there are some revisionists afoot in the family. I am one of them. She was incredibly demanding of us. Some of these standards of honesty and decency are part of me today, but also some of the intolerance of fuzzy thinking and sloppy behavior are, too. I am beginning to understand that she needed to hold herself to such a high standard and to control both herself and her children in order to save us all from the abuse she had experienced. No terror and no anger were allowed because these emotions represented a loss of control—there is nothing worse than the lack of control a child has over an abusive parent. No amount of high achievement in school or in life will relieve that terror or release that anger, but I certainly tried.

The process of revision is, I believe, part of the reason for one brother's defection from the family; he speaks politely if spoken to by my sister or me, but he has essentially cut himself out. By doing so, he deprived his own two children of their aunts and cousins, and us of them. There aren't many of us left, and we try to guard the worthwhile as we move forward. Over the past few years, my brother, sister, and I have slowly begun to reconstruct our childhood. One will contribute a funny story, another will summon the courage to tell another horror story. One will not remember one thing from a certain time (significant in itself, of course), while another can relate an incident or a season in great detail. One brother, the one who has divorced us, will not or cannot enter this dialogue. He seems to prefer an unreconstructed past to the alternative, which we each know from experience, is exceedingly painful but invaluable to our lives now. Part of this process has taken place in the therapist's office for each of us, but I have learned that the most revealing experiences have come in the process of remembering together. That remembering inevitably leads to the revision I mentioned admitting that an abusive and inadequate father may have loved each of us and contributed to each self today, or that a mother who fiercely held us together and somehow scraped together the means to send us each to prep school, who cooked up a storm for us when we returned home on vacations, also coldly rejected my sister and me at times when we needed her most. She may have been brilliant and delightful, but she was also harsh, demanding, and adept and "not knowing."

I was finally forced into this revision, which meant removing some of the blinders which enabled me to function, when my daughter began to remember the sexual abuse which tore her life to pieces. She finally confronted me with her anger, her sense that she deserved my protection and comfort. Although she and I have much more to do, her act of courage helped me begin the long, slow process of knowing that she and I were part of generations of abuse. I finally was able to see that my mother and her mother before her had been abused. This abuse has taken many forms through the years; I told you a few stories in the beginning of this piece. I am just like my mother; I somehow managed not to know most of what happened to my daughter in her teens; I was too busy being just like my mother. She was dying during this crucial period, and I left my own children often to be with her as she died slowly of cancer. Now I understand that during that same period in my own life, she was not there for me either. It is no surprise that she refused to come to me when I was twenty, in labor with my daughter, alone in another city. This pattern of refusal or inability to know or to be there with open heart at the most important times is part of the legacy of this charming family. These loving women each have a cold hard spot in their hearts. Each of us has been damaged in some brutal way and has protected herself, closed off a part.

I am beginning to understand that I may never recover lost pieces of my own past. I am beginning to understand that the myths and tattered photos may be valid and important. But I will never forget that what is hidden behind that curtain of wit and charm is just as much a part of the reconstruction I do. When I rebuild that past, I am beginning the process of inventing or maybe transforming my future. No amount of revision is going to influence that future if I cannot summon the courage to look behind that curtain.

CHILD SEXUAL ABUSE

Nicole

I can't remember the first time it happened. I know I wasn't very old though, probably about three. It continued until I reached the age of ten. Usually he just touched me. He'd call me over to his chair, it was a green recliner with his afghan thrown over the back in case he got cold. Mom and Dad were at work, Grampa in the garden, and Grammie upstairs. He'd say that he wanted some company, that he felt lonely. I knew by this time not to disobey him because he'd tell everyone what a bad, dirty girl I was. I'd go over to him and stand by the side of that awful green recliner. He'd pull my pants down and start fondling me. It always hurt a little bit, but I'd just stand there until he was finished. When he got done I'd pull my pants up and he'd grab my arm. This was when he told me that this was our secret, and if I told anyone bad things would happen. At six years old, of course, I believed him.

Unfortunately my story is not uncommon. One out of four girls and one our of six boys are sexually assaulted by the time they are eighteen (Interview Dec 2, 1992). The effects of this form of abuse are devastating. Not a day goes by that I don't think about what Karl did to me. He was my———, an old man who lived with us because he couldn't live on his own anymore. A man that supposedly I could trust, an adult authority figure.

Sexual abuse is not what I think about when I remember my childhood, but it certainly is a big part of it. I'm affected by it even now, almost ten years later. In order for this abuse to end our society needs to wake up. We have to work together, family, schools, and the legal system, to stop this heinous abuse against children.

It was a normal afternoon. Wendy and I were playing in my room. Wendy decided she wanted to watch TV. I didn't want to, Karl was out there. She insisted so we went to the family room. I don't remember exactly how it happened but Karl tried to grab Wendy and me. Wendy started screaming and Grammie ran down the stairs. Relief swept through me, I thought Karl would stop touching me forever and Grammie would kick him out for being a bad man. It didn't happen that way. I guess Karl said he would never try anything again so Grammie didn't tell anyone. Grammie called Wendy's mom. I don't know what she told her, but soon after she came to pick Wendy up. Wendy never came over again. Grammie told me that Karl was sorry and not to tell anyone. I trusted Grammie so I believed her.

I have never understood why people don't report child abuse. As I sat in a restaurant a couple of weeks ago I overheard a woman talking at the next table, and it reminded me of what happened with my grandmother. The lady said, "I thought they were abusing their kids, but I wasn't sure so I didn't report it." I wanted to scream at her. It's much better to be overly cautious than to have an innocent child hurt. According to Gail Wyatt and Gloria Powell, in 1984 200,000 child sexual abuse cases were reported in nineteen states. Only half of them were confirmed, but many more were probably legitimate. Due to a lack of social workers and the amount of work that they undertake, it is no wonder that many of the cases were overlooked (Wyatt and Powell 11). These figures don't even take into account the countless children who, like me, remain silent about their abuse. According to Elizabeth Stanko only about six percent of women sexually abused as children ever tell the authorities, and one out of five had never told anyone (25). To me this shows how prevalent sexual abuse is in our society and how hard it is for children and adult survivors to tell their experiences. In the words of Wyatt and Powell, "Children under the age of eighteen are often subjected to physical and psychological coercion to ensure their participation and silence in abusive relationships" (12).

Even if a child does speak out and say that someone has touched him/her, often no one believes the child (Wyatt & Powell 12). Many people think that children just make up stories. The SHARPP advocate that I interviewed told me that children don't make up these stories. She said that only about two percent of women who claim to be raped are lying, and the number is probably even less for children who claim to have been molested. Yet still so many people refuse to listen. For example in *Nap Time*, the true story of the New Jersey day care where children were sexually abused, no one paid attention when Johnathan, a four year old boy, told them what was going on. His mom took him to the doctor because his personality was changing. As the nurse took his temperature rectally, Johnathan told her that Kelly did that to him at the day care. The nurse knew that temperatures were taken by using plastic strips on the forehead, but she didn't say anything to the doctor. Johnathan's mother wasn't paying attention and didn't hear what Johnathan said (12).

When children tell, either right after the abuse occurs or years later, the person they tell might make light of the situation. "They (abused children) are often ignored, punished, and not supported by non-abusing adults and professionals" (Wyatt & Powell 12). Sexual abuse has been a taboo subject in our society for so long that people just don't want to deal with it and sometimes ignore its consequences. In fact, in 1952 a study by Bender and Gruett documented by Wyatt and Powell found that there were no long-term negative effects of child sexual abuse. They studied fifteen individuals who were abuse survivors and claimed all of them suffered no adverse effects as a result of the abuse. In actuality, when John Conte and John Schuerman reviewed the case reports years later, they found that only two of the fifteen hadn't experienced any major problems. The remaining went through such horrors as drug and alcohol abuse, hospitalization, and suicide (Wyatt and Powell 158).

In my case, my grandmother made light of my abuse. I couldn't visit her because she lived in the house where I was molested. Mom asked if she could tell her why I wouldn't visit. When Grammie first found out that Karl had molested me, she couldn't figure out why I was bringing up something that happened so long ago. She believed it was totally irrelevant. Since then I guess she's changed her attitude, but it will never make up for her betrayal of me. To me, it was almost like she'd taken Karl's side.

Often in cases of child sexual abuse the survivor feels great amounts of guilt (Stanko 25). Since many people don't like talking about sexual abuse, the survivor feels that it was in some way her fault. Usually, Karl told me what a good girl I was to behave and let him touch me. He tried to be soothing so I wouldn't think what he did was wrong. I remember one day, I guess I was about seven, he asked me to do something new. He wanted me to perform fellatio on him. I think this was the only time he made me do it, but it was a real turning point for me. I had to touch him now, it wasn't him touching me. I started feeling extremely guilty that I was doing this to him. It made me feel so disgusting. I still don't remember everything that I felt that day, but I do remember running to the bathroom afterward and gagging. I brushed my teeth repeatedly as if that would change what he'd made me do. It was that day that I promised myself never to tell anyone because everyone would think that I was a dirty, terrible girl.

I don't know why children and even adult survivors blame themselves. Sometimes, even now, I wonder if I couldn't have done anything to stop Karl. I know it wasn't my fault, but every once in a while I find myself thinking about why I didn't do anything. Ellen Bass and Laura Davis say in their book *The Courage to Heal* that children blame themselves for many reasons. Some children were told that they were bad and dirty. Others were punished or ignored when they did tell someone. Even never discussing the subject with children can lead them to believe it is a terrible dirty thing.

It is never the fault of the child. In the words of Bass and Davis, "It is always the responsibility of the adult to behave with respect toward children" (107). It has only been recently that children in school have been taught about good touching and bad touching (Bass and Davis 107). At least now schools are teaching children that they have control over their own bodies, and that they have the right to say no. More of these programs are necessary in order to let children know that abuse is not their fault, and it is good to tell someone.

Many times sexual abuse survivors have low self-esteem. When someone degrades you by using your body it is hard to feel good about yourself. As stated by Bass and Davis, most survivors were told that they were to blame and that they would never amount to anything. Quite a few survivors think that they have to do well all the time. This helps to compensate because they feel they "messed up" as children by being abused.

The most apparent result of my own abuse is that I feel I must always be in control. I had no control over the situation with Karl so now I try to control all other areas of my life. Like everyone else I want things to go my way, but I sometimes get a little obsessive about it. Bass and Davis say this is a very normal feeling for a survivor: "Control is a thread that runs through the lives of survivors" (43). As one survivor said, "I have an incredible attachment to things going my way. It feels like I'm going to die if I don't get my way" (43–44). Control can be positive, but its negative effects make it hard for people to be flexible. For example sometimes I find myself needing to know exactly what my boyfriend is doing and who he is with. I trust him completely, but when I'm thinking about Karl I feel I must control Mike so he can't hurt me.

It seems strange that control is a big part of survivors' lives for it is also a big part of the lives of the perpetrators. In 1989 Jane Gilgun and Teresa Connor conducted a study of fourteen male child molesters. Many said that controlling their victims made them feel good. As one perpetrator stated, "being in control of her life was a big thrill for me" (249).

When asked why they molested children, most replied that it felt good when they did it. The molesters didn't even consider the children were people while they abused them. They viewed their victims as objects with no feeling and who would suffer nothing by being abused. The perpetrators were asked why it felt good to molest children. Some said it was for the orgasm they got out of it. One molester said this: "I remember that high, and boy I wanted it." Others claimed that it felt good to touch their victims. And still others were excited about planning out the abuse itself. "The planning was almost more exciting than having sex with her. Setting everything up, just to get her alone. It took a lot of my time, a lot of energy to do that. There was a lot of preoccupation, a lot planning involved (Gilgun & Connor 250).

Perhaps no one will ever know what leads people (90–97% of them male) to commit these crimes. The SHARPP advocate I spoke with told me that many abusers were abused themselves as children and the only way they felt they could control a situation was through sex. Because they never got the help they needed, they became offenders as a way of getting back at the abuse they endured.

The media too plays a big role in the incidence of child sexual abuse. Children are often exploited by the media as sexual objects before they are old enough to realize what is going on. In December of 1981, Ellen Bass and Louise Thorton went out and bought issues of four men's magazines, *Playboy, Hustler, Gallery,* and *Oui.* At least once in all four magazines there was a reference to children being used as sex objects. *Hustler* advertised videos that featured sexually exploited children. In *Oui* readers were asked which celebrity made this statement: "I have never been able to understand how any father could tenderly love his charming daughter without having slept with her at least once." *Hustler* even depicted cartoons of "Chester the Child Molester" poking fun at molestation (243).

When males who are unstable receive these kinds of images they feel it is acceptable to abuse children. One man, a former child molester now involved in Parents United (an organization to help stop child sexual abuse) said that he grew up hearing such things as "Old enough to bleed, old enough to slaughter" (Bass and Thorton 244). No one says that child sexual abuse is moral, but the media practically condones the practice.

I wish that I had told someone when I was a kid. As it happened, I repressed the abuse and didn't remember it until after Karl died. I remember visiting him in the nursing home and not knowing why I felt the incredible urge to wash my hands every time I touched something that he touched. I know that if he were alive today I'd want to make him pay for what he did to me. Unfortunately it is very hard to convict someone of child sexual abuse. Many times survivors don't remember until years later, and then proving the abuse is difficult, if not impossible.

More states need to adopt the policy of California. Mary Williams is an attorney there and she deals with survivors of sexual abuse. As in all states, California has a statute of limitations which prevents people from suing after a certain amount of time has passed. Sexual abuse is a delicate issue and many survivors spend well over a year deciding if they want to take action against their perpetrators. A few years ago California passed a three year statute of limitations on civil actions based on abusers who are family or household members. Many survivors do not remember their abuse until years later. Fortunately the legislation does not prohibit delayed discovery which would allow for adult survivors who have just remembered the abuse to sue their perpetrators years after the abuse occurred (Bass & Davis 307–10).

Many people wonder why survivors would want to go through the hassle of a civil suit so many years after the abuse has taken place. I would do it because it would put Karl through some of the pain he caused me. To sue him and see him try to explain and lie his way out of the situation would give me a great sense of power. For once I would be in control over him. Mary Williams says that although most cases are settled out of court, survivors still feel they have accomplished something by taking action against their perpetrators (310).

Often when children tell of abuse and the abuser stands trial, not enough is done. In 1991 Marnie Rice, Vernon Quinsey, and Grant Harris conducted a study of

136 child molesters. These men had been in a maximum security psychiatric institution. When they were released, they were followed up for the next 6.3 years. Over that period, 31% were convicted of a new sexual offense, 43% were committed for a violent and/or sexual offense, and 58% were arrested for some offense or returned to the institution (381).

I spoke with a man who has been in the Indiana State Prison since 1973. He told me that child molesters and rapists were treated really badly in the prison. In his words, "No one has any respect for men who abuse women and children. They get beat up, stabbed, and pushed around." Little if anything is done to reform them. In his opinion there should be a separate institution especially designed for sex offenders so that they can received the help that they need (Interview Nov 29, 1992).

It is really sad when men like Everett Mueller escape the system for so long that they devastate many lives. As Bowes wrote, Mueller was arrested in February of 1990 for the death of ten year old Charity Powers. After his arrest the police found that Mueller had a long history of crimes against young women. In 1972 he was charged with the kidnapping of a young California woman at knifepoint. He pleaded guilty to reduced charges of pan-handling and disturbing the peace. Less than a month later he was charged with kidnapping and rape in two separate attacks. For that he spent twenty-three months in a psychiatric hospital. In July of 1976 he was convicted of the knife point rape of an eighteen year old woman. He was sentenced to forty years with a twenty year suspended sentence. He was paroled February 23, 1988 (126). It is clear that some people do not take sexual assault seriously enough.

As stated in the *Report to the Joint Ad Hoc Committee to Review New Hampshire's Rape Laws,* the Commissioner of Corrections, Ronald Powell, said, "I think we need to look at the parole process because I think there has been an expectation that has developed . . . that if a person does well in prison the expectation is that they'll be paroled at their minimum term regardless of how many times they've been there" (4). The committee is working to change the law-making. "Intentionally touching the genitals of a child under the age of thirteen with circumstances that can be reasonably construed as being for the purpose of sexual arousal" would be an incidence of aggravated felonious sexual assault, a class A felony (5). This would allow for much more serious punishment, longer jail sentences.

Child sexual abuse is a serious crime. Taking advantage of another person's body is the worst thing that we do to each other with the only possible exception being murder. I know—I've lived through the pain of being molested. For a long time I did blame myself. I don't know if society made me feel that way or if it was all Karl's doing. Maybe it was a combination of both. I do know that by believing the stories of children and adult survivors and by educating people, we can work together to stop this abuse. Already I see society changing. Women aren't so scared anymore to tell their experiences. We shouldn't be scared; we should be proud that we had the courage to survive through such horror. I wish that I had never been abused. I wish that no one ever was. Since it did happen though, I refuse to stand around and not do anything about it. By speaking out we educate. As Ellen Bass stated, "In truth itself, there is healing."

References

Bass, Ellen, and Laura Davis. *The Courage to Heal.* New York: Harper and Row, 1988.

Bass, Ellen, and Louise Thorton. *I Never Told Anyone.* New York: Harper and Row, 1981.

Bowes, Mark. "Blind to the Record." *Reader's Digest.* August, 1991, v 139 n 832 p 126.

Gilgun, Jane, and Teresa Connor. "How Perpetrators View Child Sexual Abuse." *Social Work.* May 1989, v 30 n 3 p 249–51.

Interview with SHARPP advocate, Susie. Dec 2, 1992.

Interview with prisoner, John Doe. Nov 29, 1992.

Manshel, Lisa. *Nap Time.* New York: William Morrow and Company, Inc, 1990.

Report of the Joint Ad Hoc Committee to Review New Hampshire's Rape Laws. January 27, 1992.

Rice, Marnie, Vernon Quinsey, and Grant Harris. "Sexual Recidivism Among Child Molesters Released From a Maximum Security Psychiatric Institution." *Journal of Consulting and Clinical Psychology.* June, 1991, v 59 n 3 p 381–87.

Stanko, Elizabeth. *Intimate Intrusions: Women's Experience of Male Violence.* Boston: Routledge and Kegan, 1985.

Wyatt, Gail, and Gloria Powell. *Lasting Effects of Child Sexual Abuse.* Beverly Hills: SAGE Publications, 1988.

REALITY BITES

Kristen

Weight has been an obsession of mine my entire life to date. Since the day I was born I was chubby. Although most children gradually shed away their baby fat, mine just would not budge. Not only was it frustrating as a child to be overweight, but it was difficult to find clothes that fit, and to find people that judge you on your inner being and not by just your outward appearance. As a child I was ridiculed by many, especially by the older kids at my school. I learned to ignore their comments, and often kept my feelings inside, even though they left me with a deeply wounded heart. It was not until the end of my freshman year in high school that I came to the conclusion that I was determined to lose weight. From that point on, my life completely changed from the worse to the better.

Although I have always had an excessive amount of fat on my body, it never really bothered me. This was because it was thought that the fat would shed. This process never occurred. One of the big problems was my tendency to overeat, especially at times when I was not hungry. I loved food! This was helped on because I ate almost anything that was offered to me. As a young child, my weight was not of concern to me and did not phase me in the least. That was until the comments began to arise.

By the time I entered first grade, I began to attend a public school comprised of grades one through eight. At first, this was extremely overwhelming, much like the transition from high school to college. Being away from home and my mom all day was tragic at first. I was so used to her being there for me during the day. I got used to it though and after the first few weeks I loved it! Then about a month after school began, I became the center of mockery by the older kids. When I walked by I was often referred to as "Miss Piggy," 'Fatso," or "Chubby." It was as if I had lost my real identity. It felt as if I was being stabbed through the heart each time these wicked comments arose. Each morning I would wake up crying, not wanting to face another day of insults. I eventually made it through.

By the time I had reached seventh grade, I had matured, and found my new friends, but my weight still remained a problem. I was not verbally abused anymore, but the weight had not come off either. I was uncomfortable with my self image, but did not have the stamina to change it. Not until the end of seventh grade did I come to the conclusion that weight really does matter to others. I realized this when I asked a boy I had a crush on to go to the end of the year dance with me. He turned me down, saying that he was not planning on going with anyone. Later that day, though, one of my "skinny" friends asked him to escort her to the dance. His reply: YES.

Society makes us self conscious of our bodies. We are programmed to believe that skinny is beautiful and fat is ugly. This is what leads many to anorexia nervosa and bulimia. Models in magazines supposedly have the "perfect shape." We all strive to get this form, but who is to say what this so-called shape is.

I believe it was the summer of my freshman year when I decided that I wanted to lose weight. It was an overnight transformation. I woke up one morning and told myself that I was sick of being overweight, and I was going to do something about it. From that day on my life changed forever.

The fall of my sophomore year was incredible. My friends were completely shocked with my drastic weight loss, and the guys were giving me second glances. I had yet to reach my goal weight, but over the summer I had dropped a significant amount. I had never been happier in my entire life.

The fear of gaining back my weight caused me a few problems my sophomore year. I began skipping meals and exercising rigorously in order to lose more weight. I started to become anorexic. Many of the tell-tale signs were noticeable in me: loss of hair, black outs, lack of energy, and loss of appetite. I was losing weight, though, so it did not matter to me. By the end of the tenth grade, I had dropped over seventy pounds from a size fourteen to a size five. I had never been thin in my life. For once I was getting asked out on dates and buying all new clothes.

On the downside, I was over-exercising profusely, and I was not eating enough. This caused my menstrual cycle to cease. Fortunately my mother came to the realization that I needed help. She was fearful for me and my body. I recognized that something was wrong too, and I made an appointment with the gynecologist. It was discovered that my lack of period was due to my excessive weight loss and exercising, and I was given a prescription to help me get started again. I also got back on track with my eating, and I have a well-balanced diet now.

Although living a healthy lifestyle, I still have an unhealthy image. Today, three years later, my period is irregular without the help of a pill, even though I have gained back fifteen pounds. I am extremely unhappy with this weight gain and would do anything to lose it. I don't think I'll ever be happy with my body. I wish that I could be, but I know that it is not going to happen. Even at 110 pounds, the image locked in my head was that I had fat legs, a big stomach, and a large behind. I wish that I could accept my body the way that it is, but I cannot. I am able to look at girls in magazines, or friends of mine who are tall and stick thin without wishing they were me. I think I'll always be unhappy with my self-image unless I am able to change my state of mind completely. Weight is a constant struggle, one that I encounter every single day of my life. I have gone through so much that I can relate to others who are overweight or need help on ways to lose weight. The only point I wish to stress is to lose the weight in a healthy way, no matter how long the process takes. My whole cycle is disrupted, and I do not know if I will ever get a regular menstrual period again.

Learn to love yourself and your body. Don't try to change that which you were born with and take pride in what you were given. The more you learn to accept your body, the happier your life will be.

REALITY BITES

Kristen (Research Essay)

Anorexia Nervosa is an eating disorder that afflicts every one in two hundred and fifty girls between the ages of sixteen and eighteen (Kim Cherin 13). It is an extremely harmful disease that is often not noticed until the victim has dropped an excessive amount of weight. A number of things can trigger the onset of this disease such as family problems, childhood sexual abuse, and alcoholism (Business Week 75). The major factor in many cases is a lack of self-identity (Cherin 15). Many escape this emptiness by becoming anorexic. Having an eating disorder puts you in control of your body and your actions. You are able to control the amount of food you put into your mouth at all times. For people who are weak with a poor self-esteem this is a self-image booster. On the downside, Anorexia Nervosa is an extremely dangerous disease. You have a preoccupation with food, retreat from your social life, from classes, from activities, and exercise profusely. Much time is spent reading over calorie and fat intake charts, and measuring and weighing out food portions (Cherin 21). Your mind becomes obsessed with one thing: food.

It didn't become evident to me until I entered high school how many students have eating disorders. To many it was the only way to keep a slim figure which attracted the male gender. To others it was the fear of gaining weight now or later in life. One of my friends, Kelly, is both anorexic and bulimic. Her reason: the fear of becoming the size of her mother. She loves her mother more than anything in the world, but dislikes the size of her. Her mother's image was the major reason for Kelly's eating problems. It has been identified that mothers influence daughters to become anorexic or bulimic (Cherin 42). Whether the size of the mother or her constant nagging on being thin and healthy, family is one of the factors that can contribute to the beginning of an eating disorder. Anorexia Nervosa is a very distinct illness with a remarkable feature: relentless pursuit of excessive thinness (Hilde Bruch, M.D. ix). Once the weight starts to drop, your mind set focuses on how much better you will look with the weight off and you become determined to lose even more. Many factors add to this distinction. Supermodels in magazines, movies, and TV carry the same message, every single day, that one can be loved and respected only when slender (Bruch, M.D. viii). Society makes us self-conscious of our bodies. We are programmed to believe that skinny is beautiful, and fat is ugly. This is what leads many to anorexia nervosa and bulimia. Models in magazines supposedly have the "perfect shape." Young women strive to get this form, but who is to say what this so-called shape is?

Erin, a friend of mine who attends Loomis Chafee in Connecticut, is both anorexic and bulimic. She became anorexic her junior year in high school. She is a senior now. The instigator: her mother and a younger sister. When Erin was a baby she was adopted. Obviously her bone structure is not going to be the same as her adopted mother's. By the time she was a junior, she came to the realization that she wanted to look like both her mother and sister (who was not adopted) who both had slender, small-boned figures. Her outlet was to become both anorexic and bulimic. Erin dropped a significant amount of weight, and it was not until her grades began to slip and she was down to eating six prunes a day, that she came to the realization that she needed help. She was admitted into a hospital and eats more now, but still not enough. She will probably never be completely healed. Anorexics are blind to how thin they are, because no matter how much they weigh they still claim that they are "too fat."

Three years ago I became anorexic. It began with me wanting to lose weight. As a child I was ridiculed by many because of my size and was often referred to as "Miss Piggy," "Fatso," or "Chubby." I was a fairly secure child with self-confidence until the comments arose. At this point it was as if I had lost my real identity. From that point on, my weight was of concern, and I was uncomfortable with my self-image, but it was a while before I actually had the stamina to change it. I knew at this point that weight really did matter to others, no matter what your personality was like. After numerous tries at various diet centers such as Weight Watchers and Nutri-System during junior high school, I came to the conclusion that I did not have the willpower to lose a significant amount of weight. It was not until the end of my freshman year in high school, when I arose from bed one morning with the determination that that particular morning was going to change my life forever. It was simply an overnight transformation. I told myself that I was sick of being overweight, and was going to do something about it this time. I started to exercise for at least an hour an a half every day, and I drastically cut back on my daily fat intake. Through food restriction and rigorous exercise, anorexics pursue their goal of ultimate thinness (Bruch, M.D. 5). Initially my new ways were a shock to my body, but it eventually adjusted. From then on the pounds just dropped significantly. That particular morning changed my life forever.

The fall of my sophomore year was incredible. My friends were completely shocked by my drastic weight loss, and the guys were giving me second glances. I had yet to reach my goal weight, but over the summer I had dropped a substantial amount. In less than three months, I had lost thirty-five pounds. I had never been happier in my entire life. The fear of gaining back my weight caused me a few problems my sophomore year. I began skipping meals and exercising profusely in order to lose more weight. I started to become anorexic. Every single day I woke up to the realization that I was not eating but was losing weight. The weight was so easy to lose. With enough willpower I could control my urge to eat. Besides, even though I was constantly getting hunger pains through the day, it was locked into my mind that I was full. That was the reason my stomach was upset all the time. One of the three areas of misinterpreted psychological functioning in anorexics is inaccuracy in the way hunger is experienced (Bruch, M.D. x). With anorexics the mind takes over complete control of the body, and anything "bad" that they eat, they get punished for. One time after school, after not eating anything all day, I gave in to my longing for something sweet. The culprit: a peanut butter cookie. Initially it tasted heavenly. Each bite tasted like a million dollars. After I had eaten it though, I felt like a fat slob. It was as if I had gained back twenty pounds. The fat felt like it was swelling up on my body, and I felt extreme guilt for it. Major problem characteristics of most anorexics are disturbances in the body image, in the way that they see themselves (Bruch, M.D. 85). As soon as I got home I went straight to the VCR, put in an aerobics tape, and did and hour and a half of aerobics. I was going to work that cookie off no matter how long it took. Anxiety about the fat of food results in excessive exercising (Bruch, M.D. 85). Exercise was a necessity. I could not miss a single day of it. It was really a matter of life or death. No matter what sort of dilemma was occurring, I always found the time to exercise. This caused me to separate myself from my family and friends to a point where I began to actually lose friends. One anorexic I read about actually drew a self portrait of herself as being self-divided, two-in-one. She drew herself completely surrounded by spikes, which were described as the "forcefield." This defended her against the world, hostility and friends alike (Maud Ellmann 44).

Besides my lack of eating and excessive exercising, many of the telltale signs of anorexia were noticeable in me: loss of hair, blackouts, lack of energy, and irritability. By the end of tenth grade I had dropped over 70 pounds from a size fourteen to a size five. I had never been thin in my life. For once I was getting asked out on dates and buying all new clothes. A large percentage of young adults judge you by the way that you look on the outside, not by your inner being. Being thin, I discovered, had people view me differently than before. It was as if being thin made me a better person.

Another downside to anorexia is the cessation of the menstrual period. Mine ceased completely for a long period of time. Fortunately, by this point, my mother came to the realization that I needed help. She was fearful for me and my body. Did I really need help? Was my body deteriorating right before my eyes without my knowledge? I trusted what my mother was saying and ended up taking the initiative. My first step to recovery began by making an appointment with the gynecologist. After acknowledging the disease by getting help, many anorexics confess that this cruel dieting was a way to make them the center of attention because they felt that nobody really cared for them (Bruch, M.D. 3). At the gynecologist, it was discovered that my lack of period was due to my excessive weight loss and exercising, and I was given a prescription to help me get started again. I also got back on track with my eating, and have a well-balanced diet now. Before I would not even take a bite out of a piece of chocolate or anything that was "fattening." I now realize that an occasional treat is not going to convert me back to my old unhealthy eating habits.

Today, I have finally come to terms with my real identity. Although living a healthy lifestyle, I still am not completely cured. My period is still irregular without the help of a pill, even though I have gained back fifteen pounds. I am extremely unhappy with this weight gain and would do anything to lose it. I don't think I'll ever be completely satisfied with my body. I wish that I could be, but know that it is not going to happen. Even at my lowest weight, 110 pounds, the image locked in my head was that I had fat legs, a big stomach, and a large behind. I wish that I could accept my body the way it is, but I cannot. When looking at girls in magazines or friends of mine who are tall and stick thin, I wish they were me. I think I'll always be unhappy with my self-image unless I am able to change my state of mind completely. Weight is a constant struggle, one that I encounter every single day of my life. I have gone through so much that I can relate to others who are overweight or need help on ways to lose weight. The only point I wish to stress is to lose weight the healthy way, no matter how long the process takes. My whole cycle is disrupted, and I do not know if I will ever get a regular menstrual period again.

Learn to love yourself and your body. Don't try to change that which you were born with, and take pride in what you were given. The more you learn to accept your body, the happier your life will be.

Works Cited

Bruch, Hilde M.D. *The Golden Cage.* Cambridge, Massachusetts: Harvard University Press, 1978. viii, ix, x, 3, 5, 85.

Cherin, Kim. *The Hungry Self.* New York: Times Books, 1985. 13, 15, 21, 42.

Dunkin, Amy. "When Thinness Becomes Illness." Business Week n3277 (August 3, 1992): 75.

Ellman, Maud. *The Hunger Artists.* Cambridge, Massachusetts: Harvard University Press, 1993: 44.

My Response to Lisa's Essay "AN ETHNIC SOUND"

Ann

I was so glad, practically relieved when I read through the first paragraph of Lisa's paper entitled "AN ETHNIC SOUND." I was relieved because I realized that the issue of the paper (rap music, how it is commonly stereotyped by non-rap listeners, and about the critical issues in today's society involving the quality of life of most African Americans) is being recognized. I agreed with what she had to say in her essay, and I like the way she presented these issues.

I, myself, have never been really into rap music, but I don't say that I just plain don't like it as entirely too many people, primarily white people, do. I try to listen to all music, be it country, metal, rap or folk music, if not for entertainment to hear what the song has to say. I must admit there have been times that I've said that I didn't like rap music, and that I didn't like country music, but I think that as I've become more aware through education, observing my surroundings, talking to friends and, most importantly, hearing what people have to say, my mind has become more open.

I guess you could go so far as to say that I used to be one of those people Lisa discussed in her paper that thought that all rap was about the degradation of women and that it placed little value on human life until my best friend made me listen to her "mixes" and I realized that not all of the music was really bad. I heard Queen Latifa's "Unity," and I realized that this song had a very important message. "Who you callin' bitch?" she accuses. She sings to women, telling them to demand the respect they deserve. "You ain't a bitch or a ho," she explains. I think it was this song that told me to wake up, that there was more to rap than disrespectful sex and violence, there are serious social issues addressed in rap music. I was just so glad when I read Lisa's essay to see that other people (white people) see how critical these issues are in today's society.

However, when it came time for the class to discuss the essay I was absolutely stunned when that girl, the same one who complains about everything, said that she thought that the essay was "annoying." First of all, what kind of a person has the nerve to say that she thinks her classmate's paper is annoying and secondly, how can anyone say that they're sick of hearing about this subject constantly? Maybe I live a sheltered life or something, but I really can't identify with her complaint. I really don't think that we hear enough about this stuff. I think that society has got a major problem on it's hands about the quality of life for minorities that must be addressed and isn't.

When people began to back up the "annoying" girl (I forget her name, I'll call her Sue) by saying that information on this topic is everywhere, MTV, etc., I was amazed. I suppose it is basically true that I never watch TV, but I find it really hard to believe that these issues are addressed everywhere.

I was overcome with pure frustration. I knew I should have said something in class and wanted to, but I was past frustration. I was mad. I'm not sure why I got so angry, but I even had the little tremors and hot cheeks of true anger. People in the class, not all but a lot, were the same "Chris" that Lisa wrote about who generalized all rap as just being about killing and sex. This is true of the typical gangster rap, but this conveys a message to the listener that this is an issue that must be changed. Sure, I understood when many people said that they didn't want to listen to this kind of music because it is so negative, but for goodness' sake, at least hear and be aware of what is going on! I want people to hear the words and to say that no one should have to live like that, that something must be done. I don't want them to tune themselves out and say that we hear too much about this problem. Obviously we don't hear about it enough when conditions in the ghetto persist, even worsen, as they do.

To the living conditions described in the "typical rap song" some of the students in the class said that these are the bad-ass images that rappers are constantly portraying through their music and appearance. Students said how these rappers probably don't even know what it's like in the ghetto, they probably live very rich lifestyles and just front the gangster image. I tend to disagree. I think that these rappers are conveying an insight to a life of repression, bigotry, and poor opportunity. Lisa refers to a song in which the black man's family is struggling to make ends meet and the man shares three pairs of pants between himself and his brother. The man sees his friend decked in chains of gold who gives him "$200 for a quick delivery. . . ."

These lyrics are pleading for better working opportunity. The lyrics are not glorifying drug dealing, they are saying that there isn't really any other way to turn. The sale of drugs turns big money fast, and it is hard, almost impossible to find a job that pays enough to get by. America must find a way to create more jobs. It is my opinion that this is the best way to fight the drug problem. Instead of sinking billions of dollars each year into the "war on drugs," why can't this money go toward creating jobs? Drug education is important, I know, but there will always be people that will abuse drugs no matter what anyone tells them. But for those who have nothing else to turn to (money-wise and living conditions so poor that they have no self-respect) there must be some way to create better opportunity.

The solution to these problems must start with communication. The majority of white people tune themselves out to rap for the main reason that they think the music doesn't apply to them in the first place. I see from my own experience that people tend to listen to the music that I guess you could say "applies" to them, and that they can identify with the most. For instance there is the category of the Dead Heads. These people tend to enjoy a good time in various states of mind. There are those who like classic rock such as Led Zeppelin, and some people like my roommate like country music. She likes it because she's a country girl at heart; she is a sheep farmer. All of these styles of music have so much to say either about different ways of life, feelings, social and personal concerns and even historical events and attitudes. Music is a way to understand all of these topics by hearing what the words have to say and feeling how the mood of the song affects you.

We need to talk about the problems of our society. As I noticed in the class discussion, there was a strong feeling of tension and anxiety about the issue of racism that seemed to be making everyone breathe a little more shallowly and tightened around our esophaguses like a tight turtleneck shirt. "The paper isn't about racism," said one person. But the paper is about racism in our society and the kind of lifestyle it has created. People in the class said that they didn't want to listen to rap because of its messages of hate and violence. They said that rap gave them feelings of anger and destruction.

It is absolutely crucial to listen to these messages that rap conveys because these are major problems in society everywhere. The more we don't listen to these messages either because they "don't apply to us" or we just plain don't like to hear it, the more we contribute to the problems. The more we don't talk about the issue of racism the longer it lasts. We can not afford to tolerate racism in society anywhere, anytime. There are so many brilliant minds and colorful cultures to repress any one of them. These issues do apply to us because our generation must annihilate the fist of racism and its brass knuckles of related issues. We must open our minds to hear the words of rap music and then talk about the issues.

Notes

Introduction

1. Although the perspectives of French feminism inform my readings of these student essays, I do not specifically address issues of language and the libidinal body or draw extensively on psychoanalytic theory.

2. See Sandra Harding (1987), Patti Lather (1991), and Gesa Kirsch and Patricia Sullivan (1992).

Chapter 1

1. See also Catherine Lutz (1990), and Rom Harre (1988).

2. Despite Susan Miller's (1991) contention that composition pedagogies (whether expressivist or social constructionist) have rendered all student writing "inconsequential" vis-à-vis public (59–61), rhetorical discourse, when students who have been abused and who suffer from eating disorders adopt the normalizing functions of college writing, some of them do so as a beginning rhetorical and public position from which to speak. It is often a more protected position than those outside the university, but quite consequential to them.

3. For his text, *American Cool: Constructing a Twentieth-Century Emotional Style*, Stearns (1994) studied the "prescriptive literature" available during the nineteenth and twentieth centuries—their discourses on emotion—literature that was directed to middle-class business and professional people about how to manage expressions of love, grief, jealousy, anger, and guilt. Thus, as Stearns carefully points out, the claims he makes for the shifts in emotion culture are claims about dominant middle-class ideology and its standards for responding to and constructing the meaning of various emotions. How people actually responded is less the focus of his study

than how they were *expected* by others to respond and the ways these standards defined class, gender, and race identities (4). At the same time, Stearns emphasizes the impact emotion standards had on various public policies, institutions, and relationships, illustrating that a culture's constructions of emotion are interwoven with its public and private values.

4. Students may also be counting on the "inconsequential nature" of college writing as it has developed since the nineteenth century (Miller 1991, 59–61). Although that may be true, it doesn't necessarily mean such writing cannot lead to publicly consequential writing later, once they have begun to try on an academic identity that affords necessary protection in their view (nor does all writing have to be purposeful in public ways). The subjects themselves have been so politicized and imbued with cultural critiques and issues of power that their public relevance now seems a given.

5. Many students mentioned that writing seemed to protect them from psychological scrutiny, a challenge to Susan Miller's (1991) argument about the clinical functions of college writing where attention to mechanical correctness (historically) turned students' texts into "instruments for examining the 'body' of *a* student" (57). Although some teachers fear examining a student's body *and* psyche by attending to the craft of an essay on bodily violence, some students perceive teachers quite differently.

6. I don't want to deny the effects of unconscious motivations here, but I think it is important to recognize the ways that students *do* make choices about what to disclose and what not. The fact that some students recognize the restraints of the rhetorical situation—and the influence of private disclosure on their perceived identity—suggests that they are not simply passive or reenacting an egocentric imitation of tabloid revelations.

7. Because Carole Spitzack's (1990) argument about the politics of body reduction for women depends on confession, I'll defer a discussion of this until Chapter 4.

Chapter 2

1. Marilyn Valentino (1996, 274) and Dan Morgan (1998, 322–23) assert this as well, noting that students will write about their personal experiences with a subject, whether in response to a reading or an assignment prompt, even if the teacher has explicitly avoided asking for such responses. Jeffrey Berman's text, *Diaries to an English Professor: Pain and Growth in the Classroom* (1994), explores the writing his students do in response to literature, journal responses that often connect the student's experience with incest, for example, with what the class has read for the day, using the text to reframe personal experience.

2. Students' names have been changed and, where requested, some details have been altered to respect students' privacy.

3. In this particular course, Emily and I met a total of four times in conference, and this essay was her third of five. There was little time for us to meet individually and thus little opportunity for anything close to a therapeutic relationship to even be sensed, let alone developed. During the conference when we discussed this essay, Emily was clear with me that she wanted to work on the draft as a piece of writing (although, as she says, not the grammar), that she did not want my compassion and concern to overshadow our talk about how she might shape the draft to become more effective.

4. Therapists and psychiatrists such as Judith Herman (1992) also suggest that these moves are often the first step for survivors as they begin therapy, and writing about it in a classroom setting can be an incentive to begin counseling.

5. Although many feminists have argued that speaking about one's sexual abuse can become a method of transforming the culture that condones it, doing so within a university writing course raises new issues: What in particular can be changed when a professor or students are the audience? How politically powerful can college writing be? What is the focus of the course, writing, self-analysis, and social critique?

6. According to some historians, this was common. If a man were convicted of sexual deviance, he was often reintegrated into the community within a year or two, regardless of his standing in the town. In a divorce case from the late-eighteenth century, a woman accused her husband of incest with their fourteen-year-old daughter, but then she dropped the charges and accepted him back into the family when he decided to reform (at his wife's request) (D'Emilio and Freedman 1988, 25).

7. I am indebted to Cinthia Gannett for introducing this text to me during her graduate seminar on the history and art of journal writing.

8. In the end, Asa convinces Abigail to go to New York with him to settle some land for the divorce, and, having deceived her, leaves her there. Abigail makes her way back to New Hampshire by herself, with the aid of people along the way. As soon as she returns, in June 1792, she has Asa arrested as he tries to escape. Abigail chooses an informal settlement in the divorce, apparently to avoid the emotional trauma of a trial for her family, and having sacrificed a large property settlement by avoiding a trial, she has to give her children to homes where they can be cared for. Records suggest that Phebe went to live with an uncle and eventually joined the Shaker community in Enfield, New Hampshire, under an assumed name, Phebe Huntington. It may not be surprising that Phebe joined a religious group committed to celibacy and gender egalitarianism. Their founder, Ann Lee, was herself a survivor of abuse from her husband, as well as from townspeople who rejected her message.

9. Karen McLennan illustrates this point quite powerfully in *Nature's Ban: Women's Incest Literature*.

10. When I met with Fanny two years after she had written this essay, her first comment as she reread it was, "Boy, this is dripping with anger and intense feelings. I forgot about that."

11. Carol Barringer (1992), in her article "The Survivor's Voice: Breaking the Incest Taboo," identifies several linguistic characteristics of sexual abuse narratives, one of them being the use of euphemism.

12. None of the students in my study were required to write about this abuse, contrary to what Swartzlander et al. (1993) imply. A number of therapists I interviewed asserted that someone who has been abused will not speak or write about it until she or he feels psychically able.

Chapter 3

1. These are the first two lines of a poem in Zelda Fitzgerald's novel, *Save Me the Waltz:*

Why am I this way, why am I that?

Why do myself and I constantly spat?

Which is the reasonable, logical me?

Which is the one who must will it to be? (69)

2. One of the earliest twentieth-century researchers of eating disorders, Hilde Bruch, describes how anorexic women deny their bodies' physical impulses, develop heightened sensations, and experience themselves as all mind without a body. Some of the young women she quotes say, "Everything became very intense and very intellectual, but absolutely untouchable"; "Being hungry has the same effect as a drug, and you feel outside your body. You are truly beside yourself—and then you are in a different state of consciousness and you can undergo pain without reacting" (1978, 13–17). Noelle Caskey, in discussing Bruch, emphasizes "the ecstatic nature of the anorexia experience" (1986, 184) from both a physiological and psychological perspective, but cultural theorists such as Sandra Bartky (1988) and Susan Bordo (1993) suggest this pleasure is produced because such bodily discipline gives women a sense of power and mastery—as an exaggeration of femininity in Western culture, anorexia illustrates how a woman's identity is structured around physically disciplining and mastering the unruly body.

3. See Bordo (1993, 46 and note 2 on the same page); Hastings and Kern (1994); Kearney-Cooke and Striegel-Moore (1994).

4. Noelle Caskey (1986) brings together Freudian and Jungian theories to argue that anorexia can be interpreted as both a form of "psychic incest" and a call to the mother for help. From a Jungian perspective, to reject fat is to "reject . . . the sexually mature feminine as represented by the maternal image. It is unity with the father against the mother and all that the mother represents" (187). As "psychic incest," anorexia is "a rejection of the mother and the mother's body in favor of a delusional relationship with this pure male adolescent spirit [*puer aeternus*] who has all the spiritual attributes of the divine masculine youth." This psychic incest occurs in women whose relationships with their fathers emphasize the "life of the mind" (185). In striv-

ing for order, control, and a sense of competence, anorexics internalize a "secret aspect," a separate masculine person whose masculinity commands more respect and value. Bruch says,

> Their overslim appearance, their remarkable athletic performances, with perseverance to the point of exhaustion, give them the proud conviction of being as good as a man, and keep the "little man," the "evil spirit," or some other magic force from tormenting them with guilt and shame. (1978, 55–56)

But even as anorexia "results from a psychically incestuous relationship with the father, it is simultaneously an expression of that relationship . . . and a defense against it, an attempt to escape domination." Turning to Freudian theory where anorexia is interpreted as "an oral impregnation phobia," Caskey suggests anorexia is also a warding off of the father, a fear of being impregnated by him and "imprisoned by him" completely. The disease can be a "cry to the mother for help," and treatment usually emphasizes strengthening the mother-daughter bond (1986, 187). Although most psychoanalysts now reject the oral impregnation theory, feminists such as Orbach reach similar conclusions about the anorexic's relationship with her mother: Because the mother has been socialized to suppress her desires for both "dependency gratification and autonomy," she disciplines her daughter to suppress them as well, complicating even further the separation and individuation process for both of them ("Accepting," 1985, 84–85). Feeling "emotionally unentitled and undeserving," the daughter develops anorexia as a safeguard against her neediness (Orbach, "Visibility," 1985, 136).

5. For summaries of these theories, see Brumberg (1988, 24–40) and Gimlim (1994). For more detailed discussions of particular perspectives, see Bruch (1978; 1988), Orbach (1985), Katz (1985), and Garner and Garfinkel (1985).

6. See Brumberg (1988, 25–27) and Katz (1985).

7. As with all three of the types of bodily violence that I am studying—sexual abuse, eating disorders, and physical abuse—not only are definitions of the terms equivocal, but the accuracy of statistics is questionable. Because diagnostic criteria are not standardized, it is difficult to generalize whether and by how much the number of eating disorders cases has increased in the latter half of the twentieth century (Brumberg 1988, 11), so it is hard to know who is being counted for what particular symptoms. In addition, it is difficult to determine the extent to which eating disordered behavior was prevalent before the twentieth-century focus on and dissemination of information about it.

8. Rose L. Squires and Dona Kagan (1985) conducted a study in which they concluded that compulsive eating among college women was linked to the women's desires to be more feminine, not less (as some of the psychological research has posited). Seeing this as a refutation of Orbach's theories, Squires and Kagan did not see how their conclusions further illustrated feminist cultural theories that women become so invested in achieving feminine ideals (which also require a repudiation of

the feminine—neediness, desire, and so on) that an eating disorder becomes a manifestation of such femininity.

9. I am grateful to Melody Graulich for directing me to this point.

Chapter 4

1. Because only three students who wrote about being abused by their boyfriends agreed to work with me, I am not able to draw conclusions about particular patterns in the essays. Although none of the essays about physical abuse was about long-term or ongoing violence, these three all described beatings the young women had received from boyfriends (of similar age) who lashed out at the women in often jealous anger, trying to use violence to prevent the women from leaving.

2. As I noted in Chapter 3, it is not unusual for victims of abuse to suffer from eating disorders, a way to "regulate their internal emotional states" (Herman 1992, 109) that is also a reenactment of the abuse (and a sign the victim has few methods of self-care) (Herman 1992, 166). As I discuss later, Ann came from a family in which alcoholism, verbal abuse, and possibly physical abuse were the norm, so her relationship with her boyfriend was one factor among many that may have precipitated her anorexia.

3. I thank Patricia Sullivan for drawing my attention to this point.

4. For a historical perspective on domestic violence and how it has been conceptualized, see Linda Gordon, *Heroes in Their Own Lives*.

5. For more detailed arguments than those that I present later in this chapter, see Richard J. Gelles and Donileen R. Loeske, editors, *Current Controversies on Family Violence* (an excellent text for both overview and details); Judith Herman, *Trauma and Recovery;* Gerald T. Hotaling, David Finkelhor, John T. Kirkpatrick, and Murray Straus, editors, *Family Abuse and its Consequences;* Adam Jukes, *Why Men Hate Women;* Del Martin, *Battered Wives;* Robert T. Sigler, *Domestic Violence in Context;* Murray A. Straus and Richard Gelles, *Physical Violence in American Families;* Murray A. Straus, Richard J. Gelles, and Suzanne K. Steinmetz, *Behind Closed Doors.*

6. See Maureen A. Pirog-Good and Jan E. Stets, editors, *Violence in Dating Relationships: Emerging Social Issues.*

7. Countering these individually oriented interpretations, sociological theories point to the influence of social class, gender, race, and ethnicity, and they argue that although family violence cuts across these lines, it is greater in groups who are more disadvantaged, especially economically (Gelles and Loeske 1993, 32–33). The family system also plays a role in which "the same characteristics [sociologists Straus, Hotaling, and Gelles] saw as making the family violence-prone also serve to make the family a warm, supportive, and intimate environment" (Gelles and Loeske 1993, 35).

8. Briefly, sociology has developed four primary theories to explain family violence: general systems theory, where violence is not a product of individual pathol-

ogy but of the systems; resource theory, which posits that all systems rest on the possibility of force that grows greater the more resources one has; exchange/control theory, which asserts that violence occurs when there are rewards for it; and subculture of violence theory, where subcultures are understood to construct different meanings to violence (Gelles and Loeske 1993, 36–38). Although feminist theories work from many of these theories, they emphasize that significantly more men are violent toward women and this emerges from patriarchal systems of privilege and power (although women also report—are reported to—being violent toward their partners, sometimes as much or more than men, that aggression is usually self-defensive or less threatening than male violence; see Straus and Gelles 1992). Linda Gordon is careful to point out that male dominance is not the *cause* of such violence, but that male dominance is a *basis* for it (1988, 251, 264). A number of feminists have argued that popularized theories of domestic violence, sexual abuse, or the more general state of being codependent move away from understanding how patriarchy and capitalism construct the possibilities for this violence and put more emphasis on "the problem [as] personal pathology, not societal oppression" (Brown 1990, 4).

9. My thanks go to Patricia Sullivan for drawing my attention to these shifts in agency.

10. See Swartzlander et al. (1993), and Bass and Davis (1988). Janet Leibman Jacobs refers to Judith Jordan's term *faulty empathy* to describe this: "a personality construct in which the individual's self boundaries are extremely permeable and thus she cannot easily distinguish between her needs and the needs of others" (1994, 70).

11. Personal interview, Dianne Rice, M.S., L.S.W., CCDC III of Pathways to Recovery, Centerville, Ohio.

12. As Katherine described this to me

[I try] to get them to see [context] in more concrete ways. And I use the quilt and then I use this diagram to sort of talk about that, and very much about context. And what I say is everybody has this little center, this black square that is your self and then we have all these different layers of how we view things, how we look at things, but what makes this a nice picture is when all the squares will come together and all the colors work together, . . . but it really works and then I have this actual diagram that I write out where I put different things in each of the layers and how they connect and how they overlap and how I see texts overlapping and all that.

13. This quote is from a student's course evaluation.

14. Stearns (1994) is careful, however, to avoid making direct evaluative statements like this about the impact of these new emotion standards (see Chapter 10).

15. Unlike war veterans, Ann has not been expected to use violence against others and is solely a victim of males' violence. As a woman, she also has less cultural support for writing about her abuse than O'Brien does. It seems significant, however, that Ann focused on subjects where the victims she empathized with were also, at

times, perpetrators (the Irish Republican Army, rap stars who sing about sexual and physical violence against women—although the women singers who reject these lyrics were the ones who initiated her reassessment of rap—and Vietnam veterans).

Conclusion

1. See also *I Never Told Anyone: Writings by Women Survivors of Child Sexual Abuse* (Bass and Thorton, 1983), and *Voices in the Night: Women Speaking about Incest* (McNaron and Morgan, 1982).

2. See Bell (1993, 28–30).

Bibliography

Allison, Dorothy. 1992. *Bastard Out of Carolina*. New York: Dutton.

Angelou, Maya. [1971] 1969. *I Know Why the Caged Bird Sings*. New York: Bantam Books.

Baker, Houston A., Jr. 1984. *Blues, Ideology, and Afro-American Literature: A Vernacular Theory*. Chicago: University of Chicago Press.

Bartholomae, David. 1985. "Inventing the University." *When a Writer Can't Write*, edited by Mike Rose, 134–65. New York: Guilford.

Barringer, Carol E. 1992. "The Survivor's Voice: Breaking the Incest Taboo." *National Women's Studies Association Journal* 4 (1): 4–22.

Bartky, Sandra. 1988. "Foucault, Femininity, and the Modernization of Patriarchal Power." *Feminism and Foucault: Reflections on Resistance*, edited by Irene Diamond and Lee Quinby. Boston: Northeastern University Press.

Bass, Ellen, and Laura Davis. 1988. *The Courage to Heal: A Guide for Women Survivors of Child Sexual Abuse*. New York: Harper and Row.

Bass, Ellen, and Louise Thorton, eds. 1983. *I Never Told Anyone: Writings by Women Survivors of Child Sexual Abuse*. New York: HarperCollins.

Bell, Vikki. 1993. *Interrogating Incest: Feminism, Foucault, and the Law*. New York: Routledge.

Berlin, James. 1987. *Rhetoric and Reality: Writing Instruction in American Colleges, 1900–1985*. Carbondale: Southern Illinois University Press.

Berman, Jeffrey. 1994. *Diaries to an English Professor: Pain and Growth in the Classroom*. Amherst: University of Massachusetts Press.

Berthoff, Ann. 1981. *The Making of Meaning: Metaphors, Models, and Maxims for Writing Teachers*. Montclair, N.J.: Boynton/Cook.

Bourdieu, Pierre. 1984. *Distinction: A Social Critique of the Judgement of Taste*. Trans. Richard Nice. Cambridge: Harvard University Press.

Bordo, Susan. 1993. *Unbearable Weight: Feminism, Western Culture, and the Body*. Berkeley: University of California Press.

Brown, Laura. 1990. "What's Addiction Got to Do With It?: A Feminist Critique of Codependence." *Psychology of Women: Newsletter of Division 35, American Psychological Association.* 17 (1): 2–4.

Bruch, Hilde. 1978. *The Golden Cage: The Enigma of Anorexia Nervosa.* Cambridge: Harvard University Press.

Brumberg, Joan Jacobs. 1988. *Fasting Girls: The Emergence of Anorexia Nervosa as a Modern Disease.* Cambridge: Harvard University Press.

Caskey, Noelle. 1986. "Interpreting Anorexia Nervosa." *The Female Body in Western Culture: Contemporary Perspectives,* edited by Susan Rubin Suleiman. Cambridge: Harvard University Press.

Chernin, Kim. 1981. *The Obsession: Reflections on the Tyranny of Slenderness.* New York: Harper and Row.

Clark, Suzanne. 1994. "Rhetoric, Social Construction, and Gender: Is It Bad to Be Sentimental?" *Writing Theory and Critical Theory,* edited by John Clifford and John Schilb. New York: Modern Language Association.

Cornelius, Randolph R. 1996. *The Science of Emotion: Research and Traditions in the Psychology of Emotion.* Upper Saddle River, N.J.: Prentice-Hall.

Deletiner, Carole. 1992. "Crossing Lines." *College English* 54 (7): 809–817.

D'Emilio, John, and Estelle B. Freedman. 1988. "Family Life and the Regulation of Deviance." *Intimate Matters: A History of Sexuality in America.* New York: Harper and Row.

Faigley, Lester. 1992. *Fragments of Rationality: Postmodernity and the Subject of Composition.* Pittsburgh: University of Pittsburgh Press.

Felman, Shoshana, and Dori Laub. 1992. *Testimony: Crises of Witnessing in Literature, Psychoanalysis, and History.* New York: Routledge.

Fitzgerald, Zelda. 1967. *Save Me the Waltz.* Carbondale: Southern Illinois University Press.

Foucault, Michel. 1979. *Discipline and Punish.* New York: Vintage Books.

———. 1978. *The History of Sexuality Volume 1: An Introduction,* translated by Robert Hurley. New York: Vintage.

Gannett, Cinthia. 1992. *Gender and the Journal: Diaries and Academic Discourse.* Albany: SUNY Press.

Garner, David M., and Paul E. Garfinkel. 1985. *Handbook of Psychotheraphy for Anorexia Nervosa and Bulimia.* New York: Guilford Press.

Gelles, Richard J., and Donileen R. Loeske, eds. 1993. *Current Controversies on Family Violence.* Newbury Park, Calif.: Sage Publications.

Gilman, Charlotte Perkins. 1973. *The Yellow Wallpaper.* Old Westbury, N.Y.: The Feminist Press.

Gimlim, Debra. 1994. "The Anorexic as Overconformist: Toward a Reinterpretation of Eating Disorders." *The Ideals of Feminine Beauty,* edited by Karen A. Callaghan. Westport, C.T.: Greenwood Publishing Co.

Glaspell, Susan. 1993. *A Jury of Her Peers.* Mankato, MN: Creative Education.

Goffman, Erving. 1963. *Stigma: Notes on the Management of Spoiled Identity.* New York: Simon and Schuster.

Gordon, Linda. 1988. *Heroes in Their Own Lives: The Politics and History of Family Violence, Boston 1880–1960.* New York: Penguin.

Harding, Sandra, ed. 1987. *Feminism and Methodology.* Bloomington: Indiana University Press.

Harre, Rom, ed. 1988. *The Social Construction of Emotions.* Oxford, U.K.: Basil Blackwell.

Hastings, Teresa, and Jeffrey M. Kern. 1994. "Relationships Between Bulimia, Childhood Sexual Abuse, and Family Environment." *International Journal of Eating Disorders* 15 (2): 103–111.

Herman, Judith Lewis. 1992. *Trauma and Recovery.* New York: Basic Books.

Hotaling, Gerald T., David Finkelhor, John T. Kirkpatrick, and Murray Straus, ed. 1988. *Family Abuse and its Consequences: New Directions in Research.* Newbury Park, CA: Sage Publications.

Jacobs, Hariet [Linda Brent]. 1973. *Incidents in the Life of a Slave Girl, Written by Herself,* edited by Lydia Maria Child, 1861. New ed., Walter Teller. New York: Harcourt Brace Jovanovich.

Jacobs, Janet Liebman. 1994. *Victimized Daughters: Incest and the Development of the Female Self.* New York: Routledge.

Jaggar, Alison. 1989. "Love and Knowledge: Emotion in Feminist Epistemology." *Gender/Body/Knowledge: Feminist Reconstructions of Being and Knowing,* edited by Alison Jaggar and Susan R. Bordo. New Brunswick: Rutgers University Press.

Jarratt, Susan. 1991. "Feminism and Composition: The Case for Conflict." *Contending with Words: Composition in a Postmodern Era,* edited by Patricia Harkin and John Schilb. New York: Modern Language Association.

Jay, Gregory. 1987. "The Subject of Pedagogy: Lessons in Psychoanalysis and Politics." *College English* 49 (November): 785–800.

Jukes, Adam. 1993. *Why Men Hate Women.* London: Free Association Books.

Kagle, Steven E. 1986. *Early Nineteenth-Century American Diary Literature.* Boston: Twayne Publishers.

Katz, Jack L. 1985. "Some Reflections on the Nature of the Eating Disorders: On the Need for Humility." *International Journal of Eating Disorders* 4 (4): 617–626.

Kearney-Cooke, Ann, and Ruth H. Striegel-Moore. 1994. "Treatment of Childhood Sexual Abuse in Anorexia Nervosa and Bulimia Nervosa: A Feminist Psychodynamic Approach." *International Journal of Eating Disorders* 15 (4): 305–319.

Kirsch, Gesa, and Patricia Sullivan, eds. 1992. *Methods and Methodology in Composition Research.* Carbondale: Southern Illinois University Press.

Lather, Patti. 1991. *Getting Smart: Feminist Research and Pedagogy with/in the Postmodern.* New York: Routledge.

Lutz, Catherine A. 1990. "Engendered Emotion: Gender, Power, and the Rhetoric of Emotional Control in American Discourse." *Language and the Politics of Emotion,* edited by Catherine A. Lutz and Lil Abu-Lughod. Cambridge: Cambridge University Press.

Lutz, Catherine A., and Lila Abu-Lughod. 1990. "Introduction: Emotion, Discourse, and the Politics of Everyday Life." *Language and the Politics of Emotion,* edited by Catherine A. Lutz and Lil Abu-Lughod. Cambridge: Cambridge University Press.

Martin, Del. 1976. *Battered Wives.* New York: Pocket Books.

Maasik, Sonia, and Jack Solomon. 1994. *Signs of Life in the USA.* Boston: Bedford Books.

McLennan, Karen Jacobsen. 1996. *Nature's Ban: Women's Incest Literature.* Boston: Northeastern University Press.

McNaron, Toni A. H., and Yarrow Morgan, eds. 1982. *Voices in the Night: Women Speaking about Incest.* Pittsburgh: Cleis Press.

McNay, Lois. 1991. "The Foucauldian Body and the Exclusion of Experience." *Hypatia* 6 (3): 126–139.

Miller, Richard. 1996. "The Nervous System." *College English* 58 (3): 265–286.

Miller, Susan. 1991. *Textual Carnivals: The Politics of Composition.* Carbondale: Southern Illinois University Press.

Morgan, Dan. 1998. "Ethical Issues Raised by Students' Personal Writing." *College English* 60 (3): 318–325.

Murphy, Ann. 1989. "Transference and Resistance in the Basic Writing Classroom: Problematics and Praxis." *College Composition and Communication* 40 (2): 175–187.

Newkirk, Thomas. 1996. "Seduction and Betrayal in Qualitative Research." *Ethics and Representation in Qualitative Studies of Literacy,* edited by Peter Mortensen and Gesa E. Kirsch. Urbana: National Council of Teachers of English.

Newkirk, Thomas. 1992. "The Narrative Roots of the Case Study." *Methods and Methodology in Composition Research,* edited by Gesa Kirsch and Patricia A. Sullivan. Carbondale: Southern Illinois University Press.

O'Brien, Tim. 1990. *The Things They Carried.* New York: Penguin.

O'Leary, K. Daniel. 1993. "Through a Psychological Lens: Personality Traits, Personality Disorders, and Levels of Violence." *Current Controversies on Family Violence,* edited by Richard J. Gelles and Donileen R. Loeske. Newbury Park, CA: Sage Publications.

Orbach, Susie. 1985. "Accepting the Symptom: A Feminist Psychoanalytic Treatment of Anorexia Nervosa." *Handbook of Psychotherapy for Anorexia Nervosa and Bulimia,* edited by David M. Garner and Paul E. Garfinkel. New York: Guilford Press.

Orbach, Susie. 1985. "Visibility/Invisibility: Social Considerations in Anorexia Nervosa—A Feminist Perspective." *Theory and Treatment of Anorexia and Bulimia: Biomedical, Sociocultural, and Psychological Perspectives,* edited by Rev. Steven Wiley Emmett, Ph.D. New York: Brunner/Mazel.

Pfeiffer, Kathleen. 1993. "Comment and Response." *College English* 55 (6): 669–671.

Pirog-Good, Maureen A., and Jan E. Stets. 1989. *Violence in Dating Relationships: Emerging Social Issues.* New York: Praeger Publishers.

Remmler, Karen. 1994. "Sheltering Battered Bodies in Language: Imprisonment Once More?" *Displacements: Cultural Identities in Question,* edited by Angelika Bammer. Bloomington: Indiana University Press.

Rice, Dianne, M.S, L.S.W, CCDC III. Personal Interview. April 15, 1995.

Roiphe, Katie. 1995. "Making the Incest Scene: In Novel After Novel, Writers Grope for Dark Secrets." Review. *Harper's Magazine* November: 65–71.

Rosaldo, Michelle Z. 1980. *Knowledge and Passion: Ilongot Notions of Self and Social Life.* Cambridge: Cambridge University Press.

Scarry, Elaine. 1985. *The Body in Pain: The Making and Unmaking of the World.* New York: Oxford University Press.

Sigler, Robert T. 1989. *Domestic Violence in Context: An Assessment of Community Attitudes.* Lexington, M.A.: Lexington Books.

Sommers, Nancy. 1980. "Revision Strategies of Student Writers and Experienced Adult Writers." *College Composition and Communication* 31 (4): 378–388.

Spilka, Mark. 1992. *Eight Lessons in Love: A Domestic Violence Reader.* Columbia: University of Missouri Press.

Spitzack, Carole. 1990. *Confessing Excess: Women and the Politics of Body Reduction.* Albany: SUNY Press.

Squires, Rose L., and Dona M. Kagan. 1985. "Sex Role and Eating Behaviors Among College Women." *International Journal of Eating Disorders* 4 (4): 539–547.

Stanko, Elizabeth. 1985. *Intimate Intrusions: Women's Experience of Male Violence.* Boston: Routledge and Kegan.

Stearns, Peter. 1994. *American Cool: Constructing a Twentieth-Century Emotional Style.* New York: New York University Press.

Straus, Murray A., and Richard Gelles. 1992. *Physical Violence in American Families: Risk Factors and Adaptations to Violence in 8,145 Families.* New Brunswick: Transaction Publishers.

Straus, Murray A., Richard J. Gelles, and Suzanne K. Steinmetz. 1981. *Behind Closed Doors: Violence in the American Family.* Newbury Park, CA: Sage Publications.

Swartzlander, Susan, Diana Pace, and Virginia Lee Stamler. 1993. "The Ethics of Requiring Students to Write About Their Personal Lives." *The Chronicle of Higher Education* 17 February, B1–2.

Tal, Kali'. 1996. *Worlds of Hurt: Reading the Literatures of Trauma.* Cambridge: Cambridge University Press.

Taves, Ann, ed. 1989. *Religion and Domestic Violence in Early New England: The Memoirs of Abigail Abbot Bailey.* Bloomington: Indiana University Press.

Thompson, Roger. 1986. "Sexual Deviance and Abuse." *Sex in Middlesex: Popular Mores in a Massachusetts County, 1649–1699.* Amherst: University of Massachusetts Press.

Ulrich, Laurel Thatcher. 1991. *Good Wives: Image and Reality in the Lives of Women in Northern New England, 1650–1750.* New York: Vintage Books.

Valentino, Marilyn. 1996. "Responding When a Life Depends on It: What to Write in the Margins When Students Self-Disclose." *Teaching English in the Two-Year College* 23: 274–283.

Worsham, Lynn. 1992–1993. "Emotion and Pedagogic Violence." *Discourse* 15.2 (Winter): 119–148.

Index

160